*Evolving Paradigms
in Interpreter Education*

*Interpreter Education Series*

CYNTHIA B. ROY, SERIES EDITOR

ELIZABETH A. WINSTON AND
CHRISTINE MONIKOWSKI,
*Editors*

# Evolving Paradigms
# in Interpreter Education

GALLAUDET UNIVERSITY PRESS
*Washington, D.C.*

Interpreter Education
A Series Edited by Cynthia B. Roy
Gallaudet University Press
Washington, DC 20002

http://gupress.gallaudet.edu

*Library of Congress Cataloging-in-Publication Data*

Evolving paradigms in interpreter education / Elizabeth Winston and Christine Monikowski, editors.

pages cm

Includes index.

ISBN 978-1-56368-569-9 (hardcover : alk. paper) – ISBN 978-1-56368-570-5 (e-book)

1. Interpreters for the deaf–Education. 2. Sign language–Study and teaching.
3. Translating and interpreting–Study and teaching (Higher) I. Winston, Elizabeth A. II. Monikowski, Christine.

HV2402.E86 2013

419'.7071–dc23

2013028761

♾ The paper used in this publication meets the minimum requirements of American National Standard for Information Sciences–Permanence of Paper for Printed Library Materials, ANSI Z39.48-1984.

# CONTENTS

# EDITORIAL ADVISORY BOARD

# CONTRIBUTORS

Claudia V. Angelelli
Professor
Department of Spanish and
Portuguese
San Diego State University
San Diego, California

and

Chair of Multilingualism and
Intercultural Communication
Heriot-Watt University
Edinburgh, Scotland, United
Kingdom

Karen Bontempo
Honorary Associate
Department of Linguistics
Macquarie University
Sydney, Australia

Terry Janzen
Associate Professor and
Department Head
Department of Linguistics
University of Manitoba
Winnipeg, Manitoba, Canada

Lorraine Leeson
Professor and Director of the
Center for Deaf Studies
Department of Linguistic,
Speech, and Communication
Sciences
Trinity College Dublin
Dublin, Ireland

Ester S. M. Leung
Associate Professor
Translation Program
Hong Kong Baptist University
Hong Kong, China

Ian Mason
Professor
Department of Languages and
Intercultural Studies
Heriot-Watt University
Edinburgh, Scotland,
United Kingdom

Christine Monikowski
Professor
Department of American Sign
Language and Interpreter
Education
Rochester Institute of
Technology/National Technical
Institute for the Deaf
Rochester, New York

Jemina Napier
Chair of Intercultural
Communication
Department of Languages and
Intercultural Studies
Heriot-Watt University
Edinburgh, Scotland, UK

Rico Peterson
Assistant Dean and Director
NTID Access Services
Rochester Institute of
Technology/National Technical
Institute for the Deaf
Rochester, New York

David Quinto-Pozos
Assistant Professor
Department of Linguistics
University of Texas, Austin
Austin, Texas

Debra Russell
Director
Western Canadian Centre of
Deaf Studies
Department of Educational
Psychology
University of Alberta
Edmonton, Alberta, Canada

Barbara Shaffer
Associate Professor

Signed Language Interpreting
Program, Department of
Linguistics
University of New Mexico
Albuquerque, New Mexico

Christopher Stone
Associate Professor
Department of Interpretation
Gallaudet University
Washington, DC

Helen Tebble
Adjunct Associate Professor
School of Languages, Cultures
and Linguistics
Monash University
Melbourne, Victoria, Australia

Beppie van den Bogaerde
Professor
Faculty of Education
Hogeschool Utrecht /
University of Applied Sciences
Utrecht, The Netherlands

Elizabeth Winston
Director
Center for Teaching
Interpreting Educators and
Mentors
Loveland, Colorado

# FOREWORD: INTERPRETING AND INQUIRY

HERE IS a book of scholarship on interpreting and the education of interpreters. It is a collection of thoughtful perspectives on different aspects of our craft. These pages offer ample evidence that *inquire* and *interpret* are thick as thieves: It is difficult to pursue either without needing the other. They are comrades in arms in the ancient struggle to see things clearly and unequivocally. The twin urges to know precisely and to communicate precisely drive the work of interpretation just as they drive the work of scholarship.

In the happy dreamland of interpreters, all things are visible and audible, and *who* is saying *what* to *whom*, *why*, and *where* are always known. In this place, apprehensions blossom into comprehensions. Confidence finds purpose and takes hold. Grounded in this basic information, interpreters can direct their attention to *how* best to facilitate communication.

There is, to be sure, a less hospitable dreamland, a place interpreters hardly dare speak of. In this grim quarter, apprehension blossoms into anxiety as the unknown and unknowable run riot. Here the seeds of *who*, *what*, and *why* can find no purchase and neither inquiry nor interpreting stands much of a chance.

The festival of person, place, and purpose is the landscape of interpreting, a place so changeable that one moment our predictions prove accurate and we speak with authority and the next moment the simple construct "the baby with the bathwater" remains suspended, untouched by our blinkered probing, a piñata just out of range.

Inquiry into who we are, what we do, and how we ought to behave has long been a source of fascination. Estela Herrera (2002) mines this rich vein in her essay "What Can Interpreters Learn from Aristotle and

Stanislavsky?" Herrera offers applications of Aristotle's notions on talent and *techne* and Stanislavsky's techniques for being present "in the moment." Herrera deserves praise for expanding the workbench of interpreters to include these useful perspectives.

Inquiry into identity has serious ramifications for interpreters. Knowing about myself, about *who* I am and *why* I am present, is every bit as important as knowing those things about the people for whom I interpret. Sometimes I am present as the interpreter. Sometimes I am the interpreter/aide and sometimes the employee. The rules in each of those settings are quite different. It well behooves our practice to consider formally *who* we are and *why* we are *where* we are.

In the funhouse mirror of interpreting, every "who are you?" reflects back "who am I?" and "what do you want?" glimmers with "what do I want?" Just as perceptions of Self and Other morph and morph again, so do the roulette wheels of Role, Motivation, and Setting spin out the parameters of interpreting, combining and recombining kaleidoscopically, sometimes rewarding our wagers and sometimes not.

The role confusion of "who am I?" is bred into interpreters. In an earlier telling of our tale, we were half-bloods or cross-marrieds, commanded into service on incursions into hostile territory. Another time before that, we were tonsured monks translating in number and obscurity for an audience of elites. In this part of our heritage, we knew ourselves simply as employees.

Castaño (2005) quotes Jane's (1930) translation of the journal of Christopher Columbus, just as Columbus has an inspiration upon having been in first contact with the Arawak people:

> It had appeared to [me] that it would be well to take some persons, in order to carry them to the sovereigns, that they might learn our language, in order to discover what there is in the land and that, on their return, they might be tongues for the Christians and adopt our customs and the things of our faith.

Castaño (2005, 49) continues,

> Indian interpreters filled a role of servants and were exposed to an immersion method to learn Spanish. After his second journey, Columbus wrote in a letter addressed to the Catholic kings in 1495: "there are now sent with these ships some of the cannibals, men and women and boys and girls. These their highnesses can order to be

placed in charge of persons so that they may be able better to learn the language, employing them in forms of service."

Count Columbus, then, was an early proponent of service learning in the education of interpreters. Indeed, interpreters and translators among our forebears have been pressed into service as slaves and hailed as diplomats,[1] canonized as saints, and reviled in eponym,[2] "symbols of treachery and vile behavior … stereotypes of the liar, traitor and promiscuous lover" (Castaño 2005, 47). From our current vantage point it might seem quaint to consider "the low position most interpreters occupied in society as servants, slaves, [and] members of inferior castes" (Delisle and Woodsworth 1995, 244), as quoted in Castaño.

Role confusion is far from the only ambiguity with which interpreters struggle. In discussing the complexity of translating the 1995 *Dayton Framework for Peace in Bosnia-Herzegovina* from its original English version into Croatian and Serbian, Pehar (2006, 3) describes the dilemma of ambiguity:

> An ambiguous text is not fully meaningful yet—it is only potentially meaningful, and to attribute ambiguousness to it is to underline the fact that one has not yet determined its meaning. Therefore, one cannot translate ambiguity from a text written or spoken in one language into a different language; literally, one has nothing to translate. The authors have not offered any meaning that one should take from one language and transfer to, and house, in another.

With our roles and texts at times ambiguous, the *who* and the *what* in interpreting can easily lack focus. At those times, the *where*, *when*, and *why* of interpreting take on greater significance. Courtroom, doctor's office, and staff lounge flicker on one screen while the spinning hands of a clock and the fluttering pages of a calendar zoom by on another. Headlines blare about mass layoffs, legal wrangling, and the rising cost of health care.

Inquiry has long been employed as an antidote to ambiguity. In the early organization of public inquiry in the Western world, we saw the development of "three paths," a trivium of grammar, logic, and rhetoric put forward as the building blocks of a liberal education. This sine qua non

---

1. See Roland (1999).
2. See definition and etymology for *Felipello*.

for free people to participate fully and meaningfully in their societies is also an historic representation of the human desire to think and communicate effectively and clearly.

With this book, the corpus of what is known about interpreting and how well it is known continues to grow apace. Interpreting education, once the province of families and communities, is now an established academic discipline. Our curiosity and creative energies have wrought an impressive number of books, journals, articles, and media. We are well provisioned with theories and models, paradigms and schema.

Questions about who interpreters are and what interpreters want are more easily addressed. Not that long ago, it was rare to see an interpreter working. Nowadays, interpreters are public fixtures, reliably present in many community and private events. In addition to a growing corpus of thought, we have a large body of work done publicly. Both our theories and our practices are readily available for scrutiny.

The path from "low position" to respected practice has seen some dramatic twists and turns. Indeed, one of the most significant recent changes is seen in the code of ethics espoused by the Registry of Interpreters for the Deaf. In its latest iteration (2005), we see the exaltation of the word *professional*, which appears more than 30 times, an eight-fold increase from the 1979 version. In the 26 years between codes, professionalism gained such cachet among interpreters for the Deaf that we added it to the title of our code of conduct!

No sooner do interpreters fix the badge of professionalism to their coats than inquiry demands its due. What does it mean to be a professional? How best to determine standards for professional conduct? In the course of our work as interpreters, are there circumstances within which professional standards ought not apply to our work? What then?

Once again, we find inquiry and interpretation neatly juxtaposed. Careful consideration of who we have been in the past, and who we are now, is our best chance at self-determination over who we become and what we do in the future.

If you are interested in such things, this is the book for you.

Rico Peterson
Pittsford, NY
March 2013

# REFERENCES

Castaño, Victoria Ríos. 2005. Fictionalising interpreters: Traitors, lovers, and liars in the conquest of the America. Special issue, *Linguistica Antverpiensia* 4:47–61. Retrieved March 26, 2013, from http://www.lans-tts.be/img/NS4/Rios.PDF.

Delisle, Jean, and Judith Woodsworth, eds. 1995. *Les traducteurs dans l'histoire*. Ottawa: les Presses de l'Université d'Ottawa/Éditions UNESCO.

Herrera, Estela. 2002. What can interpreters learn from Aristotle and Stanislavsky? *ATA Chronicle*, September: 31–37.

Jane, C., trans. and ed. 1930. *The voyages of Christopher Columbus being the journals of his first and third, and the letters concerning his first and last voyages*. London: Argonaut Press.

Pehar, Dražen. 2006. *Is a translator of ambiguity necessarily a traitor?* Retrieved March 26, 2013, from http://www.academia.edu/2701186/Is_a_Translator_of_Ambiguity_Necessarily_a_Traitor.

Roland, Ruth. 1999. *Interpreters as diplomats: A diplomatic history of the role of interpreters in world politics*. Ames: University of Iowa Press.

# ACKNOWLEDGMENTS

We acknowledge the enthusiasm with which all of our contributors responded to our concept when approached to participate in this project. Their inspired work and attention to timelines helped make this an enjoyable experience for all of us.

We especially appreciate the encouragement from Dr. Cynthia Roy to pursue this project at a time when we most needed it. We doubt this volume would have come to fruition without her.

We also are grateful for the time and energy of our colleagues Laurie Swabey and Brenda Nicodemus, who had developed a writing project that involved all of our chapter authors. Indeed, they nurtured the seminal ideas for these chapters.

We also thank Ivey Wallace for her enthusiastic response to our proposed ideas; she guided us through the editing and publication of this volume.

Last but never least, we thank our sweet husbands who—as always—support our work and keep us grounded at the same time: Gene Michieli and Rick Monikowski.

ELIZABETH A. WINSTON AND
CHRISTINE MONIKOWSKI

# *Introduction*

This volume invites educators and researchers of interpreting education to bridge the widening gap between research and teaching and to infuse each with the other to inform the future of our field. Each chapter in this volume is written by a leading researcher/educator and addresses how research in interpreting must impact our teaching. Each chapter is accompanied by two commentaries prepared by internationally renowned leaders in interpreting education and research. The commentaries bring new dimension to this volume, offering a starting point for reflection and discussion about growing needs and evolving paradigms in interpreting education. Each author and commentator invite you, our colleague, to reflect and consider additional perspectives on the topics. We hope that you will join this crucial discussion!

Chapter 1, "The Academic's Dilemma: A Balanced and Integrated Career," highlights the dramatic increase in American Sign Language (ASL) / English interpreter education programs in institutions of higher education across the United States. This increase in programs requires educators who can succeed in the academy, which increasingly means completing doctoral degrees and ongoing research and practice. Monikowski shines a light on the evolving responsibilities of and challenges faced by interpreting educators in the academy—teaching, practice, and research—and reflects on the need to achieve a balanced and integrated career for interpreter educators.

In chapter 2, "Researching Medical Interpreting: An Applied Linguistics Perspective," Tebble uses systemic functional linguistics along with a variety of research concepts and methods from other relevant disciplines. She provides theoretical insights into both the language used in interpreted specialist medical consultations and the practical outcomes, especially for the education of medical interpreters and physicians who use the services of medical interpreters. The chapter is also a case study of empirical research in hospitals for medical interpreters and applied linguists who intend to undertake research into aspects of medical interpreting or other dialogue interpreting and can provide material for educational courses.

In chapter 3, "The Impact of Linguistic Theory on Interpretation Research Methodology," Janzen examines why the interpretation researcher needs both a well-developed, useful theory of linguistic structure and a viable theory of interpretation. He emphasizes that these can work together as tools to benefit the most from interpretation research. Basic to this discussion is that a theory of language must underlie assumptions about language, even if that theory is not consciously or overtly explicated. This is basic because such assumptions exist regardless of an educator's awareness and profoundly impact the researcher's work.

Shaffer offers a review of our history with an emphasis on the metaphors that inform, influence, and perhaps even plague us in chapter 4, "Evolution of Theory, Evolution of Role: How Interpreting Theory Shapes Interpreter Role." She predicts that we as interpreters are obligated to rid ourselves of the conduit metaphor of meaning and view decision-making processes more clearly. She further argues that if we finally consider the message from a linguistic and cultural perspective, we will find that we need to revisit how we describe our role.

Finally, in chapter 5, "Infusing Evidence into Interpreting Education: An Idea Whose Time Has Come," Winston explores the pressing need for, the rich potential of, and the challenges associated with infusing effective evidence-based teaching practices into sign language interpreting education. She argues for a comprehensive and principled approach to interpreting education that is founded on the principles of effective evidence-based practices.

We invite you to explore this volume and ponder the challenges discussed in each chapter and the stimulating questions raised in the commentaries. Do they reflect your experiences and needs? Have you been struggling with similar issues? What can you do in response to the need for and emergence of these evolving paradigms in our field? What can we as a field do to inspire ongoing evolution and to embrace necessary changes with enthusiasm, wisdom, and humor?

CHRISTINE MONIKOWSKI

# The Academic's Dilemma: A Balanced and Integrated Career

## Abstract

The study of interpreting between American Sign Language (ASL) and English is a relatively new discipline linked to linguistics, communication, sociology, and studies of social interaction. Scholarship is key in this "academization." The dramatic increase in ASL/English interpreter education programs in institutions of higher education across the United States requires instructors who can succeed in the academy, which often means completing doctoral degrees and navigating through the tenure and promotion processes. As a "practice profession," our constituencies expect us to interpret; as academics our constituencies expect us to teach and conduct research. In this chapter I address the challenges faced in the academy—teaching, practice, and research—and reflect on a balanced and integrated career for interpreter educators making their way through this culture of teaching and learning.

A BALANCED and integrated career filled with intellectual stimulation, a continued sense of learning, respect and recognition from colleagues and students, financial reward (one must be realistic), and a happy and fulfilled life—is this not what we all want?

I became a teacher because I enjoyed being a student but could not financially afford to be a perennial student; teaching seemed to be the next best thing. I could continue to read, learn, conduct research, interact with like-minded colleagues, influence the next passionate generation, and earn a living at the same time. That was what I wanted to do and, to a certain

1

extent, it is what I still strive to do. My life in the academy is a good one and I am afforded many opportunities to keep my energy flowing. The real challenges are how to organize my time, how to identify appropriate topics for research and writing, with whom to collaborate, and when to say "no."

Legato's classic "three-legged stool" (2006, 71) for a faculty member in higher education describes the three primary responsibilities: teaching, practice, and research. (Legato's work specifically addresses physicians who teach in medical school, but the model applies to other disciplines, especially interpreting, regardless of the languages involved.) ASL/English interpreting has a history in teaching and practice. As we continue to move into higher education, we are coming to grips with the importance of research; it is "the heart of what [teaching in the academy] is all about" (Boyer 1990, 1). I strive to be a scholar and maintain a balance in my professional life; addressing these three responsibilities requires its own amount of time and attention.

As I approach my 30th year in higher education (seven years in a lecturer position at a major university in the American Southwest prior to the tenure-track position I now hold), I appreciate the opportunity to reflect upon the time and energy I have expended to arrive at the rank of full professor (which required one tenure portfolio and two promotion portfolios over the years) and the choices I have made along the way.

## INTERPRETER EDUCATION PROGRAMS (IEPs) IN INSTITUTIONS OF HIGHER EDUCATION

## Where Are We Now?

Although the field of translation is a well-established, well-respected, and venerable area of academic inquiry, interpreting between American Sign Language (ASL) and English is a relatively new interdisciplinary area of academic study linked to a variety of disciplines such as linguistics, communication, sociology, and studies of social interaction. This is manifested in the qualifications for faculty positions in this discipline in institutions of higher education (IHEs); the required qualifications are not consistent.

The differences between typical two-year and four-year IHEs in the United States make the issues even cloudier. According to the U.S.

Department of Education National Center for Education Statistics (2010),[1] there are 1,180,153 full-time faculty employed in four-year IHEs (colleges and universities) and 216,756 full-time faculty employed in two-year IHEs (most commonly called community colleges) in the United States.

The American Association of University Professors (AAUP) lists five categories of higher education institutions in the United States: category I, those that offer doctoral degrees; category IIA, that offer no higher than master's degrees; category IIB, that offer only baccalaureate degrees; category III, that offer only associate's degrees and have academic ranks for faculty; and category IV, that offer only associate's degrees and do not have any academic ranks for faculty (AAUP 2009, 45). Only the institutions in category I are considered research institutions, where faculty are expected to conduct and publish research for tenure and promotion. Other IHEs are often considered teaching institutions with the emphasis on effective teaching and scholarship associated with teaching and learning.

The tenure process at community colleges typically does not require the faculty member to publish articles or book—and therefore does not require research—although "evidence of good teaching" is required because that is the primary responsibility. "Most community colleges do offer some version of tenure—and it's often relatively easy to get. Unlike their counterparts at four-year institutions, who may be required to publish numerous articles and perhaps even a book to be considered for tenure, community-college faculty members have no such mandate" (Jenkins 2003, 1).

The advertisement for my current tenure-track position required a master's degree but I was only a few months away from completing my doctorate when I was hired. The level of research I was comfortable producing carried over into my pursuit of tenure. Coming from a huge state university where tenure-track positions required doctoral degrees, I was amazed at the number of faculty members in IEPs with master's degrees, but at that point in time most IEPs offered two-year degrees. Things have changed somewhat since then.

Today interpreter educator positions in four-year IHEs tend to indicate "doctoral degree preferred," whereas other disciplines require that

---

1. Most recent data available.

candidates "must hold an earned PhD." The doctoral degree serves two purposes: First, it produces faculty who are at the top of their knowledge base in their field, and second, it produces faculty (i.e., potential scholars) who can contribute to the research and body of writing in their specific area of expertise, moving the field—and hence the practice—forward. We bemoan the fact that there are too few qualified applicants with doctoral degrees but do little to advance the promise of those degrees. Higher education specifically for ASL/English interpreters is almost nonexistent. For example, in 2005, a graduate program was established at Boston's Northeastern University: the master's in interpreting pedagogy. It was a small online degree developed by leading interpreting educators and researchers but was eliminated after only a few years. Gallaudet University recently established a doctoral program in interpreting "designed to prepare interpreter educators and researchers" (Gallaudet University 2012); their master's degree in interpretation is well established. In addition, two other programs have since been established. Western Oregon University (Monmouth) offers a master's in interpreting studies online during the traditional academic year and onsite during the summer. The University of North Florida (Jacksonville) offers a similar blended approach for their master's, which includes a partnership with a video relay service agency, an innovative collaboration. Yet, when we argue that there is no terminal degree in our field, we relegate our field to sit and wait for a PhD in ASL/English interpreting rather than embracing the varied seemingly tangential disciplines that are part of what interpreters need to know. Those who have already completed doctoral degrees in our field have a wide variety of expertise and knowledge: adult learning, communication, curriculum and instruction, education, and linguistics. The expertise we have gained from these disciplines has given us a broad view of our field, and we should continue to encourage our students to pursue such degrees.

Ninety-one IEPs[2] report a total of 367 faculty who teach interpreting courses; 103 of them (28%) are in tenured or tenure-track positions (Cokely and Winston 2008, 7). The challenge for us is to make our way through this culture of teaching and learning in a balanced and realistic

---

2. The Conference of Interpreter Educators, the professional organization for instructors in IEPs, reports a total of 130 IEPs in the United States.

way, but as latecomers to IHEs we are hard-pressed to catch up with the established disciplines of higher education.

Although no data could be found on this topic, in talking to numerous faculty in IHEs, there is a clear bias against online doctoral degrees. Many colleges and universities in the United States offer online coursework and degrees, but many in the academy see the online or distance doctoral degree as "less than" the traditional one. Perhaps this will change as more brick-and-mortar IHEs offer comparable online degrees.

Some would argue that we are still involved in an evolution from the early training programs that offered two-year degrees. This is often evident in how we designate interpreter *training* programs (ITPs) and interpreter *education* programs (IEPs). Indeed, my own program is housed in an IHE of technology that offers "career-oriented studies" rather than liberal arts. Most students here are accepted into an already-declared major, allowing little time for exploration and the typical liberal studies approach to courses. Although there is a definite shift toward four-year degrees (my program changed from two-year to four-year in 2001), there are still vestiges of the original training-program approach (i.e., two years or less) established in the 1970s when the first six federally funded programs offered "basic interpreter education" (Frishberg 1990, 13).[3] The establishment of those original programs ushered in "a dramatic increase in the academic institutionalization of [teaching ASL], the language of the [American Deaf] Community (Cokely 2005, 14)."

By 1980, there were more than 50 colleges or universities in the United States that housed interpreter training programs (Cokely 2005, 14–15). In 2008, 91 IEPs participated in a national survey (out of a reported 130 IEPs) and 64 (70%) still offer two-year degrees and/or certificates of study (Cokely and Winston 2008, 4). Currently, 70% of our IEPs are housed in IHEs that fall into either category III or IV, where all faculty members are referred to as "instructors" or "professors" but in reality there is no distinction (AAUP 2009, 45).

---

3. The Rehabilitation Services Administration of the federal government funded the National Interpreter Training Consortium (NITC), which included six institutions: California State University, Northridge; Gallaudet College; New York University; St. Paul Technical Vocational Institute; Seattle Central Community College; and the University of Tennessee, Knoxville.

According to the U.S. Department of Education, approximately 19% of full-time faculty at community colleges hold doctoral degrees, compared to almost 79% of full-time faculty at category I and IIA four-year colleges and universities (National Center for Educational Statistics 2004b). Because 70% of our IEPs are in community colleges, it seems clear that expectations for faculty are different in these two kinds of institutions.

The recent changes in the requirements for the national Registry of Interpreters for the Deaf (RID) certification process are having an impact on the preparation of interpreters. As of June 2012, RID requires a baccalaureate degree before one sits for certification; the degree need not be in interpreting. As a result, many of the two-year programs are exploring "two-plus-two" options with nearby four-year degree colleges/universities, are refocusing to offer degrees in ASL or Deaf studies, or are making the change to four-year interpreting degrees, although it is unclear how many will either close or adapt. Therefore, we are moving away from "training" programs that had a "distinctly vocational profile" (Pöchhacker 2004, 31), and we need faculty who can represent that discipline in the academy and address the slow "academization" (30) in our field. It is unclear how many two-year programs are really going to make the change.

This shift toward four-year degrees in IHEs requires qualified faculty members with terminal degrees: doctoral degrees in appropriate disciplines. Although this is normal for well-established disciplines, this is still new for faculty members in interpreting education. Typical faculty members in other disciplines are required to teach, publish, and provide service, most often in the form of committee work, to their departments and universities. As IEPs move from community colleges to universities—in established departments of linguistics, education, communication, modern languages—our faculty must be able to hold their own among their colleagues in the academy. Instructors hired in our early IEPs were well-respected interpreters who had experience in the day-to-day business of interpreting, may have achieved an undergraduate/graduate degree in a "related" field, but tended not to have doctoral degrees.

Cokely stated that the "pivotal 1972–1975 period" in ASL/English interpretation offered "activities that were mistaken for accomplishments" and "one is struck by the virtual absence of research" (2005, 18). Although reliable research in our field continues to be intermittent and sparse, there is a nascent canon of work, mostly produced by those few individuals who have earned doctorates. Despite this, Pöchhacker (31–32) maintains that the United States is a "paragon" for education and research related to interpreting, especially the master's degree program at Gallaudet University, which has "proved seminal to the promotion of research on sign language interpreting." Be that as it may, the dearth of graduate programs in interpreting in the United States contributes to the production of interpreters who can practice the profession but who do not have the appropriate credentials to secure tenured employment in IHEs; consequently, they are not the scholars we desperately need to conduct research and move us forward. Our current undergraduate IEPs prepare students to interpret; employment is the goal, not graduate school nor research. The disconnect is clear. Perhaps what limits the growth of graduate programs is the question, Who would enroll in them? Another factor is that IHEs are hiring more part-time faculty, not only in our field but in general.

## CHALLENGES FACED IN THE ACADEMY

Historically, full-time tenured faculty appointments constitute the core of an institution of higher education: "academics value tenure, and tenure remains the prototype of the ideal academic career" (Gappa et al. 2007, 54). Regardless of egalitarianism, there is a pecking order within the academy; the rights and responsibilities that come with tenure do not come with alternative appointments. Tenured faculty have the potential to move a discipline forward by conducting and disseminating research. The permanency connected with tenure can allow for a more balanced life; the pressure to prove oneself abates and the freedom to make choices increases. Academic freedom allows for creativity in teaching, for individuality in research, and for innovation in service.

In the 21st century, higher education in the United States and worldwide faces many important issues, including but not limited to intellectual property rights, national/international security, economic belt-tightening, and rising tuition rates. One of the primary issues in the United States is the changing demographics of the faculty: We know that 68% of all faculty appointments in the academy are non-tenure-track positions (AAUP n.d.). We know that 35% of full-time faculty members are in non-tenure-track positions (Gappa et al. 2007, 66). And we know that in our institutions of higher education, there are 1.4 million full-time professionals who have instructional responsibilities. Only 47% (approximately 658,000) of them had faculty status and only 30% of those 47% (approximately 197,000) either had tenure or were on the tenure track (Knapp et al. 2009, 3). Regardless of which statistic one accepts, "the majority of faculty members teaching in American colleges and universities today are not on the tenure track" (Gappa et al. 2007, 82). The American Association of University Professors (AAUP) believes that

> Because faculty tenure is the only secure protection for academic freedom in teaching, research, and service, the declining percentage of tenured faculty means that academic freedom is increasingly at risk. Academic freedom is a fundamental characteristic of higher education, necessary to preserve an independent forum for free inquiry and expression, and essential to the mission of higher education to serve the common good. (AAUP 2003)

This move toward *contingent faculty*[4] (sometimes labeled "alternative appointments," a term that includes both part- and full-time faculty who are appointed off the tenure track) brings its own issues of working conditions and pay, but the requirements for achieving tenure are still quite stringent, allowing institutions of higher learning to become more selective—all the more reason for our signed language interpreting discipline to have faculty with doctoral degrees. The ranks of contingent faculty continue to grow and their working conditions continue to deteriorate. The contingent faculty members hired are overwhelmingly in long-established disciplines and departments where there are already a number of tenured/tenure-track faculty; the lament is strong in English, history, psychology, and so forth. However, interpreter educators have long been contingent faculty in a contingent discipline, with too few among us having attained

---

4. "The term 'contingent faculty' calls attention to the tenuous relationship between academic institutions and the part- and full-time non-tenure-track faculty members who teach in them. For example, teachers hired to teach one or two courses for a semester, experts or practitioners who are brought in to share their field experience, and whole departments of full-time non-tenure-track English composition instructors are all 'contingent faculty'. The term includes adjuncts, who are generally compensated on a per-course or hourly basis, as well as full-time non-tenure-track faculty who receive a salary" (AAUP, n.d.).

tenure appointments. As stated previously, 72% of our IEP faculty are not tenured or in tenure-track positions. We do not have much research to support our pedagogical approaches, our curricula, or our course development. Although we are latecomers, there is still an important place for us. We need a core faculty who can contribute to the canon, who can set the standards for the field, who can contribute to the academy, and show that we are a discipline worthy of research and publication. A glaring example of the pitfalls is that all the faculty for the online degree offered at Northeastern University were contingent, which probably contributed to its demise.

The first hurdle we face is to earn the doctoral degrees that prepare us with a strong foundation in a discipline and a clear understanding of the rigors of research and publication. As of this writing, Gallaudet offers the only doctoral degree in interpreting, which is certainly a step forward for our field, but it is not necessarily the preferred degree for all our faculty of the future. There are many options, such as doctoral degrees in adult learning, curriculum, and linguistics. It is time we stop whining about the lack of terminal degrees in our field and raise our heads to see the many possibilities that could support our academization!

# THE NEXT GENERATION IN HIGHER EDUCATION

## The Academy

Given the move toward contingent or alternative faculty positions in the academy, it gives one pause to consider whether completing a doctoral degree is realistic. Who will replace the current tenured faculty in our IEPs and how can we ensure the future of our field? The love of learning is not enough in our world today, unless one is financially independent. Most of us need to ask what kind of job awaits after the doctoral degree. Life in the academy is not what it used to be: Everyone is expected to do more with less. Contingent faculty members are increasing while the number of tenure-track positions are decreasing at an alarming rate. If our field is to continue its march toward academization, research needs to be the heart of our work. However, at a recent webinar, directors of the three master's programs in the United States were asked about potential employment for their graduates. The consensus was that earning such a degree would allow for advancement in nonacademic settings; teaching positions were not mentioned as the primary goal.

There has been a "vision of the ideal worker" in higher education for quite some time. "Ideal academic workers moved from their doctoral programs ... directly into tenure-track faculty positions" and they "dedicated themselves fully to their work, particularly during" the pretenure period. This mindset was true for the "middle-class white men" who composed the faculty in higher education "from approximately the middle of the nineteenth century to the middle of the twentieth" (Gappa et al. 2007, 26–27). Although the demographics of the academy have changed in recent years, this view remains. "One of the most significant demographic changes for faculty is the increasing presence of women"; in 2003, women were 44% of new faculty members, up from 20% in 1969 (59). In addition, "in 2003, for the first time, women earned 51% of all doctoral degrees awarded" (61).

## ASL/English Interpreting

Gappa et al. (2007, 29) continue: "Although men and women alike are expressing concern about their personal lives [and the strain of balancing work/home], women in particular have a difficult time finding a satisfactory balance between home and work." This seems to be of particular importance to our field, given that the majority of interpreters are women. The RID reports a total membership of 13,778; approximately 85% are females (personal correspondence, Erica White, January 25, 2010). The Conference of Interpreter Trainers (CIT; the professional organization for interpreter educators in the United States) reported 272 members in 2002–2003, 185 of whom responded to that year's demographic survey. Of those 185 participants, 156 (84%) were female (CIT 2004, 1). (See table 1.) Is this part of the reason why we have so few scholars with doctoral degrees? Did the field of ASL/English interpreting miss out on the era of middle-class white men as a core group of scholars? The scales tipped in higher education in 2003, with more women earning doctoral degrees than men. The scales in our field tipped a long time ago toward women, but we have not kept pace with the trend in higher education. For the most part, our female educators, although a majority of the organization, do not have doctoral degrees.

Table 1. Conference of Interpreter Trainers 2002–2003, Demographic Survey

| Total responses to survey | 185 | Percentage (%) |
|---|---|---|
| Female | 156 | 84 |
| Male | 25 | 14 |
| Members holding PhDs | 20 | 11 |
| Members holding MA/MS/Med | 109 | 59 |
| Members holding BA/BS | 44 | 26 |
| Members holding AA/AS | 4 | 2 |
| Members, "college in progress" (no indication which degree) | 3 | 1 |

Unfortunately, given a few minutes, it is possible to name all those in our field who do have doctoral degrees. I daresay it would be impossible for an English professor at any American college or university to create a list of his/her peers in a comparable amount of time.

I have no data to explain why individuals—female or male—do not pursue doctoral degrees in our field, only anecdotal comments that are familiar to us all: high tuition, no local programs, family responsibilities, no future positions, etc. Many sacrifices need to be made by and for the doctoral student—family, financial, social; we have all made them and survived. I have yet to meet anyone in our field who regrets the degree and the opportunities it affords (although I am sure there is someone out there). We are, after all, in the business of education. What we, as a field, must address is how to encourage our next generation to pursue terminal degrees. Every single graduate with a doctorate leads us further in the academization process.

## Reflections on My Career

## Teaching

The first leg of that three-legged stool (teaching, practice, research), and the most important for me, is teaching: "For the truth is that teaching is frequently a gloriously messy pursuit in which surprise, shock, and risk are endemic" and "all teachers worth their salt regularly ask themselves whether or not they are doing the right thing" (Brookfield 1990, 1–2). I work hard and enjoy the work immensely, but I also enjoy thinking about teaching, reflecting on what I do, mulling over my approach to a topic, and talking to like-minded colleagues about the paths we have chosen. My philosophy of teaching is straightforward, although it has evolved—thankfully—over the years. With time and experience, I have come to know that teaching is more about learning and thinking than about content. If I can just help my students understand how important it is for them to reflect upon their work—in both skill and content courses—then I have succeeded. I thoroughly enjoy interpreting between ASL and English and I enjoy the interaction the process requires. I want my students to become confident and comfortable so they, too, can enjoy the process.

I have experienced the gloriously messy pursuit; faculty who say they have not are not being honest with themselves. The challenges to grading have been few, but they drain my energy. The incidents of cheating have been sparse, thank goodness. The drama of many students' lives is ongoing. I have questioned whether I help or hinder students' success. I have been stung by remarks on course evaluations and I have been inspired by notes from current and former students. I have dreaded watching the recordings of student projects. I have basked in the successful presentations of final projects. A bumpy ride, indeed!

I continue to be challenged by keeping my courses interesting and up to date; it is sometimes difficult when I continue to teach the same course year after year, but that is what also inspires me to read and write. The issues in my class and the challenges with which my students struggle motivate me to seek out solutions and in-depth understanding of those struggles. One of the most rewarding aspects of my position is academic reading. I read and attend conferences with other like-minded faculty whose disciplines are far removed from mine but with whom I share a passion for teaching and learning. I read about what it takes to be a successful teacher, from how to organize successful groups to introspective works that challenge my life's choices (Brookfield, Dewey, Freire, Palmer, McKeachie, Millis among others). I have found solace and stimulation for my teaching with colleagues in other IEPs around the country. Teaching and learning is not what I do; it is who I am.

## Practice

In recent years, most interpreter educators and working interpreters have begun to call ourselves a "practice profession,"[5] which involves practice of the actual work during the educational experience, attempting to claim our place among the fields of education, social work, law, and medicine by requiring practicum or internship opportunities. We also have begun to discuss the professional consultation and our concerns about confidentiality. This implies that the educator in an IEP needs to also be a practitioner. Our resemblance to the aforementioned professions is a bit murky. Not all law professors are practicing lawyers, nor are all medical professors practicing physicians. However, we believe if one is going to teach interpreting, one needs the bona fides, the ongoing practice, to give credibility in the classroom. We certainly have had definitive research from individuals who are not practicing interpreters, but those who do practice often have underlying and unmentioned doubts about the work of those who do not, perhaps because there is no clear connection to the Deaf community and to those interpreters who practice the profession on a regular basis. The other half of this practice approach to our profession is teaching; where do we practice that? More colleges and universities are offering opportunities for doctoral students to practice their teaching in those very programs (beyond the traditional responsibilities for the teaching assistants). This is an issue that the academy continues to face and that our field needs to acknowledge.

As we attempt to hire faculty with credentials to prepare them for success, we must also be cognizant of the fact that those faculty need to be practitioners in the interpreting community. Many of our early educators were successful and well-respected working interpreters, and as a field we still recognize the importance of that practice. It is imperative that our faculty continue to have contact with Deaf consumers. In fact, at a recent conference of the Association of Visual Language Interpreters of Canada,[6] it was quite clear that Deaf faculty and Deaf interpreters are finding their place in the field. The collaboration between hearing interpreters and

---

5. This has come to the fore most notably through the work of Robyn Dean and Robert Pollard in their demand–control research and publications.

6. Association of Visual Language Interpreters of Canada 2012 in Calgary, Alberta: Creativity and Collaboration.

these members of the Deaf community is an intellectual endeavor that reflects mutual respect.

Classroom instruction can then resonate with veracity; we understand the issues, not just from our distant past but from yesterday. If we experience the process of interpreting on a regular basis, we can share the successes and failures with students in an active, exciting way that transcends articles and in-class activities. If they cannot see our passion for the work, how can we expect them to be passionate? Observations allow for reality and integrity, the "wholeness … [that] is integral to my selfhood" (Palmer 2007, 14). In reality, interpreting is about connections (video-relay interpreting notwithstanding). Interpreters tend to be people who are about the connections with individuals. What better way to contemplate our interactions than interpreting and facing the challenges of those interactions on a regular basis? What better way to connect with students than to have them observe our work and to see us face reality?

The practice of interpreting should inform our teaching. If we want thoughtful students, then reflection on our own work as interpreters is crucial. Palmer (2007, 30) asks, "How did it come to be that our main goal as academicians turned out to be performance?" We should not simply perform; we should share, reflect, and learn while teaching. For me, the best way to continue to learn about interpreting is to practice it on a regular basis. After all these years as an interpreter, I continue to find events and/or interactions that challenge my thinking. I continue to reflect on the work I render and the decisions I make. Interpreting keeps all of us honest and connected to the community, engendering credibility among consumers and colleagues (i.e., working interpreters). Does our teaching reflect our experiences? Are discussions in an ethics course grounded in reality? A cursory review of current job listings for faculty in IEPs shows that, if not required, then at minimum "preference will be given" to applicants with certification from the national professional organization in the United States, the Registry of Interpreters for the Deaf (RID), indicating the importance of experience in the field. There is no data available on this concept, but conventional wisdom indicates this is de rigueur for our faculty.

This is where the issue of time rears its head. When pressed to consider priorities, how does one account for the time involved in accepting interpreting assignments? When one is preparing a tenure portfolio, into which category does this activity fall: scholarship, professional activities, service to the institute, or service to the community? Will a tenure-review committee understand the importance of this activity? If we present it as important, then the tenure committee will probably see it the same way. If our interpreting informs our teaching, then it is vital to our portfolio.

Before the onset of video-relay interpreting, my institution was purported to be the largest employer of signed language interpreters in the world; there are more than 100 full-time interpreters on our campus and numerous other part-time or freelance interpreters. I have often interpreted classes in the evenings after my faculty responsibilities were fulfilled. I am fortunate because these assignments were usually within walking distance of my office, but they still required time. This work serves to keep me humble, to remember what a challenge it can be, and to show my students that my in-class self is not "performance" but real. If appropriate permission is granted, they come to observe me and see a completely different side of me. It is not my class and I am subordinate to an unknown faculty member who may or may not share my approach to teaching. At that point, I am not a faculty member; I am an interpreter whose primary goal is successful communication between individuals who are not using the same language. Oh, what discussions I have with my students! The underclassmen see me interact with Deaf consumers, being "personable but not personal" (Witter-Merithew 1982, 12). The upperclassmen can see how I, too, struggle with complicated classifiers, how I need time to comprehend the signs and fingerspelling before I attempt to voice in English, and how I handle my mistakes. Sometimes they take a turn interpreting and everyone revels in the experience, including the deaf consumers. This keeps my teaching grounded in reality and helps me understand my students' fears and emotions as they prepare for their future. These experiences also keep me grounded in the community of approximately 1,200 Deaf students we have on campus.

These experiences also have an impact on my teaching in both skills courses and content courses. For example, the small-group activities I use for my ethics class come from dilemmas I experience when interpreting on campus. I use my role as instructor, with which my students are familiar, to illuminate my role as interpreter. This is often a good place to begin our discussion because my students' peers (i.e., the Deaf students on campus) will one day become their consumers.

## Research

The third leg of that academic stool is research (again, historically viewed as the most important); publish or perish still holds true. Tenure-track positions at category I IHEs require research, regardless of how it is defined. (See Boyer 1997 for an excellent discussion of the four elements of scholarship.)

Published research (i.e., scholarly work) is the foundation of a discipline. It should inform our curriculum and our approach to teaching. For lack of a better term, we have "flown by the seat of our pants" far too long. We need research to give us credibility, but I have no answers for how to increase the research we produce. Our field has pseudoscholars who present workshops not grounded in theory and who pontificate their point of view without sufficient knowledge of the discipline. We also have one-shot scholars (as does every discipline) who produce research, earn a degree, and then settle into an academic rut. Unfortunately, we all too often assume that if something is in print, it is indisputable.

Perhaps this is because we are a relatively young and small field of study, and we are not *expected* to be scholars. We have neither the history nor the credibility of many other disciplines, and we have so few faculty with terminal degrees that the academy seems to view us as special and therefore does not impose the same rigor on our faculty or afford us the same status when establishing new programs and positions. This is not where I want us to be.

Although teaching is my primary activity, I am expected to "engage in significant scholarship as measured by external disciplinary and professional standards as acknowledged by department and program practices of faculty review." Our tenured and tenure-track faculty are expected to engage in scholarly work and to disseminate their work by the normal means; ultimately, the goal of this scholarship is to "enhance the education of our students" (Rochester Institute of Technology [RIT] 2006). There is much flexibility in our definition of research because we are an institute of higher learning that includes a variety of technical disciplines ranging from our School of American Crafts, to our College of Science, to our College of Business. However, it is quite clear to all that scholarship is important. When I began my career here at RIT, I knew the first thing I had to do was publish an article from my dissertation, something expected by my dissertation advisor. My involvement with and my knowledge of my professional organizations gave me a built-in audience. I published several articles from the dissertation, including Monikowski 1995a and 1995b, and also was invited to present the information at several national conferences. These venues also introduced me to those in my field who conducted research and were forward-thinking leaders. Given my understanding of the march toward tenure, I welcomed the opportunities that my newly minted "paper" afforded me.

In my career, I have produced at least one publication per year, in addition to completing refereed presentations for my peers and workshops for working interpreters. My scholarship includes book reviews (I relish the opportunity to keep current: Monikowski 1996, 2001, 2004), primary authorship (language acquisition, my favorite: Monikowski 2005), secondary authorship (finding someone to write with—when it works—is a treat: Monikowski and Winston 2011, Monikowski and Peterson 2005, Winston and Monikowski 2004), collaborative presentations, data collection, reports on special projects and/or innovative curriculum, linguistic analysis of ASL, and research with my undergraduate students—Herrera, Orr, Williams, and Monikowski[7]—fairly typical for a faculty member in the humanities.

I also look to my teaching to guide my research. Technology and the explosion of using computers to enhance coursework led me to meet several colleagues not in my department but at my greater institution, which then led to other possibilities. Online courses and programs in ASL/English interpreting are quite common today, but when I first began in this tenure-track position, there was nothing. I had the good fortune to participate in a project that delivered professional development to educational interpreters living in rural areas of the Midwest.

I also seek out colleagues who are more experienced, more involved in research, more knowledgeable about a topic, and more energized than I am. Interacting with those people keeps me excited and challenged; I do

---

7. Such as a refereed presentation, "Educational interpreting: Insights from the field," presented at the New York State Educational Support Service Personnel Conference, Niagara Falls, NY, May 5, 2007, with my students Denise Herrera, Emily Orr, and Courtney Williams.

my best work when I know the bar is set high. I become excited to learn what they know and to think about things from their perspective. Because one of the reasons I wanted to secure a position as a faculty member in higher education was that I enjoyed learning, as I began my tenure-track career I sought out those who were "more."

One last comment about research and the doctoral degree. We do have—as does every discipline in every institution of higher learning— faculty with doctorates who see the degree as an end, rather than as a beginning, and the attainment of tenure represents the opportunity to ease up on the work. Certainly, the mere attainment of a doctoral degree does not prove anything; the passion and the desire to teach and to learn supersedes any degree. I have no solution for these individuals and neither, it seems, does anyone else in the academy, but I seek to align myself with faculty who motivate students and maintain a level of scholarship that ethically represents teaching and learning.

## MY BALANCED LIFE

## The Doctoral Degree: Entry Into the Academy

As stated by Sorcinelli, Austin, Eddy, and Beach (2006, 106), "The greatest complaint voiced by new faculty is lack of time—being overwhelmed by multiple responsibilities" and even experienced faculty members who are tenured point to not having "enough time to do my work" as a top complaint. Full-time faculty work approximately 53 hours a week with 58% of that time devoted to teaching, 20% to research, and almost 21% to "other" (U.S. Department of Education NCES 2008). These data are culled from 681,000 full-time faculty across 6,700 two- and four-year degree-granting institutions in the United States. We bring work home; we read students' papers on Sunday afternoon; we grade tests at midnight and at dawn. Despite this heavy burden, a substantial number of doctoral degrees are awarded annually: "U.S. academic institutions awarded 48,802 research doctorate degrees in 2008, the sixth consecutive annual increase in U.S. doctoral awards and the highest number ever reported" (National Science Foundation 2009). I assume many of these individuals plan to seek positions in the academy. Why are there so few seeking work in the field of

ASL/English interpreting? What mindset allows us to think we can continue to hire faculty who are not comparable to those in other fields and still think we are a true profession? How long are we to be mired in the academization process before we are ostracized by the academy? Conventional wisdom offers two thoughts to ponder: If one's dissertation is not completed within three years of the approved proposal, it will not be completed, and approximately 85% of candidates who have completed all required course work for the degree but not yet begun the dissertation never complete the dissertation. Across all disciplines more than 48,000 doctoral degrees were completed in 2008.

For four years (2005–2008) I was the coordinator for new faculty in my college; this included all new hires in a variety of academic departments, not just those in my own department. Each fall, approximately twelve new hires arrived (two or three tenure track, nine or ten contingent of one kind or another). My primary responsibility focused on those in the tenure-track positions: help them get settled, establish priorities, become familiar with the university resources, and begin a plan for tenure. Administrators told me it costs more than $2 million (including benefits) for a tenured faculty member, from hiring to retiring—a substantial investment. Many IHEs have some kind of entity that offers support for the new hires, including professional development opportunities, teaching and learning centers, mentoring experiences. In addition, more and more doctoral programs, not in education, are offering graduate students who work as teaching or graduate assistants a variety of experiences to develop their teaching skills. This helps those who are focusing on their content areas to consider a variety of pedagogical issues that can better prepare them for tenure-track positions in IHEs; topics may include how to develop a course, assess student work, etc. Faculty development is a growing field that addresses those already in the academy but also those just entering. Membership in the Professional and Organizational Development Network in Higher Education (POD Network), established in 1974, continues to increase every year. Numerous other organizations recognize the importance that faculty development plays in "promoting and disseminating effective educational practices" (Sorcinelli et al. 2006, xiv). The support this field offers to faculty also helps to promote scholarly work that Boyer (1990) discussed, a broader approach to research that recognizes the importance of successful teaching.

My dilemma was that we hired faculty members who had neither doctoral degrees nor experience teaching in higher education. Attempting to mentor individuals without some kind of underlying philosophical structure was quite challenging. I see a difference between content knowledge and ability to teach. Unfortunately, because there are so few individuals who are truly prepared, we are left to teach them how to teach. Certainly, a new teacher needs time and support to become successful, but most doctoral programs offer students the opportunity to gain knowledge about content (be it curriculum, learning styles, whatever) so the actual practice of teaching can become the focus of those first few years. I am at a loss to understand how an inexperienced faculty member without a doctoral degree can hope to earn tenure in either a category I or II IHE; he/she would be truly exceptional.

In our field we make too many exceptions and delude ourselves into thinking that our faculty are more qualified than their degrees indicate. Attend our professional conferences and you will find presentations in the program that purport to be research when in reality they simply represent data collection, lacking any analysis. Or worse, presentations are offered that represent an individual's opinion with no supporting literature or research. More than forty years after the establishment of those original IEPs, we still mistake "activities for accomplishment." Unfortunately, this does not earn us the respect we need from other members of the academy. This puts us on unequal footing and makes collegiality within the IHE difficult. Gappa et al. already reported that "the lack of collegiality that some tenure-track faculty now experience" is a challenge for new faculty (2007, 78). "Good teaching requires colleagueship" (Rice 2000, 15). Lacking the standard doctoral degree is one more barrier to that collegiality.

## Tenure and Promotion

My current university has a very clear set of guidelines for tenure and promotion. When I interviewed for an assistant professor position, I inquired about the process and was immediately presented with several documents on policies and procedures for tenure and promotion; I found that very heartening. The process was not easy, but it was quite clear. It was not a checklist but it offered enough information to help me understand what was expected. From my date of hire, I knew I would achieve tenure and I developed a plan that would take me there. Those first few years required a discipline that mirrored the work I did during my doctoral program; I sacrificed many Sunday afternoons trying to stay ahead of the work but I also enjoyed the process. It was what I wanted to do and I was happy to be doing it. I had always wanted to teach; my undergraduate work prepared me to teach high school English but that never happened. Along the way, my interest and experiences in signed language interpreting focused my studies on linguistics and education because I thought I could help interpreters learn how to be more successful.

I sought out tenured faculty to learn about their experiences and developed a five-year plan that would lead to a successful tenure review. My IHE requires an annual plan of work every fall and an annual appraisal at the end of the academic year; each faculty member reflects on his/her work in four areas: (1) primary area of responsibility; (2) professional development and communication plan; (3) professional activities and scholarship; and (4) campus and community service. Consequently, every fall I develop an overarching plan for the year, itemizing possible activities, committees, opportunities for service, etc. At the end of the academic year, I reflect on my plan and then write a review of how well I think I accomplished that plan. It is not meant to be a simple checklist; the act of reflecting upon one's year is important because next year's plan needs to include a continuation of one's goals. This is the importance of a long-term plan. When it was time for the actual tenure review process, the committee wanted to see how I documented evidence of "tenurability": "the major criterion for awarding tenure should be excellence in his/her primary area of professional responsibility" (Rochester Institute of Technology 2006, 5).[8] Excellence in teaching is an elusive target, and hence the importance of a comprehensive plan that includes a philosophy of teaching that evolves with experience. I needed to reflect on my daily work and show how I attempted to improve the areas of weakness and develop my strengths. Preparing my portfolio for the tenure committee was made easier because of my annual appraisal documents.

---

8. Unfortunately, a lot of this documentation is done to stave off lawsuits in the event that an individual is denied tenure, but for many department chairpersons, it really is seen as an important part of one's growth.

The promotion process was also quite clear, although again not easy. When I earned tenure, my IHE did not automatically include promotion from assistant to associate professor (this has since been changed). The promotion process to full professor will continue to be separate, continue to recognize the candidate as one who shows "evidence of superior performance in his/her academic and professional qualifications" and who is recognized "as a role model in the primary area(s) of job responsibility and demonstrate outstanding professional accomplishments and service within and outside" our IHE (Rochester Institute of Technology 2007, 13–14). One must truly demonstrate leadership in a variety of areas, most notably one's primary area of responsibility within our IHE and in the greater domain of one's area of expertise. Even after one is promoted to full professor, annual appraisals are used by administrators to determine merit pay increases.

## Life's Pleasures

There is a rhythm to the academic calendar, and learning how to manage its ebb and flow is important. Autumn holds all the promise and hope of new students, new classes, and new projects. It also includes anxiety about the unknown—a change in administration, perhaps, or curriculum revision, or a different office. The excitement I experience always brings me back to my childhood and those days of new pencils and new books. The depth of winter in this area is quite remarkable and spring often comes later than in other parts of the country; everyone's energy wanes. Then graduation day arrives and we all celebrate our students' achievements. The years fly by and the work continues, unceasingly it seems at times. Because of this, it is even more important to attend to oneself and one's personal needs.

My time away from work is special to me; my husband, my family, and my friends support me and give me great joy. My exercise time is important to me and I am careful to guard it because it keeps me happy and healthy. These forays into the real world energize me to return to my daily tasks. A side note … during my doctoral program, every once in a while, my advisor could not be found in his office or in the student union or in the library. I later learned that he would disappear—to the movie theater in the middle of the day. It was his escape and now, having experienced some of what he experienced, I think of him and although I do not go to the movies, I do escape.

To the uninitiated, working in the academy affords "summers off" (you can hear the envy when you talk to friends and family in the business world). The scholar knows that is not true. Summer is a time to write the articles, plan for the presentations, and read the journals that have accumulated during the academic year. Those days do have a different energy and need to be enjoyed because the ability to refresh oneself is important, but sometimes it comes from presenting at a conference where you meet energetic colleagues who stimulate your thinking. Sometimes it comes from participating in a campus workshop for new faculty, and sometimes it comes from an early morning bicycle ride along the canal with the love of your life!

Perhaps the lament about "time" should be balanced with an understanding of the importance of "time management." A balanced life is a healthy and happy life; there is time for family and friends, time for exercise, and time for rejuvenation and relaxation. In many ways, my work is not compartmentalized into a "job"; it is a huge part of my life and it is who I am. Occasionally, I relegate some things to the far corners of my mind because I would rather play, but I always return to my life in the academy. Thomas Jefferson said it best: "I cannot live without my books" (Cappon 1998, 441).

## Conclusion

I cannot snap my fingers and create a critical mass of individuals who have doctoral degrees in disciplines that complement the field of ASL/English interpreting. I do have serious concerns about the future of our field, of *my* field. My colleague Rico Peterson eloquently shares these concerns (personal correspondence, January 21, 2010):

> Our field is a lovely mongrel of a thing. Mothered by necessity and fathered by chance we have made our way in the world mainly by pluck. Those of us who teach feel this, I think, most poignantly. We made it up as we went along. I remember that with nostalgia as I watch us continue to this day to make it up as we go along.

And we do continue to make it up. The establishment of interpreter *training* opportunities by companies that provide video-relay service should cause us to question the value or benefit or usefulness of a four-year degree. It seems that we need to "produce" more "warm bodies" (i.e., interpreters) to fill positions, but where is the research that shows us how to produce more and *better*? In my heart, I believe that a well-rounded education is important if an interpreter is to be successful; a little bit of knowledge (i.e., a four-year degree) is not necessarily a dangerous thing— it can lead to lifelong learning and self-reflection. Students need to learn to think for themselves, but they also need guidance and a helpful perspective. We have not begun to explore mentoring for graduate students: Do they even think about pursuing doctoral degrees? Do they even know it is a possibility? Do they think about it but are clueless on how to pursue such a dream? It is incumbent upon us to accept this "senior faculty" responsibility.

I wonder whether some of my undergraduate students will one day take my place at the front of the classroom to experience the excitement of teaching and learning that I so enjoy. Over the years, a few of my students have gone on to pursue master's degrees, although the preferred discipline seems to be Deaf education. One former student completed a doctoral degree and is an assistant professor of linguistics at a large state university. Two others are in the doctoral program at my alma mater.

I said I became a teacher because I really wanted to be a perennial student. I have told my students this; some seem fascinated to imagine this for themselves. Those students are my future, our future.

## References

American Association of University Professors (AAUP). n.d. *Contingent faculty*. Accessed August 22, 2012, from http://www.aaup.org/AAUP/ issues/contingent/.

———. 2003. *Contingent appointments in the academic profession*. Accessed August 22, 2012 from http://www.aaup.org/AAUP/pubsres/policydocs/ contents/conting-stmt.htm.

———. 2009. The annual report on the economic status of the profession, 2008–09. *Academe* 95 (2): 45.

Bell, Brenda, John Gaventa, and John Peters, eds. 1990. *We make the road by walking: Conversations on education and social changes, Myles Horton and Paulo Freire*. Philadelphia: Temple University Press.

Boyer, Ernest. 1990. *Scholarship reconsidered: Priorities of the professoriate*. San Francisco: Jossey-Bass.

————. 1997. Scholarship a personal journey. In *Scholarship assessed: Evaluation of the professoriate*, edited by C. Glassick, M. Huber, and G. Maeroff, 1–4. San Francisco: Jossey-Bass.

Brookfield, Stephen D. 1990. *The skillful teacher*. San Francisco: Jossey-Bass.

Cappon, Lester J., ed. 1988. *The Adams-Jefferson letters: The complete correspondence between Thomas Jefferson and Abigail and John Adams*. Chapel Hill: University of North Carolina Press. Accessed on August 22, 2012, from http://catdir.loc.gov/catdir/toc/becites/main/jefferson/88014258.toc.html#11.

Cokely, Dennis, and Elizabeth A. Winston. 2008. National Consortium of Interpreter Education Centers, *Interpreter Education Programs Needs Assessment—Final Report*. Boston: Northeastern University.

Cokely, Dennis. 2005. Shifting positionality: A critical examination of the turning point in the relationship of interpreters and the Deaf community. In *Sign Language Interpreting and Interpreter Education: Directions for Research and Practice*, edited by Marc Marschark, Rico Peterson, and Elizabeth A. Winston, 3–28. New York: Oxford University Press.

Conference of Interpreter Trainers (CIT). 2004. *CIT Demographic Survey Results for 2002–03*. Boston: Author.

————. n.d. Job Postings/Advertisements. Accessed August 22, 2012, from http://www.cit-asl.org/members/jobs.html.

Dewey, John. 1990. *The school and society and the child and the curriculum*. Expanded ed. Chicago: University of Chicago Press.

Frishberg, Nancy. 1990. *Interpreting: An introduction*. Rev. ed. Silver Spring, MD: Registry of Interpreters for the Deaf Publications.

Gallaudet University. n.d. Graduate programs. Accessed August 22, 2012, from http://www.gallaudet.edu/Interpretation/PhD_Program.html.

Gappa, Judith M., Ann E. Austin, and Andrea G. Trice. 2007. *Rethinking faculty work: Higher education's strategic imperative*. San Francisco: Jossey-Bass.

Jenkins, Rob. 2003. Not a bad gig. *The Chronicle of Higher Education*. November 103. Accessed June 24, 3013, from http://chronicle.com/article/Not-a-Bad-Gig/45224.

Knapp, Laura G., Janice E. Kelly-Reid, and Scott A. Ginder. 2009. *Employees in postsecondary institutions, Fall 2008, and salaries of full-time instructional staff, 2008–09*. Washington, DC: National Center for Educational Statistics (NCES), U.S. Department of Education.

Legato, Marianne J. 2006. Balancing the three-legged stool: Which faculty are most important in our academic medical centers? *Gender Medicine* 3 (2): 71–72.

McKeachie, Wilbert J., and Marilla Svinicki. 2006. *Teaching tips: Strategies, research, and theory for college and university teachers.* 4th ed. Boston: Houghton Mifflin.

Miller, Charles, Simon Hooper, and Susan Rose. 2008. Avenue ASL: Transforming curriculum through design and innovation. *TechTrends* 52 (2): 27–32.

Millis, Barbara J., and Phillip G. Cottell, Jr. 1998. *Cooperative learning for higher education faculty.* Phoenix: The Oryx Press.

Monikowski, Christine. 1995a. Proficiency: Issue paper. *Proceedings from the Conference of Interpreter Trainers' 1995 Convention,* 31–49.

———. 1995b. Assessing second language proficiency of interpreters. *Proceedings from the Conference of Interpreter Trainers' 1995 Convention,* 83–96.

———. 1996. Review of *Language contact in the American Deaf community,* by Ceil Lucas and Clayton Valli. *Anthropological Linguistics* 38 (3): 575.

———. 2001. Review of *Storytelling and conversation: Discourse in Deaf communities,* by Elizabeth A. Winston. *Studies in Second Language Acquisition* 23 (4): 566–67.

———. 2004. Review of *Language, cognition, and the brain: Insights from sign language research,* by Karen Emmorey. *Studies in Second Language Acquisition* 26 (3): 497–98.

———. 2005. First language, second language, what language? In *Educational interpreting: How it can succeed,* edited by Elizabeth A.Winston, 48–60. Washington, DC: Gallaudet University Press.

Monikowski, Christine, and Elizabeth A. Winston. 2011. Interpreting and interpreter education. In *Handbook of deaf studies, language, and education,* edited by Marc Marschark and Patricia Spencer, vol. 1, 2nd ed., 367–79. New York: Oxford University Press.

Monikowski, Christine, and Rico Peterson. 2005. Service learning in interpreting education. In *Interpreting education: from research to practice,* edited by Marc Marschark, Rico Peterson, and Elizabeth A. Winston, 188–207. New York: Oxford University Press.

National Science Foundation (NSF). 2009. Awards of U.S. doctorate degrees rise for sixth straight year. Press Release 09-227. Accessed August 22, 2012, from http://www.nsf.gov/news/news_summ.jsp?cntn_id=115964.

Palmer, Parker. 2007. *The courage to teach.* 10th anniversary ed. San Francisco: Jossey-Bass.

Pöchhacker, Franz. 2004. *Introducing interpreting studies.* London: Routledge.

Rice, R. Eugene, Mary Deane Sorcinelli, and Ann E. Austin. 2000. *Heeding new voices: Academic careers for a new generation.* Washington DC: American Association for Higher Education.

Rochester Institute of Technology (RIT). n.d. *Policies and Procedures Manual.* Accessed August 22, 2012, from http://www.rit.edu/~w-policy/ alpha.shtml.

————. 2006. RIT *Tenure Policies and NTID Administrative Guidelines and Criteria for tenure of full-time faculty.* Rochester, NY: Author.

————. 2007. *Guidelines, Procedures, and Qualifications for Promotion in Rank of Full-Time NTID Faculty.* Rochester, NY: Author.

Sorcinelli, Mary Deane, Ann E. Austin, Pamela L. Eddy, and Andrea L. Beach. 2006. *Creating the future of faculty development: Learning from the past, understanding the present.* Boston: Anker.

U.S. Department of Education, National Center for Education Statistics (NCES). 2004. National study of postsecondary faculty, NSOPF:04. Table 14. Accessed August 22, 2012 from http://nces.ed.gov/das/library/ tables_listings/showTable2005.asp?popup=true&tableID=2114&rt=p.

————. 2008. National Study of Postsecondary Faculty, Table 250, 2008. Accessed August 22, 2012, from http://nces.ed.gov/programs/digest/ d08/tables/dt08_250.asp.

————. 2010. Employees in postsecondary institutions and salaries of full-time instructional staff, 2009–10: First look. Table 3. Accessed August 22, 2012, from http://Nces.ed.gov/pubs2011/2011150.pdf.

Winston, Elizabeth A., and Christine Monikowski. 2004. Marking topic boundaries in signed interpreting and transliterating. In *From topic boundaries to omission: New Research on interpretation,* edited by Melanie Metzger, Steven Collins, Valerie Dively, and Risa Shaw, 187–227. Washington, DC: Gallaudet University Press.

Witter-Merithew, Anna. 1982. The function of assessing as part of the interpreting process. *Registry of Interpreters for the Deaf Journal* 1 (2): 8–15.

COMMENTARY

# Changing Our Attitude and Position
*Beppie van den Bogaerde*

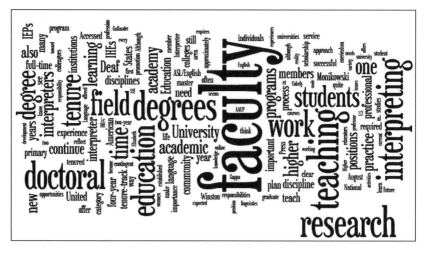

Figure 1. Wordle of Monikowski chapter (this volume).

CHRISTINE MONIKOWSKI's chapter on the challenges faced by interpreter educators when planning their career in the United States fits with the developments that have been going on in Europe since the 1990s. I briefly discuss these and review her chapter in relationship to these developments.

## DEVELOPMENTS IN EUROPE

The Bologna Declaration is a pledge by 29 European countries to reform the structures of their higher education systems, which was intended to be fully implemented by 2010 (CEURC / CRE 2000). A 2012 report mentions that easily readable and comparable degrees and a two-cycle system are now being implemented in the 47 countries constituting the European Higher

Education Area (European Commission 2012, 4).[9] Among other things, this meant that all institutes of higher education (IHEs) in the member countries would adhere to the bachelor/master/doctorate system. The many varieties of higher vocational schooling were also to be adapted to this system in the form of universities of applied sciences (De Weert and Soo 2009).

In Europe there are currently more than 65 training programs for sign language interpreting (SLI), as described by the respondents[10] of a recent survey by de Wit (2012). She lists 14 baccalaureate programs, 24 master's programs, 66 vocational training programs (4 of which are on a certificate/course level), 10 differently specified programs, and 1 temporary program (2012, fig. 2.3). Teachers affiliated with the baccalaureate and master's programs in universities of applied sciences are often working interpreters in their local spoken and signed languages, Deaf native signers, and other professionals who come from the practical domain of Deaf studies, for example, teachers of the deaf, educationalists, or speech therapists. Many of these hold vocational degrees from before the time of the Bologna agreement, and although qualified, they do not always have experience with research. Many programs do not have any or have only a few staff members who have a doctorate in linguistics, communication, or other related fields. Faculty members in traditional universities hold doctoral degrees. Because educators working in SLI programs need to be working within the triangle mentioned by Monikowski (this volume, 2), all factors she listed also apply to the IHE SLI education programs in the European union, specifically in universities of applied sciences; in the traditional universities the focus on interpreting techniques and skills on the job might prove challenging to implement in the curriculum. However, no research has been done on this aspect, to my knowledge.

---

9. http://www.ehea.info/article-details.aspx?ArticleId=65.
10. Respondents were from 40 countries and regions of EU, which currently consists of 47 countries: Albania, Austria, Belgium (Flanders), Belgium (Wallonia), Bosnia and Herzegovina, Croatia, Czech Republic, Cyprus, Denmark, United Kingdom (and Wales and Northern Ireland), Estonia, Finland, France, Germany, Greece, Hungary, Iceland, Ireland, Italy (ANIMU and ANIOS), Kosovo, Latvia, Lithuania, Malta, Netherlands, Norway, Poland, Portugal, Romania, Russia, Scotland, Serbia (ATSZJ and UTLOSS), Slovenia, Spain, Sweden, Switzerland (French, German, and Italian regions), and Ukraine.

## CHALLENGES

Monikowski's description of the challenges facing academia in the United States can be applied seamlessly to the situation in Europe, even though the tenure track system varies significantly in the different countries (Batterbury 2008). What struck me most of Monikowski's argumentation was not that we need practical research to support our pedagogical approaches or our curricula development (this volume, 9). This has been discussed by Pöchhacker (2010), Nicodemus and Swabey (2011), and many others. No, it is that "we need faculty who can represent [this new] discipline in the academy and address the slow 'academization' … in our field" (this volume, 6).

Being of the same mind, the European Forum of Sign Language Interpreters (EFSLI) organized three seminars for trainers on curriculum development for SLI education in IHEs, with reference to the European Qualification Framework (2008), which in turn is closely related to the qualifications framework for the European Higher Education Area (2005/2007). During the international seminars, where usually more than 20 countries were represented, it became very evident that we needed more research *and* researchers to justify the choices we are making in the professionalization of our teachers and in our didactical choices regarding language education and interpreting skills of our students. Most important, we agreed that our students need to adopt an academic attitude toward their profession and realize that research is part of being a good professional. To that end, we need faculty who can be their role models, as much as in research and interpreting as in the discourse and attitudes that go with these.

The advantages of working within the triangle appear to be self-evident (Hazelkorn 2010) but are perhaps less so for traditional universities. By doing practice-oriented research both teachers and students contribute to the improvement of their profession, to a deeper and wider knowledge Ginstance, at the institute in the Netherlands where I work, half of the staff are involved in research, either by pursuing studies, coaching students, or actively participating in research. This has substantially contributed to our new curriculum, which we started to develop in 2010 and which will be fully implemented by 2014. Evidence-based practice and practice-based evidence are both necessary to justify our decisions in accreditation procedures. The cycle of research is an excellent way to make students (and educators) realize that being a professional means lifelong learning. In this respect new technologies make it easier to incorporate blended learning in our approach of active learning, which is suited to our modern way of life (and learning), and calls for actively doing, experiencing, and working together to enhance learning outcomes. To serve learners optimally, in my view, the education system starting from (pre)primary school to post-doctoral learning needs innovation and reconsideration of goals and approaches (see, e.g., Robertson 2010). We are not the only discipline that needs reflection and focus to prepare our students better for future society.

## The Future

In Dutch we have an expression which literally translates to a "feast of recognition," the feeling when hearing that someone else's experiences closely match you own. Reading Monikowski's chapter was such a feast of recognition for me both as a teacher and as a researcher. Starting today, we should make sure that our students and successors become better prepared for research than we were, and, to carry the profession to a new level, to become perennial students (this volume, 24) and thus serve the Deaf community and the academy to the best of their ability. This begins by improving our curricula and providing an excellent teaching and research environment to enable our students to become excellent professionals.

Figure 2. Wordle of this review.

# REFERENCES

Batterbury, Simon. 2008. Tenure or permanent contracts in North American higher education? A critical assessment. *Policy Futures in Education*, 6(3), 286–97. Accessed from http://dx.doi.org/10.2304/pfie.2008.6.3.286.

CEURC / CRE. 2000. *The Bologna declaration on the European space for higher education: An explanation.* Accessed December 1, 2012, from http://ec.europa.eu/education/policies/educ/bologna/bologna.pdf.

De Weert, Egbert, and Maarja Soo. 2009. *Research at universities of applied sciences in Europe: Conditions, achievements, and perspectives.* Twente, the Netherlands: University of Twente. Accessed December 1, 2012, from http://www.kfh.ch/uploads/doku/doku/HBO-UASnet%20rapport-C%20(2).pdf?CFID=29497469&CFTOKEN=57440950.

De Wit, Maya. 2012. *A comprehensive guide to sign language interpreting in Europe.* London: Author.

European Commission. 2012. *Press briefing: The European higher education area in 2012: Bologna Process implementation report.* Accessed January 18, 2013, from http://eacea.ec.europa.eu/education/eurydice/documents/thematic_reports/138EN_HI.pdf.

European Qualification Framework (EQF), 2008. Accessed from http://ec.europa.eu/dgs/education_culture.

European Higher Education Area (EHEA), 2005/2007. Accessed from http://www.ehea.info/article-details.aspx?ArticleId=65.

Hazelkorn, Ellen. 2010. Teaching, research, and engagement: Strengthening the knowledge triangle. Paper presented at the EUA Sirus Conference, Vienna, Austria, November.

Kahneman, Daniel. 2011. *Thinking fast and slow.* New York: Farrar, Straus and Giroux.

Nicodemus, Brenda, and Laurie Swabey, eds. 2011. *Advances in interpreting research.* Amsterdam: John Benjamins.

Pöchhacker, Franz. 2010. The role of research in interpreter education. *Translation and Interpreting* 2 (1): 1–10.

Robertson, Ken. 2010, October. *Changing education paradigms.* Accessed December 15, 2012, from http://www.youtube.com/watch?v=zDZFcDGpL4U.

# The Chicken and the Egg Dilemma: Academizing a Semiprofession
## *Karen Bontempo*

In her chapter, Monikowski outlines the challenges facing interpreter educators affiliated with higher education institutions today. The move toward the academization of signed language interpreter education in the United States, and indeed in several other countries around the world, has led to new demands of interpreter educators. Interpreter educators are now increasingly situated in universities, resulting in an expectation that in addition to teaching they will also conduct research and continue their practice as interpreters. Of concern to Monikowski, however, is the low number of faculty members in interpreter education programs in the United States holding doctoral degrees and actively contributing to the scholarly knowledge of the field. Indeed, she is honest that there is little to teach without research, as for too long our sector has encouraged interpreter education and training based on intuition and not evidence—scholarship is the hallmark of a profession and our field has far to go in this regard.

Speaking plainly about the employment of interpreter educators in higher education institutions, Monikowski asks, "What mindset allows us to think we can continue to hire faculty who are not comparable to those in other fields and still think we are a true profession?" Monikowski is referring to the pattern of appointment of interpreter educators to key positions in higher education institutions without doctorates, or sometimes even without master's degrees, as higher degrees are listed as desirable rather than essential criteria in many job advertisements. This does not happen in other disciplines situated in academia. Perhaps being held to a different standard reflects a cold, hard truth for our sector. We are not a true profession. Not yet. We are clearly not an established profession, such as medicine or law: We cannot fully regulate who practices, control entry to the profession, or universally suspend people from practice after wrongdoing. We do not have uniformly applied standards of practice, years of requisite training with a significant intellectual component, or registration boards with legal authority. We also do not have community sanction, broad societal acceptance, or formal induction systems in the field, all traits suggested by Tseng (1992) as markers of a profession.

Our journey toward professionalization has moved beyond infancy but has not yet reached maturity, a source of frustration for Monikowski. Perhaps reservation about the impact of academization has delayed professionalization of our field? For example, Winston (2005, 209) notes "as interpreting education has shifted into academia, it has, albeit unintentionally, lost much of the experience and expertise of the Deaf community." Kent (2004), Turner (2004), and Cokely (2005) also all express concern about the risk of increased social distance between interpreters and the Deaf community as a consequence of the steps taken toward the academization of our field and the potentially negative implications of professionalization in terms of our relationship with the Deaf community. Brunson (2006, 1) reinforces these concerns, suggesting the current trajectory of professionalization could lead to "further estrangement between deaf people and sign language interpreters." Have these concerns influenced our journey?

Perhaps it would be more accurate to describe our current status as a semiprofession, an occupational group that has achieved some of the characteristics of a profession but to a lesser extent (Hudson 2002). We are slowly but surely acquiring systematic knowledge about our practice; we have formal interpreter associations; we have systems of assessment, certification and licensure; we have codes of conduct; and in some countries we also have recommended working conditions and education and training programs of variable quality and duration, including university-level studies in some cases. The winding path we have slowly tread toward professionalization and academization has been commented on by others in our sector for example, Turner and Harrington (2002) in the United Kingdom; Witter-Merithew and Johnson (2004) and Winston (2005) in the United States, and Fenton (1993) in New Zealand. We have much yet to do, however, particularly in relation to Monikowski's call for greater scholarship and doctoral studies in the field.

Germane to the issue of scholarly activity is that there has also been a groundswell of research initiated by intellectually curious interpreting practitioners who are not full-time academics as such. Essentially they have an interest in a topic or an area of concern informed by their own practice as interpreters, which draws them into conducting and publishing research (Napier 2011). A term for this phenomenon was coined by Gile (1994) when it first occurred among spoken language interpreters, describing practioner-researchers as practisearchers. Given the relatively low number of academics in full-time positions at universities involved in signed language interpreting research in various countries around the world, the contribution of practisearchers has been critical in terms of growing the international scholarship of our field and must be acknowledged.

Despite the burgeoning scholarly activity in recent years by academics and by practisearchers in our field, Monikowski is right to challenge the status quo. It is unacceptable that we do not hold ourselves to task as a field and demand more of ourselves in teaching and training the next generation of interpreters. Monikowski argues our relative youth as a field is no longer a justifiable cause for expecting less of our interpreter educators of today in terms of the qualifications they hold or the contribution to scholarship they should be making, when considered in parallel with academics in other disciplines. The initial reasons for practitioners being foisted into teaching roles in institutions and teaching based on their intuition alone no longer exist.

Although our field may still be maturing, a wide range of qualifications and study options are now available to interpreter educators in many countries, and a culture of research and publication is being strongly encouraged. The chicken and the egg problem should no longer be used as an excuse to hold our field back. While we wait for suitable interpreting-specific doctoral programs to appear and forego opportunities to publish the good work we are doing, the rest of academia is whizzing by, leaving us behind stuck in a vicious cycle in semiprofessional land, with a significant impact on our teaching and our practice. Hale (2007, 166) reinforces this view, referring to the spoken language interpreter education sector when she notes, "the unavailability of academic degrees impacts of the development of research in community interpreting, which in turn impacts on the quality of training and eventually the practice."

Insightfully, Monikowski also touches on the issue of gender in her chapter, raising it as one of the possible reasons for the slow academization of our field. There is a recognized link between gender and the journey to professionalization, with occupations such as teaching, nursing, and social work hindered in their growth and recognition as they have been historically viewed as "women's work" and subject to paternalistic treatment in the academy and in society. Bolton and Muzio (2008) note the preponderance of women in these occupations and the helping nature of this kind of work have impacted on the social standing and material rewards of these professions. Effectively bringing interpreting in line with these other practice professions, Monikowski identifies the overrepresentation of women in the interpreting and interpreter education fields in the United States. Monikowski's statistics are mirrored in the global picture, with 89% female and 11% male signed language interpreters represented by data collected from more than 2,000 signed language interpreters from 38 different countries (Bontempo and Napier 2012). Has the significant gender imbalance in our field of expertise impacted on our journey toward professionalization, as it historically has with other semiprofessions?

Turning to the global context, it is worth noting that many countries view the situation of signed language interpreter education in the United States with envy. Monikowski's concerns are valid, yet the United States has more than 100 programs and so many teaching resources in comparison to other countries. Despite Australia being a similar size geographically to mainland United States, no undergraduate university degree for interpreters exists anywhere in Australia at present, despite efforts to gain institutional support for one (Bontempo and Levitzke-Gray 2009). Instead, our entry-level interpreting students undertake an 18-month part-time training course in one of just five vocational colleges around the nation that offer interpreter education programs.

The only postgraduate university program for Auslan[11]/English interpreters was established in 2002 at Macquarie University, Sydney, which also conducts master's degrees in interpreting and translating, and in interpreting pedagogy. A Doctor of Philosophy (PhD) program is an option for interpreters pursuing research interests. Most doctoral research

11. Auslan is Australian Sign Language.

programs are subsidized by the Australian government for citizens and permanent residents, so students do not pay any tuition fees. Programs are available via distance learning, there are scholarships available to support living expenses, and students can complete an exclusively research-based doctorate rather than including any coursework. A relatively new initiative in Australia being adopted by many universities is a "thesis by publication" option, a nontraditional format that allows the candidate to publish different slices of their research results across several self-contained articles or book chapters as they proceed through their candidature, contributing to the body of knowledge in the field as they go. Such pragmatic support for PhD candidates in Australia suggests a different picture from that painted by Monikowski regarding doctoral studies in the United States, where tuition fees are high and coursework is required along with a traditional dissertation, potentially limiting distance PhD candidacy.

Just as Monikowski suggests she could name those in the field in the United States holding doctoral degrees because the numbers are so low, similarly at present in Australia only three interpreter educators regularly involved in sign language interpreter education programs hold doctorates and none of them are employed as full-time academics. Another nine interpreters hold or are currently completing PhDs, but these are not necessarily linked to interpreting. Significant gains have been made in Australia in a relatively short time, considering a postgraduate university program for interpreters has only been available since 2002 and the relatively small population of Australia. For us, the question remains that, with so few full-time university-based teaching positions available in Australia for interpreter educators (i.e., one position at present, recently vacated and open to signed or spoken language interpreter educators/scholars), why would trainers, educators, mentors, or practitioners necessarily pursue doctoral degrees, other than for personal reasons and out of professional curiosity? There is not a great deal of incentive. Critically though, the role of PhD theses in "fueling the development of interpreting studies as an academic discipline can hardly be overestimated" (Pöchhacker 2004, 31).

It is clear that in Australia we face the same issues elucidated by Monikowski regarding the state of play in the United States, yet the United States has had nearly 50 years to reach its current position in the trajectory toward the professionalization of signed language interpreters and interpreter education. Outside the United States, the interpreting profession is considerably younger,[12] so it is no surprise that the community of scholars is relatively few in number. In New Zealand, for example, an undergraduate baccalaureate degree in signed language interpreting established in 2011 has had difficulty attracting a scholar with a doctorate in the field to head the new program. Similarly in Sweden, successful advocacy resulted in moving an interpreter education program from a vocational college to a university setting. This led to the creation of a professor position in the program in 2012, which had not been permanently filled at the time of writing. In the United Kingdom, only a handful of British Sign Language/English interpreters hold doctorates and work as academics in university-based sign language interpreter education programs. Other countries present a similar picture or fare less well.

If there is no expectation of a higher standard of education and qualification from prospective and current interpreter educators, they may not see the need to aspire to doctoral studies. However, a key issue is if there is not the number of suitable jobs available in academia for PhD holders in our field, it may be hard to convince practitioners and educators that they should undertake doctoral studies. There may not be enough motivation for individuals to take on the commitment of a PhD, regardless of an acknowledgment that more doctoral faculty should be involved in interpreter education and in practice, as well as in proactively publishing relevant research in the field.

Monikowski has been brave to hold a mirror up to our field in this way, as it is somewhat difficult examining the reflection staring back at us. The significant lack of doctorally prepared faculty, or even those with advanced degrees, employed in interpreter education programs in higher education institutions is likely to continue to negatively impact the research agenda for our field on an international scale, and something should be said about it, even though it may be an uncomfortable dialogue. The paucity of doctorates, and even master's degrees, among interpreter educators in universities surely impacts pedagogical practices and our capacity to build

---

12. Notwithstanding the contribution of early interpreters such as family members and teachers, nor the role of some members of the Deaf community in functioning as language brokers and sight translators in an informal capacity for many years prior to the milestone recognized as the start of "professional interpreting" in each country (Adam and Stone 2011).

and disseminate scholarly knowledge, and likely influences the preparedness of our interpreter program graduates. Monikowski has presented us with a call to arms to transform our field, recommending we increase the doctoral expectations and academic standards of our field and that we engage in a more proactive culture of research and scholarship.

Further to this, I add my voice to that of Napier (2011), who noted the research that is being conducted must actually be published, not just presented at provincial conferences, for us to gain traction as a profession. To move away from remaining a semiprofession, effectively and broadly sharing systematic knowledge among our field must become a priority. University-based undergraduate and postgraduate interpreting programs and studies should be the standard. Greater occupational and academic rewards should be available to students who complete an academic rather than vocational program of study, providing a meaningful pathway to master's and PhD level studies for those in our field. Positioning ourselves more securely in academia should provide us with a way forward.

Innovative efforts to develop higher education and doctoral programs that have an international flavor, allow for distance delivery, and encourage collaboration and the sharing of resources between institutions are worth considering, given the size and nature of our field.[13] Within a university context, the standards expected of other professions should be a reality for our field to create greater sustainability, scholarly respect, and a stronger profession. We must lift the bar in regard to the quality of the education and research opportunities we offer and in the skills, knowledge, and philosophy we share with our students. As educators, we should prepare our students better by planting the seed for their further academic pursuits, while we nurture their interpreting practice as novices. If we can lead and influence them to participate in life-long learning and contribute to the academization of our profession from the beginning, surely our field will reap the benefits in the future.

---

13. A commendable example of such collaboration is the innovative European Master in Sign Language Interpreting (EUMASLI), a program conducted by a collective of three European universities based in Scotland, Germany, and Finland between 2009 and 2011. A new EUMASLI program is due to commence in September 2013: http://www.eumasli.eu/.

# REFERENCES

Adam, Robert, and Christopher Stone. 2011. Through a historical lens: Contextualising interpreting research. In *Advances in interpreting research: Inquiry in action*, edited by Brenda Nicodemus and Laurie Swabey, 225–39. Amsterdam: John Benjamins.

Bolton, Sharon, and Daniel Muzio. 2008. The paradoxical processes of feminisation in the professions: The case of established, aspiring, and semiprofessions. *Work, Employment and Society* 22(2): 281–99.

Bontempo, Karen, and Patricia Levitzke-Gray. 2009. Interpreting down under: Signed language interpreter education and training in Australia. In *International perspectives on signed language interpreter education*, ed. Jemina Napier, 149–70. Washington, DC: Gallaudet University Press.

Bontempo, Karen, and Jemina Napier. 2012, December. Exploring personality, pedagogy, and practice: An international study of interpreters. Paper presented at the AUSIT National Conference, Sydney, Australia.

Brunson, Jeremy L. 2006. Commentary on the professional status of sign language interpreters: An alternative perspective. *Journal of Interpretation* 1–10.

Cokely, Dennis. 2005. Shifting positionality. In *Sign language interpreting and interpreter education: Directions for research and practice*, edited by Marc Marschark, Rico Peterson, Elizabeth A. Winston, Patricia Sapere, Carol M. Convertino, Carol Rosemarie Seewagen, and Christine Monikowski, 3–28. New York: Oxford University Press.

Fenton, Sabine. 1993. Interpreting in New Zealand: An emerging profession. *Journal of Interpretation* 154–65.

Gile, Daniel. 1994. Methodological aspects of interpretation and translation research. In *Bridging the gap: Empirical research in simultaneous interpretation*, edited by Sylvie Lambert and Barbara Moser-Mercer, 39–56. Amsterdam: John Benjamins.

Hale, Sandra B. 2007. *Community interpreting*. Basingstoke, UK: Palgrave Macmillan.

Hudson, Bob. 2002. Interprofessionality in health and social care: The Achilles heel of partnership. *Journal of Interprofessional Care* 16(1): 7–17.

Kent, Stephanie Jo. 2004. Why bother? Institutionalization, interpreting decisions, and power relations. In *The Critical Link 4: Professionalisation of interpreting in the community*, edited by Cecilia Wadensjö, Birgitta Englund Dimitrova, and Anna-Lena Nilsson, 193–204. Amsterdam: John Benjamins.

Napier, Jemina. 2011. If a tree falls in a forest and no one is there to hear it, does it make a noise? The merits of publishing interpreting research.

In *Advances in interpreting research: Inquiry in action*, edited by Brenda Nicodemus and Laurie Swabey, 121–52. Amsterdam: John Benjamins.

Pöchhacker, Franz. 2004. *Introducing interpreting studies*. London: Routledge.

Tseng, Joseph. 1992. Interpreting as an emerging profession in Taiwan: A sociolinguistic model. Unpublished master's thesis. Fu Jen Catholic University, Taiwan.

Turner, Graham. H. 2004. Professionalization of interpreting with the community: Refining the model. In *The Critical Link 4: Professionalisation of interpreting in the community*, edited by Cecilia Wadensjö, Birgitta Englund Dimitrova, and Anna-lena Nilsson, 181–92. Amsterdam, the Netherlands: John Benjamins.

Turner, Graham H., and Frank J. Harrington. 2002. The campaign for real interpreting. *Deaf Worlds* 18(2): 69–72.

Winston, Elizabeth. A. 2005. Designing a curriculum for American Sign Language/English interpreting educators. In *Sign language interpreting and interpreter education: Directions for research and practice*, edited by Marc Marschark, Rico Peterson, Elizabeth A. Winston, Patricia Sapere, Carol M. Convertino, Carol Rosemarie Seewagen, and Christine Monikowski, 208–34. New York: Oxford University Press.

Witter-Merithew, Anna, and Leilani Johnson, Leilani. 2004. Market disorder within the field of sign language interpreting: Professionalization implications. *Journal of Interpretation* 19–56.

HELEN TEBBLE

# Researching Medical Interpreting: An Applied Linguistics Perspective

## Abstract

This chapter describes a substantial research project into medical interpreting, which makes use of systemic functional linguistics and a variety of research concepts and methods from other relevant disciplines to provide both theoretical insights into the language used in interpreted specialist medical consultations and practical outcomes, especially for the education of medical interpreters and physicians who use the services of medical interpreters. This work can also serve as a case study of empirical research in hospitals for medical interpreters and applied linguists who intend to undertake research into aspects of medical interpreting or other dialogue interpreting. Applied linguistics research can provide new insights about the way language is used in communication within specific types of contexts or events of a given profession. Such research findings can then provide new information to apply to the pre-service and in-service education courses and pedagogical materials for the specific profession.

IN THIS chapter I describe the Medical Interpreting Project conducted initially at Deakin University and subsequently at Monash University in Melbourne, Australia, with staff and patients at a major teaching hospital in Melbourne and more widely within a regional network of hospitals in Melbourne. It is written with the intention of providing a case study for prospective doctoral students and postdoctoral scholars of community interpreting[1] (Hale 2007, 30–33, 60; Wadensjö 1998), also known as public

---

1. Community interpreting in this chapter includes interpreting for members of deaf communities.

42

service interpreting, particularly in the United Kingdom and Europe (e.g., Corsellis 2008; Graham 2012). Because I have received numerous requests for advice from prospective and current doctoral candidates from around the world and have seen interpreter educators attempt to set up medical interpreting research projects, this chapter provides details about both preliminary preparation and basic procedures for undertaking research in community interpreting, which is more than would typically occur in an academic paper reporting on a research project. Taking the classical pathway of training in research methods and conducting independent investigations from undergraduate to master's level as preparation for the PhD is not the experience of all who move into interpreter education. The chapter nevertheless outlines the research that was undertaken to design a new type of syllabus for community interpreting that is genre based (Tebble 1996, forthcoming) and theoretically accountable for sequencing, as well as for the linguistic components (structures, functions) that enable the medical professional, patient, and interpreter to participate in the professionally interpreted consultation.

Near the end of my own doctoral program, I accepted a dual appointment in separate programs in linguistics and interpreting. In my new position I observed that much of the theory from linguistics and conversation analysis that I had become aware of during my PhD research (Tebble 1991a) was being enacted in the community interpreting classes in the BA (Interpreting and Translating) program. Here the pedagogy utilized role play within a very good contextual studies framework but which at that stage lacked a strong theoretical communication- or linguistics-based framework, but I could see its potential for being updated by recent research in discourse analysis and conversation analysis. In addition, after undertaking the research for a sociolinguistic profile of undergraduate and graduate students of interpreting (Tebble and Hirsh 1997), it was clear to me that most of these students had very little to no personal experience of the specialist medical consultation. It became imperative for me to know what was going on linguistically in professionally interpreted consultations and to be able to provide a theoretical account of them in order to justify the study and practice of dialogue interpreting in university courses (Tebble 1991b).

## APPLIED LINGUISTICS

Applied linguistics is the application of insights from linguistics and other relevant disciplines to the solving of language in communication problems. It is both

> an approach to understanding language issues in the real world, drawing upon theory and empirical analysis [and]

> an interdisciplinary area of study focused on language and communication, in which linguistics is combined with issues, methods, and perspectives drawn from other disciplines. (ALAA 1998)

According to the Association Internationale de Linguistique Appliquée (AILA 1999), interpreting and translating are one major category of applied linguistics, alongside about twenty-three other categories such as communication in the professions, language for special purposes, discourse analysis, lexicography and lexicology, language planning, literacy, foreign language teaching methodology and teacher education, child language, and language and the media.[2] Some applied linguistics projects have a tangible product as their goal such as the development and production of language tests or language teaching materials. Others identify communication problems, say, in an emergency hospital ward (e.g., Slade et al. 2008), and after completing ethnographic and linguistic analyses make recommendations for ways of overcoming the problems. In the legal domain the inexperienced interpreter may not have the procedural knowledge of how a refugee tribunal meeting is conducted and so would not have any useful frame or schema to understand the significance of the phrasing or its timing by the tribunal member. The interpreter educator needs to impart to the interpreting student what the genre of such a professional interpreting event entails. In the medical domain knowing the medical terminology, medical procedures, organizational structure of the health system and their counterparts in the culture from which the patient has come demonstrates an understanding of the *contexts of cultures*

---

2. These and other categories represented the 24 Scientific Commissions of AILA in 2005. Numerous introductory books and handbooks of applied linguistics provide definitions and overviews of the field and subfields.

(Halliday and Hasan 1985). However, to interpret accurately and fully what the physician and patient say to each other in the medical consultation, the medical interpreter needs to also understand what is called the *context of situation* (Halliday and Hasan 1985). Such information comes from understanding the nature of the discourse, including its structure, cohesion, and coherence; what the physician and patient are using language to do; and how they are using language to relate to each other. That is, the medical interpreter needs to understand how the physician and patient use language at all stages of the consultation so as to relay their intentions, content, and attitudes to actually enable the practice of medicine to occur. By understanding the structure and functions of the languages they employ and how participants use them in specific interpreted genres, the interpreter—and interpreting student with practice—will be able to interpret competently and be able to account for their own professional performance. Such knowledge about the genres of interpreted events drawn from applied linguistics projects is required of the interpreter educator. The researcher making use of applied linguistics to study community interpreting needs to be very familiar not only with the professional work of interpreters but also with the work of the professional and paraprofessional clients of the interpreter such as general medical practitioners, dentists (e.g., Hirsh 1997), physiotherapists, solicitors, nurses and paramedics, and *their* own clients who need the services of interpreters. Understanding the work of these professionals and paraprofessionals entails understanding how language is used to constitute much of their work. Professional interpreters need this information. Applied linguistics research goals should have practical outcomes that can be of benefit to the subjects of the study or to similar cohorts, for example, to enable them to overcome or avoid repeating the identified problems. Other types of practical outcomes, say from the findings from an investigation into the nature of a specific interpreted genre, can be incorporated into interpreter education syllabuses, interpreter education teaching and learning materials for professional and in-service education, and professional publications.

The applied linguistics researcher's core discipline knowledge is linguistics and its various branches such as sociolinguistics, psycholinguistics, pragmatics, contrastive linguistics, and corpus linguistics. Other relevant disciplines and areas of knowledge that the researcher may need can be academic and practical ones such as ethnomethodology; sociology; social psychology; interpersonal, small group, and organizational communication; nonverbal communication; statistics; policies pertinent to the specific profession under study; economics, immigration policies; curriculum design; materials development; adult learning; and competing current theories in one or more relevant disciplines. The application of the researcher's informed insights from relevant professions such as medicine and other academic disciplines to the way the research is conducted and the way the findings are made available can affect the quality and impact of the research. The type of research implied in this chapter is qualitative research within the tradition of descriptive linguistics and is recognized as one main approach within applied linguistics. The specific approach(es) and methodology adopted depend on the goals of the research project.

## PRELIMINARIES TO THE APPLIED LINGUISTICS PROJECT

To avoid wasting time in the short period of full-time doctoral study imposed by many universities, prospective students need to have done a considerable amount of preliminary work in preparing their application for PhD candidature. They need to have found their context; identified a topic or problem to study; completed preliminary reading to ensure the work has not already been done elsewhere; described how their study will build upon previous research, identified a need for their research if evidence for it is published in government and professional reports or academic papers; investigated the professional context to elicit the informal views of current professionals; identified some of the areas of knowledge and skills needed to conduct the research; identified potential sponsors and sources of subjects; considered the methods of research, the source of the data, and the costs; considered how the research will contribute to new knowledge (its significance); and discussed the value and feasibility of their ideas with experienced scholars and professional practitioners. All of this preliminary work can take months before the aims and objectives of the study, its planning, and assessment of its feasibility can be formulated into a convincing research proposal.

Preparing the groundwork is vital for writing a successful application for admission to PhD candidature. A well-thought-out PhD application provides information under headings such as background/context, aims, significance, brief literature review, methodology (of both data collection and analysis), potential findings, timetable, budget, and references for the literature review. In some cases the information provided is changed as the PhD research evolves. In other cases, as per postdoctoral studies, such as the Medical Interpreting Project, the goals and plans were so clear that the research grant applications provided the blueprint for the study. Projects rarely attract funding if their applications are not very clear in all aspects of the design, feasibility, and potential to contribute new knowledge.

## The Medical Interpreting Project

## Overview

The main goals and time frame of the Medical Interpreting Project were more extensive than the typical scope of a PhD project, and it attracted successive research grants from university and national grant funding sources as well as a funded fellowship. The main goals were to describe the linguistic nature of the interpreted medical consultation and to apply the findings to the education of community interpreters and to the education of medical practitioners who worked with medical interpreters. The costs were substantial for research in the humanities in Australia because most of the data were actual professionally interpreted medical consultations which were video recorded by professional film crews with a sound technician. The transcripts of the data were prepared by research assistants and professional translators of eight community languages. The project had enormous goodwill from several key organizations and individuals including the dean of medicine at Monash University and academics from various universities, government administrators, and the Australian Institute of Interpreters and Translators. The research students who were attached to the project were highly motivated. An applied linguistics project of this magnitude entailed recruiting and coordinating many people over a number of years.

## Ethics Application

All human research in Australia is influenced by the National Health and Medical Research Council's 2007 National Statement on Ethical

Conduct in Human Research and its precursors. In addition Australian applied linguistics researchers follow their professional association's Statement of Good Practice (ALAA 1998), which draws upon that of the British Association of Applied Linguistics and the "Linguistic Rights of Aboriginal and Islander Communities," endorsed by the Linguistic Society of Australia. No Australian institutional research using human subjects may commence without the approval of a human research committee. Given that data for the medical interpreting project involved mainly actual interpreted medical consultations conducted mainly in the various outpatient clinics of a major public teaching hospital, two sets of ethics applications were required, one for the university human ethics committee and another for the hospital's ethics committee.

Apart from providing a detailed description of the research already stated in the concomitant research application, the ethics application forms address all the likely ethical issues that can arise in both quantitative and qualitative research. The ethics requirements are a confirmation of respect for the human rights of the subjects who freely consent to participate and have the right to withdraw from the research at any time without penalty. The potential subjects cannot give their informed consent until after they have received and have understood both a clearly written statement and an oral explanation in their own language about the aims, method, benefits, and possible risks of the research study and safe storage of the data. Their informed consent also acknowledges that results of the research usually will be presented in academic forums and published in academic and professional publications often as aggregated results, that confidentiality will be maintained, and that their specific authorization is required for release of personal information. The ethics application forms must have appended to them copies of each type of consent form with certified translations where applicable. The Medical Interpreting Project used separate information sheets and consent forms for interpreters, physicians, and patients. Three documents for patients were provided in English and translated by an accredited professional translator into each patient's community language. The first document was an information sheet written in plain English that covered requirements as described previously. The second form was a standard consent form for participants. The third was an additional consent form that requested the use of the recordings and findings for adaptation into teaching materials.

Immediately prior to the consultation, the researcher reviewed the translated documents with the patient in their community language, using the services of the interpreter, to ensure that the patient fully understood what was required before signing the consent forms. When the researcher was fully satisfied that the patient understood all and had freely given their consent the patient signed the form and the interpreter witnessed the signature. Physicians and interpreters brought their signed consent forms to the consultation. All of the members of the video recording crews undertook to ensure complete confidentiality of each consultation at which they were present. Translators, research students, and assistants also consented in writing to maintain the confidentiality of the transcriptions.

## Recruitment Procedures

Physicians were made aware of the project through information disseminated about the project sent to hospital committees and informal networks. The physicians were approached to participate by the researcher, the project's medical liaison consultant, or the chief interpreter. The 11 physicians (eight male and three female) who agreed to participate were six senior medical staff (consultant physicians and one consultation liaison psychiatrist) and five senior medical registrars (specialist physicians who attended patients in both hospital outpatient clinics and hospital wards). Their areas of specialty were neurology, nephrology, oncology, palliative care, psychiatry, and vascular medicine and hypertension. None of the physicians had been trained to work with interpreters.

The interpreters were recruited through recommendations from AUSIT and either worked full time at the hospital or were freelance medical interpreters. All but one were NAATI-accredited professional interpreters and all were members of AUSIT. The interpreter for the palliative care component of the project was a NAATI-accredited paraprofessional interpreter and a member of AUSIT. He was an experienced hospital interpreter. The experience of the interpreters ranged from mainly highly experienced to early career. In all, two male and nine female interpreters participated in the study. The project paid them for two hours of work per consultation and a transportation fee. All interpreters were given their clients' names and the contact details of the physician in advance to help them prepare their briefing.

Except for the patient in palliative care and two ward patients, the patients were identified either by the chief interpreter through the outpatient booking system, which signaled automatically the patient's need for an interpreter in a specific language, or via a research nurse who knew the patient and which community language they spoke. The community languages of the patients were Greek, Italian, Spanish, Serbian, Cantonese, Mandarin, Khmer, and Vietnamese. There were 14 patients, 2 male and 12 female, whose ages ranged from approximately mid-30s to early 70s. All were attending a specialist medical consultation as distinct from an emergency ward, an acute care ward teaching round visit, or a primary care (general practitioner's) appointment.

Once the documents (as part of the ethics application) were approved, they were mailed to all prospective participants and given to the three ward patients. To confirm the participation of the outpatients, a follow-up telephone call was made by a research nurse or a hospital interpreter in the cases of the patients and some physicians and by the researcher in the cases of the interpreters and other physicians. After they expressed interest in participating in the project they were sent the full set of the ethics documents. All subjects brought their consent forms to the consultation.

## Data Collection Procedures

As soon as the patient, physician, and interpreter had agreed to have the consultation recorded, the physician's consulting room or a room big enough to accommodate the camera crew was booked for the morning or afternoon of the consultation. Three camera people and the sound technician assembled their equipment at least an hour in advance of the recording. Each camera, mounted on a mobile tripod, was assigned to record one specific participant. The equipment to monitor the video and sound was placed in an adjacent room or behind a large curtain, blocking off the sound technician and researcher, who watched the consultation on monitor screens and listened through headphones. Having access to the audio-visual monitoring equipment out of the participants' view enabled the researcher to take useful ethnographic notes.

After the ethics documentation had been signed but prior to the consultation, the participants were introduced to the camera crew, shown the equipment, and told what would happen. A lapel microphone was attached to the clothing of each participant. The interviews commenced with the greetings and introductions, which sometimes occurred with the entrance of the patient and interpreter at the door and otherwise from their seated positions at the physician's desk (Tebble 1998b). The physician sat at the middle of one side of his or her desk and the patient and interpreter sat at the opposite corners of the desk, creating a triangle whereby all participants could see each other clearly. During the physical examination the physician stood close to the patient, who was usually lying on the examination couch (otherwise she or he was in different sitting positions on the couch), and the interpreter stood near the foot end of the couch (except for one who sat near the patient's head to be able to hear the patient speak). There were different configurations for the psychiatric and palliative care consultations. None of the interpreters took notes during the interpreted consultations. The only interruption by the camera crew was before the start and at the end of the major sections of the consultation, that is, after video recording the patient's and interpreter's entrance through the doorway and before and after the physical examination. This was for the use of the clapper board to synchronize the time coding of the three cameras. There was minimal impact on the actual style of participation of all three participants because they were in genuine interpreted medical consultations. The impact only occurred at the start of the recording for one physician and the interpreter who both had a short period of self-consciousness. On one occasion, after the consultation, an interpreter reported making what she considered to be a few minor errors. The impact of the so-called observer's paradox (Labov 1972, 209) seemed to be quite minimal as all of the participants were engaged in serious professional matters concerning the health of each patient. They were all participating in actual medical consultations that could not be repeated.

The camera crews were highly professional, courteous, respectful, and unintrusive. They were usually all male crews, although there was one female camera person on two occasions. All outpatient consultations were recorded and postproduced by the camera crew, who were university audio-visual personnel. The interpreted palliative care consultation was recorded and postproduced by an external film crew whose director was known to the university audio-visual production staff.

For each consultation, the three video recordings—one each of the patient, physician, and interpreter—were postproduced into one video recording and time coded to microseconds. It was this composite video of the three pictures presented in a triangle on the screen that was used for the analysis. In addition three copies of an audiotape of the composite video were produced for use by the transcriber, translator, and researcher. In all, 14 interpreted medical consultations, each of approximately 50 minutes duration, were video recorded in addition to a video-recorded briefing session and an audio-recorded family meeting.

## Preparation of the Transcriptions

The choice of transcription system is part of research methodology. This view is supported by Niemants (2012). For the Medical Interpreting Project a modified version of the transcription system of the conversation analysts Sacks, Schegloff, and Jefferson (1977) was used (Tebble 1992). Utterances were transcribed to the level of the tone group (Halliday 1994), which is the unit of intonation. First the researcher and research assistants transcribed and checked the transcriptions of the English spoken by the physician and the interpreter. Then a NAATI-accredited professional translator using an audiotape transcribed the community language spoken by the patient and the interpreter. For the sake of anonymity the translators were not given a copy of a videotape, but occasionally when something was unclear, access to a videotape was provided. In addition the translator provided a back translation of the interpreter's rendition as well as a literal translation and/or a morphological gloss and their own translation when needed. Non-Roman scripts also were transliterated. The researcher and student researchers checked the translators' transcriptions, translations, and glosses. Thus the length of a full transcription with translations and glosses was typically about 100 pages, ranging from 80 to 240 A4 pages.

## Methods of Analysis (With Some Findings)

This section briefly introduces the concept of the generic structure that was identified in all of the transcriptions of the interpreted specialist medical consultations recorded during the data-gathering phase of the Medical Interpreting Project. It also refers to the units of analysis adopted from a variety of disciplines for the analysis of the transcriptions and video recordings. This section is not exclusively an exposition of the units of analysis but a brief statement of what they are, (or sources from which new researchers can gain some information about them) and some of the findings obtained from their application to the Medical Interpreting Project data.

## Units of Analysis to Identify the Generic Structure

Having established that the discourse structures of the two main genres of the systems analysts' professional interviews were those outlined in figure 1 (Tebble 1991a), it was appropriate to see how far the methodology was applicable to the interpreted medical consultation. The

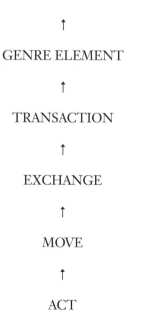

GENRE

↑

GENRE ELEMENT

↑

TRANSACTION

↑

EXCHANGE

↑

MOVE

↑

ACT

Figure 1. Hierarchy of discourse structures constituting the professional consultation or interview. (After Tebble 1991a, 1999, 184)

method of analysis of the transcriptions was the application of concepts (Taylor Torsello et al. 1997; Tebble 1993a, 1999), introduced and used by two different groups of systemic functional linguistics (SFL) scholars, Sinclair and Coulthard (1975) of the Birmingham SFL school and Hasan (1978) of the Sydney SFL school. Sinclair and Coulthard took a bottom-up approach to the analysis of spoken discourse from the smallest unit, the speech act (adopted into semantics from the philosophy of language), to the move, the exchange, and the transaction (a sequence of exchanges). These major structural discourse categories were applicable to the transcriptions, but given that Sinclair and Coulthard analyzed the discourse of teacher-pupil classroom language, some of their subcategories and discourse functions did not apply to interpreted medical consultations. Even so, the speech act (Austin 1980; Searle 1970) was conveyed by two obligatory moves—the initiating (I) and responding (R) moves (corresponding to the first and second pair parts of an adjacency pair used in conversation analysis)—and an optional follow-up (Fu) move. These two or three sequential moves **I^R^(Fu)** comprise the core structure of the exchange. Two additional nonobligatory moves, the framing and focusing moves, provide for metalinguistic marking of the organizational features of the discourse, particularly of the transaction. Sequences of exchanges related to subtopics provided the transaction.

Hasan (1978) and Halliday and Hasan (1985) took a top-down approach to the analysis of the discourse of genres and identified the genre element. This approach, when applied to each complete transcription, could reveal the large elements of the text as equivalent to the social stages of the interpreted consultation such as the exposition (Tebble 1999) or the conclusion of the actual speech event of the interpreted consultation. Tebble (1991a, 1999), using also a bottom-up approach—an analysis of ranked discourse components from the smallest, the tone groups and speech acts, to moves in every turn at talk, to the sequence of the moves in specific exchanges, to the transaction, Sinclair and Coulthard's (1975) largest discourse unit—showed that in professional interviews one or groups of transactions on one topic provided the genre element. By combining the sequence of structures of both Sinclair and Coulthard (1975) and Hasan (1978) and Halliday and Hasan (1985), Tebble demonstrated that the discourse of the particular genre, the lengthy professional

Greetings

Introductions
(Contract)

Stating/Eliciting the Problem

Ascertaining the Facts
(Diagnosing the Facts)

Stating the Resolution/Exposition
(Decision by Patient)

Clarifying any Residual Matters

Conclusion

Farewells

Figure 2. Generic structure of interpreted medical consultations.
(After Tebble 1999, 185)


interview, comprises all the discourse structures shown in figure 1. The method of analysis was applied to the very substantial transcriptions of the interpreted medical consultations with their translations and glosses to identify each speech act, each move, each exchange, and each transaction, thereby showing how they made up the genre element at each social stage of the genre of the interpreted medical consultation. This method of analysis was able to demonstrate the eight obligatory and three optional stages that constitute the genre of the interpreted medical consultation as shown in figure 2.[3]

These stages shown in figure 2 are socially identifiable and are different from each other linguistically. They form the procedural path for the conduct of the interpreted medical consultation. Understanding the purpose of these stages and when they occur helps the interpreter keep on track and not

---

3. An additional optional stage ("dictating letter") may eventually be included in the genre to account for the practice of the physician dictating a letter that summarizes the consultation in a letter to the referring doctor. This stage did not occur in the data referred to in this chapter even though it is a practice of some consultant physicians.

lose energy or focus, as happens with inexperienced interpreting students, who think that all they should do is just try to keep up by interpreting the main content of turns at talk. The main purpose of the specialist medical consultation is for the referred patient to present with symptoms to a medical expert who diagnoses the patient's particular condition, recommends a plan of treatment, and informs the referring professional about this. Because the physician and patient do not speak each other's language sufficiently well enough to understand each other in this professional context, they require the services of a professional medical interpreter to relay accurately everything that they say to each other. The specialist consultation has a beginning and an end bounded by greetings and farewells. The introductions ensure the name and identity of the participants. The interpreter during the contract stage (Tebble 1998a, 1998b, 2012) usually takes the floor to specify his or her role. The stage of ascertaining the facts can have two parts (Hirsh 2001), the actual interview and the medical examination. Stating the resolution or the exposition is the climax of the consultation (Tebble 1998a, 1998b, 1999). Opportunity is given for the patient and physician to clarify any uncertain matters before the physician draws the consultation to a conclusion.

## Role of Knower

Given that the genre of the interpreted medical consultation is one that entails information seeking and exchange, the role of who knows what with regard to each item of information can be tracked following the work of Berry (1981), a SFL scholar. She identified which speakers held the most and least knowledge in exchanges and showed that a person asking for information may already hold that information but can be testing the knowledge of their interlocutor. K1 is the "primary knower," the person with the most knowledge on that micro-item of information, and K2 is the "secondary knower," the interlocutor with less knowledge, revealed on that item of information in that exchange. The roles of K1 and K2 can change according to the type of move that the interlocutors use.

## Further Application of Units of Analysis (With Some Findings)

Figure 3 shows the layout (usually in "landscape") of the method of analysis of a sample text, an exchange, which was applied to the complete batch of transcriptions (please see appendix b). The translation and gloss have been removed from figure 3 to enhance readability. The initiating move in this exchange is made by the doctor, who in the role of the secondary knower, K2, asks a yes/no question. The given literal translation of the interpreter's relay is "*You you remember how was it first detected, the diabetes?*" The patient's answer in the responding move (2) shows her in the role of primary knower, K1. The doctor uses a follow-up move (3) to acknowledge the patient's answer and expresses her surprise at the answer nonverbally by laughing. Having received this new information (that the patient was bitten by a dog) the doctor now also is a primary knower at least on the micro-topic of what triggered the detection of the patient's diabetes.

| MOVE | ACT | ROLE | SPKR | MOVE No. | TEXT |
|------|-----|------|------|----------|------|
| IN | Q | K2 | Dr | 1 | do you recall how they first detected the diabetes ↑ |
|  |  |  | Int |  | usted se acuerda cómo fue que primero detectaron la diabetes |
| R | Ans | K1 | P | 2 | un perro me morDIÓ |
|  |  |  | Int |  | I was bitten by a dog |
| Fu | Ack | K1 | Dr | 3 | right ((laughs)) |

(Sp/VM/54)

Figure 3. Analysis of a sample eliciting exchange.

The speech acts can be listed and classified into categories (e.g., after Allan 1986) for their typical frequencies of type such as directives or acknowledgments, direct and indirect speech acts, and communicative functions. These categories can then be viewed according to medical specialty; speaker (physician, patient, interpreter); idiolect; and using the back translations and glosses, the translatability of what was said. The speech act as a performative utterance can be analyzed for the syntactic expressions and the message design (using theme–rheme structure for each utterance). The moves show the type of communicative turn the speaker takes, whether they initiate the exchange or respond to the initiating move or follow up the response. The framing and focusing moves can also show the metalinguistic organization of an interpreted consultation

(Tebble 2009). The types and frequency of occurrence of auditor back-channel responses (*mm, uhuh*) (e.g., Duncan 1974) as potential full moves or back fillers can be examined for their contribution to the interpersonal metafunction as signals indicating, for example, continuing listening or an empathic attitude (Tebble 2010). The analysis of direction of gaze can show the style of attention and involvement (Hirsh 2001; Martin 1998; Mason 2012) or disengagement of the listener when taking up, taking over, using, and relinquishing turns at talk. Attributing the roles of K1, holder of the knowledge, or K2, holder of less or no knowledge on the specific information, in these moves during the interpreted consultation can reveal the distribution and exchange of knowledge in the exchange and what information needs to be checked. The number and types of transactions can show the subtopics covered and how they constitute a social stage or genre element in the consultation (Tebble 1999, 183–84).

Cocker (1999), using Tebble's "scale of certainty" (Tebble 1991a; 1994, 269–72; 2009, 212–13), analyzed the checking strategies of the physicians in the eliciting exchanges of five interpreted medical consultations. Methods of analysis drew upon SFL, using genre theory as previously discussed, the analysis of cohesion (Halliday and Hasan, 1976), and theme-rheme structure (Halliday 1994); as well as the concepts of the adjacency pairs of the formulation and decision, and of the observation and decision from conversation analysis (Heritage and Watson 1979; Tebble 1993b). His analysis of the cohesion of the checking strategies in the eliciting exchanges of five interpreted medical consultations found that all of the formulations and their decisions occurred in the history-taking section of the genre element, ascertaining the facts (see figure 2). The observations and their decisions were found in both this stage and in subsequent stages of the consultations. Rarely was the decision one that neither confirmed nor disconfirmed the formulation or observation. The most senior consultant physician used more checking strategies than the senior registrars. Quite a number of checking strategies on the rank of significant uncertainty were used to clarify matters. Apart from providing accurate information for the consultant physician, the use of the formulation has an effect on the tenor of the consultation as it demonstrates to the patient that the physician has been listening and is genuinely interested in the resolution of their problem by ensuring that he or she has complete and accurate information on which to base his or her diagnosis and subsequent advice (Cocker 1999, 141).

Interpreters in training need to understand the pragmatic and syntactic features of the formulation exchanges and where they occur in the genre of the interpreted medical consultation to ensure cohesive and accurate interpreting. From Cocker's project additional exemplars were added to Tebble's "scale of certainty," which provides ranks of expressions used to check a speaker's degree of certainty about what has been said in the preceding or previous discourse.

## Interpersonal Features of Interpreted Medical Consultations

Concerning the principle of "accuracy" within the code of conduct of the Australian Institute of Interpreters and Translators is the requirement that interpreters and translators

> provide accurate renditions of the source utterance or text in the target language. Accurate is defined for this purpose as optimal and complete, without distortion or omission and preserving the content and intent of the source message or text. (AUSIT 2012, 10)

Within SFL each utterance is treated as comprising three metafunctions: the ideational, the interpersonal, and the textual (Halliday and Matthiessen 1999). Most effort in interpreting has tended to be given to the *ideational*, the so-called content of the message, but because the speaker also expresses an attitude toward what they say and/or to their interlocutor, the *interpersonal* must also be conveyed by the interpreter to meet the ethic of rendering a complete interpretation. The rapport between physician and patient is vital to the patient's respect for and trust of the physician, which in turn affects the patient's compliance with the recommended medical treatment. Patient-centered care as a contemporary philosophy of medicine requires the physician not only to practice competent clinical skills of diagnosis and treatment but also to use high-quality interpersonal skills, which include empathic listening (e.g., Rider and Nawotniak 2010). The nuances of attitude of both patient and physician need to be interpreted accurately. Appraisal Analysis within SFL, which is used to examine the discourse semantics of a text, provides the methodology for analyzing the interpersonal metafunction (e.g., Martin and Rose 2007; Martin and White 2005; White 1999). Tebble

([1996] 2004, 1999), applying the early categories of Appraisal Analysis from Martin (1992, 1998),[4] demonstrated analyses of tenor in interpreted medical consultations. Using the generic structure described previously, Tebble ([1996] 2004) demonstrated the tenor of the physician, patient, and interpreter throughout an interpreted neurology consultation by analyzing the discourse for occurrences of grammatical mood, modalization, modulation, person, forms of address, politeness lexis, and comment, including laughter. Tebble (1999) provided a detailed description of the interpersonal metafunction and demonstrated its application to the tenor of two medical consultant physicians during the exposition, the genre element that is the climax of their interpreted medical consultations. It illustrates the interpersonal nuances that interpreters need to be aware of and know how to interpret.

Willis (2001) advanced the methods used by Tebble ([1996] 2004, 1999) and analyzed the linguistic features of the rapport of two consultant physicians in two interpreted medical consultations using the method of Appraisal Analysis after White (2001). Willis (2001) applied the discourse semantic appraisal categories of attitude (affect, positive and negative judgment, and appreciation), features of engagement, and features of graduation. Willis found that besides the numerous interpersonal features prevailing in the genre elements of introductions, greetings, and farewells, the history-taking section of the ascertaining the facts genre element (Tebble 1992, 1999) had a high occurrence of the appraisal engagement category "optionalize," which is a subcategory of "probabilize." This showed the open-mindedness of the physicians when seeking information about the patient's medical history and the potential for the patients to feel confident to offer correct information. The Appraisal Analysis also showed the importance of interpreting the positive feedback of "good" and "ok" given to the patient during the physical examination as expressions of rapport in the ascertaining the facts stage (Tebble [1996] 2004). Such expressions can also occur within the metalingual function of the discourse structure as discourse markers or framing moves (Tebble 2009, 211–12).

---

4. Pedagogic applications of more recent developments in Appraisal Analysis (Martin and Rose 2007; Martin and White 2005; Tebble 2005; White n.d.) have been used in the Master of Arts Interpreting and Translation course at Monash University.

Hirsh (2001) analyzed four interpreted medical consultations for generic structure and in particular for their interpersonal features. She extended the Medical Interpreting Project's categories of analysis of the interpersonal features of talk to include not only those proposed by Martin (e.g., 1996, 1998, 2000) and White (1999) but also some pragmatic features of politeness, the pragmatic expression "I think" (Simon-Vandenbergen 1998), Mishler's (1984) "voice of the lifeworld," and a way of studying the relationship between gaze and taking turns (as mentioned earlier). She found variable use of personal pronouns with some physicians (untrained in working with interpreters) using "you" while speaking and looking at the patient and "she" and "her" when looking at the interpreter. Patients were addressed by their names and titles during the introductions, commencement of the stage stating/eliciting the problem, and at the start of the exposition stage. All of the physicians introduced themselves using at least their first names; two included their surnames, and one included her title and surname. These forms of address relate to the status, authority, and degree of professional distance that the physicians expressed about themselves. A variety of conventional politeness expressions were used by all physicians to show deference. The voice of the patient's lifeworld was encouraged by the physicians in the two oncology consultations in this set of four consultations of the Medical Interpreting Project. The issue of the frequent nonrelaying by the interpreter of the physicians' feedback also occurred in Hirsh's (2001) findings. The use of modality in the physician's talk was considerable, and interpreters need to be able to relay its nuances into the respective community languages to ensure complete and accurate interpreting to convey the physicians' politeness and respectful attitudes. The use of tagging (types of question tags) for content and expression of interpersonal concern were also important in conveying the physician's tenor.

The uses of the categories for the analysis of tenor (e.g., Martin 1992, 1998, 2000) and subsequently of Appraisal Analysis, the discourse semantic analysis of the interpersonal metafunction of a text (e.g., Martin and Rose 2007; Martin and White 2005; White 1999), are also ways of applying SFL units of analysis to the discourse of interpreted consultations. They have been separated here from other units of analysis because of their specific use in the analysis of the interpersonal metafunction, which has not yet been given the recognition it deserves in interpreting studies.

# Broad Findings

In summary the discourse analyses of the interpreted medical consultations have provided a substantial linguistic description of the genre of the interpreted medical consultation. They have focused in particular on its generic stages and features of each of these stages, be they types of speech acts; types of eliciting and checking strategies, their syntactic structures, and places of occurrence; features of cohesion within exchanges; the metalinguistic features of the organization of the consultation and the way they reveal the operational code of AUSIT's Code of Conduct including the briefing and contract (Tebble 2012, 28–35); the information flow between speakers; the length and structure of utterances comfortable for professional dialogue interpreters to interpret; and a glossary of plain language expressions for neurological examinations.[5] Use of eye contact and gaze is a challenge for the physician and patient, who may look at the interpreter rather than each other (Tebble 1998a). The interpreter needs to address this issue during the briefing and the contract stage and/or nonverbally during the consultation to help participants maintain rapport and make smooth transitions when relinquishing turns at talk. The interpersonal metafunction has been shown to have different types of instantiation depending on the pragmatics relevant to the generic stage. Forms of address (names and pronouns) and politeness expressions occur in specific stages of the interpreted consultation and are easy to interpret. However, the nuances of some of the lexicogrammatical features of modalization; the discourse semantics that reveal attitude, judgment, alignment, and distance; and adverbs and adjectives of graduation are challenging for the interpreter when relaying the tenor of the participants. The experienced interpreters were not found particularly wanting in most of these areas. Nevertheless, such information needs to be made explicit to interpreters in training so that as the consultation unfolds they can relay not only the content of what is said but also the level of rapport being expressed by the physician and patient in the two languages.

---

5. The occurrence of technical jargon throughout the interpreted consultations was minimal. A rapid method used during a neurological examination provided a useful exemplar of informal style switching by the neurologist.

## Application of Findings

As an applied linguistics project the Medical Interpreting Project has had both theoretical and practical outcomes. It has contributed to genre theory in linguistics an example of professional interviews. It has contributed to the linguistic description of professional interpreting practice. This research has provided a one-semester genre-based curriculum and pedagogy for pre-service education (e.g., Tebble 1996, forthcoming) and material for professional development of community interpreters (e.g., Tebble 1999, 2003, 2008, 2009, 2012; see appendix A). In addition to providing a new way of educating interpreters, a further outcome has been the design and implementation of a short course and materials to train physicians in how to work effectively with interpreters (Tebble 1998a, 1998b, 1999, 2003; see also appendix A). An unanticipated outcome has been the extensive use of this material (video and book) for the training of other professionals both in health care and beyond in how to work effectively with interpreters. The production and use of the video, book, and short course for the education of physicians was the second phase of this major project and attracted several development grants and the award of an industry fellowship. Appendix A lists conference papers (1990–2012) whereby findings from the project were disseminated.

## CONCLUSION

This chapter has described the Medical Interpreting Project conducted at Deakin University, Monash University, and Southern Health in Melbourne, Australia, particularly for interpreters, interpreter educators, early career researchers, and prospective doctoral candidates planning to investigate aspects of community interpreting. The project has been conducted within the domain of applied linguistics, making particular use of the very comprehensive theory of SFL and drawing upon ethnographic fieldwork, ethnography of communication, sociolinguistics, ethnomethodology, and conversation analysis; philosophy of language and speech act theory; pragmatics, social psychology, and nonverbal communication studies; adult learning curriculum design; and film production. It was also situated within the two professions of medicine and interpreting. The research has provided a solid description of what happens linguistically in the genre of an interpreted medical consultation conducted by consultant physicians who work in a highly regarded medical faculty attached to a major teaching hospital. None had been trained to work with interpreters, but their consultations all followed a similar structure that had been influenced by their medical communication education beliefs and philosophy of medical practice. They conducted and led the consultations, displaying respect and empathy for their patients and inviting them to contribute not only answers but to ask any questions about any concerns they may have had. The interpreters as professionals willingly allowed their performances to be scrutinized to help us understand the work of contemporary, qualified, and accredited professional medical interpreters. Three extensions of this project at Monash University will focus on patients and carers; interpreters; and physicians respectively. The study of empathy in interpreted medical consultations for elderly Italian-speaking patients with an accompanying adult will add to our knowledge of the interpersonal metafunction and how to interpret it. The interpreters will study recordings of their own performances to apply the findings reported in this chapter and accordingly develop self-reflective skills and a checklist to monitor their work. An additional study of physicians' colloquialisms and their challenge for the interpreter will provide some helpful guidance for physicians to plan what they are going to say while others talk (as per Tebble 1998a). This project was conducted with English as the professionals' language. Future genre studies could show interpreters how these linguistic metafunctions, structures, and communication strategies operate in different language pairs. Describing the generic structure of the same type of speech event is a critical starting point for providing the contextualization and the structural and metalinguistic framework for research into professionally interpreted events. Generic structures enable replication and generalization of findings and contribute more to understanding than just the anecdote of the individual. Interpreter education is desperately in need of detailed linguistic descriptions of other types of interpreted professional interviews and meetings. An applied linguistics approach makes use of a theory of linguistics that is focused on language in communication rather than on language just as a code draws upon insights from other relevant disciplines and understands the sociocultural context out of which the data are drawn. It is an approach I strongly recommend to obtain much of the information needed to educate interpreters who interpret for social and welfare workers, police, public service bureaucrats, solicitors, local bankers, estate agents, school principals and teachers, and the many others in the health-care profession beside the consultant physician.

## ACKNOWLEDGMENTS

I sincerely acknowledge the contributions to the Medical Interpreting Project made by the patients; physicians; nurses; interpreters; Sandra Nestoridis, former chief interpreter, Southern Health; Professor Barry McGrath, the liaison medical consultant to the project; Michael Ashby, professor of palliative care; translators; research assistants; secretaries; The Walrus Says ... video recording and production team; Deakin University Learning Services audiovisual, editing, and graphic design teams; Adolfo Gentile, former head, interpreting and translating program at Deakin University; research students; and AUSIT colleagues. The project was funded by grants from Deakin University, Language Australia, the Australian Research Council, and the Australian Commonwealth Government. More recent support has been provided by Monash University.

## REFERENCES

AILA (Association Internationale de Linguistique Appliquée). 1999. *AILA Scientific Commission on Discourse Analysis home page.* Accessed April 2010, http://www.ling.mq.edu.au/nlp/aila/othercom.htm.

ALAA (Applied Linguistics Association of Australia). 1998. *Statement of good practice.* Accessed May 2010 from http://www.alaa.org.au/.

Allan, Keith. 1986. *Linguistic meaning.* Vol. 2. London: Routledge and Kegan Paul.

AUSIT (Australian Institute of Interpreters and Translators). 2012. AUSIT Code of ethics and code of conduct. Accessed May 2013 from http://www.ausit.org/AUSIT/About/Ethics___Conduct/Code_of_Ethics/AUSIT/About/Code_of_Ethics.aspx.

Austin, J. L. 1980. *How to do things with words.* Edited by J. O. Urmson and Marina Sbisà. 2nd ed. Oxford: Oxford University Press.

Australian Government National Health and Medical Research Council. 2007. *National statement on ethical conduct in human research.* Accessed November 2009 from http://www. nhmrc.gov.au/_files_nhmrc/publica tions/attachments/e72.pdf.

Berry, Margaret. 1981. Systemic linguistics and discourse analysis: A multilayered approach to exchange structure. In *Studies in discourse analysis*, edited by Malcolm Coulthard and Martin Montgomery, 120–45. London: Routledge and Kegan Paul.

Cocker, Rodney. 1999. *Physicians' checking strategies: An analysis of the formulations and observations used by physicians in interpreted specialist medical consultations*. Unpublished BA(Hons) thesis. Deakin University.

Corsellis, Ann. 2008. *Public service interpreting: The first steps*. Basingstoke, UK: Palgrave Macmillan.

Duncan, S. 1974. On the structure of speaker-auditor interaction during speaking turns. *Language in Society* 2:161–80.

Graham, Anne Marie. 2012. *Training provision for public service interpreting and translation in England*. Accessed September 2012 from http://Finalreport-on-PSIT-provision-Sept-2012-LLAS-1.

Hale, Sandra B. 2007. *Community interpreting*. Basingstoke, UK: Palgrave Macmillan.

Halliday, M. A. K. 1994. *An introduction to functional grammar*. 2nd ed. London: Edward Arnold.

Halliday, M. A. K., and Ruqaiya Hasan. 1976. *Cohesion in English*. London: Longman.

———. 1985. *Language, context, and text: Aspects of language in a socialsemiotic perspective*. Geelong, Australia: Deakin University.

Halliday, M. A. K., and Christian M. I. M. Matthiessen. 1999. *Construing experience through meaning: A language-based approach to cognition*. London: Cassell.

Hasan, Ruqaiya.1978. Text in the systemic functional model. In *Current trends in textlinguistics*, edited by Wolfgang U. Dressler, 228–46. Berlin: de Gruyter.

Heritage, John, and D. R.Watson. 1979. Formulations as conversational objects. In *Everyday language: Studies in ethnomethodology*, edited by George Psathas, 123–62. New York: Irvington.

Hirsh, Dianne. 1997. Discourse analysis of dental consultations. Unpublished BA(Hons) thesis, Deakin University.

———. 2001. Interpersonal features of talk in interpreted medical consultations. Unpublished MA thesis. Deakin University.

Labov, William. 1972. The study of language in its social context. In *Sociolinguistic patterns*, 183–259. Philadelphia: University of Pennsylvania Press.

Martin, J. R. 1992. *English text: System and structure*. Amsterdam: John Benjamins.

———. 1996, July. Getting inter/personal: Construing value in text. Paper presented at the International Systemic Functional Congress, University of Technology, Sydney.

————. 1998, July. Communities of feeling: Positive discourse analysis. Plenary paper presented at the 10th Euro-International Systemic Functional Linguistics Association Workshop, University of Liverpool, Liverpool, UK.

————. 2000. Beyond exchange: APPRAISAL systems in English. In *Evaluation in text: Authorial stance and the construction of discourse*, edited by Susan Hunston and Geoff Thompson, 142–75. Oxford: Oxford University Press.

Martin, J. R., and David Rose. 2007. *Working with discourse: Meaning beyond the clause*. 2nd ed. London: Continuum.

Martin, J. R., and P. R. R. White. 2005. *The language of evaluation: Appraisal in English*. Basingstoke, UK: Palgrave Macmillan.

Mason, Ian. 2012. Gaze, positioning and identity in interpreter-mediated dialogues. In *Coordinating participation in dialogue interpreting*, edited by Claudio Baraldi and Laura Gavioli, 177–200. Amsterdam: John Benjamins.

Mishler, Elliot G. 1984. *The discourse of medicine: Dialectics of medical interviews*. Norwood, NJ: Ablex.

Niemants, Natacha, S. A. 2012. The transcription of interpreting data. *Interpreting*, 14(2): 165–91.

Rider, Elizabeth, and Ruth Nawotniak. 2010. *A practical guide to teaching and assessing the ACGME core competencies*. 2nd ed. Marblehead, MA: HCPro.

Sacks, Harvey, Emanuel Schegloff, and Gail Jefferson. 1977. A simplest systematics for the organization of turn taking in conversation. In *Studies in the organization of conversational interaction*, edited by Jim Schenkein, 7–55. New York: Academic Press.

Searle, John, R. 1970. *Speech acts: An essay in the philosophy of language*. London: Cambridge University Press.

Simon-Vandenbergen, Anne-Marie. 2000. The functions of *I think* in political discourse. *International Journal of Applied Linguistics* 10(1): 41–63.

Sinclair, John McH., and R. M. Coulthard. 1975. *Towards an analysis of discourse: The English used by teachers and pupils*. London: Oxford University Press.

Slade, Diana, Hermine Scheeres, Marie Mandis, Rick Iedema, Roger Dunstan, Jane Stein-Parbury, Christian Matthiessen, Maria Herke, and Jeanette McGregor. 2008. Emergency communication: The discursive challenges facing emergency clinicians and patients in hospital emergency departments. *Discourse and Communication* 2(3): 271–98.

Taylor Torsello, Carol, Sandra Gallina, Maria Sidiropoulou, Christopher Taylor, Helen Tebble, and A. R. Vuorikoski. 1997. Linguistics, discourse analysis, and interpretation. In *Conference interpreting: Current trends in research: Proceedings of the International Conference on Interpreting: What do we know and how?* edited by Yves Gambier, Daniel Gile, and Christopher Taylor, 167–86. Amsterdam: John Benjamins.

Tebble, Helen. 1991a. The systems analyst's interview: A linguistic study of spoken discourse. Unpublished PhD thesis. Monash University.

———. 1991b. Towards a theory of interpreting. In *CITEAA XIII Proceedings of the 13th Conference of the Interpreter/Translator Educators' Association of Australia*, edited by Paul Hellander, 54–59. Adelaide: South Australian College of Advanced Education.

———. 1992. The genre element in the systems analyst's interview. *Australian Review of Applied Linguistics* 15(2): 120–36.

———. 1993a. A discourse model for dialogue interpreting. In *Proceedings of the First Practitioners' Seminar*, Australian Institute of Interpreters and Translators, 1–26. Canberra: NAATI.

———. 1993b. Formulations and observations in professional interviews: Systems analysis. In *Proceedings of the XVth International Congress of Linguists*. Vol. 3, edited by André Crochetière, Jean-Claude Boulanger, and Conrad Ouellon, 265–68. Sainte Foy, Quebec: Les Presses de l'Université Laval.

———. 1994. The systems analyst's interview. In *Text and talk in professional contexts*, edited by Britt-Louise Gunnarsson, Per Linell, and Bengt Nordberg, 269–72. Uppsala, Sweden: Swedish Association of Applied Linguistics.

———. (1996) 2004. Research into tenor in medical interpreting. *Interpreting Research 10* 6(1): 33–45. Republished in *Collected papers from* Interpreting Research, 37–49. Tokyo: Japan Association for Interpretation Studies. Citations refer to the JAIS edition.

———. 1996. A discourse-based approach to community interpreter education. In *New horizons: Proceedings of the XIVth World Congress of the Fédération Internationale des Traducteurs (FIT)*, 1: 385–94. Melbourne: Australian Institute of Interpreters and Translators.

———. 1998a. *Medical interpreting*. Geelong, Australia: Deakin University and Language Australia.

———. 1998b. *Medical interpreting* [video]. Geelong, Australia: Deakin University and Language Australia.

———. 1999. The tenor of consultant physicians: Implications for medical interpreting. *Translator* 5(2): 179–200.

———. 2003. Training doctors to work effectively with interpreters. In *The Critical Link 3: Interpreters in the community: Selected papers from the Third International Conference on Interpreting in Legal, Health and Social Service Settings*, edited by Louise Brunette, Georges Bastin, Isabelle Hemlin, and Heather Clarke, 81–95. Amsterdam: John Benjamins.

———. 2004, May. Discourse analysis: Its relevance to ethical performance in medical interpreting. Paper presented at Critical Link 4:

International Conference on Community Interpreting, Stockholm University, Stockholm.

———. 2005, September. Interpreting the generic and the interpersonal. Paper presented at the International Conference on Translation, Solo, Java, Indonesia.

———. 2008. Using systemic functional linguistics to understand and practise dialogue interpreting. In *Proceedings of the 35th International Systemic Functional Conference (ISFC): Voices around the world*, edited by Canzhong Wu, Christian M. I. M. Matthiessen, and Maria Herke, 146–51. Sydney: Macquarie University.

———. 2009. What can interpreters learn from discourse studies? In *The Critical Link 5: Quality in interpreting—A shared responsibility*, edited by Sandra Hale, Uldis Ozolins, and Ludmila Stern, 201–19. Amsterdam: John Benjamins.

———. 2010, June. Interpreting empathy in medical consultations. Paper presented at Critical Link 6: Interpreting in a Changing Landscape conference, Aston University, Birmingham, UK.

———. 2012. Interpreting or interfering? In *Coordinating participation in dialogue interpreting*, edited by Claudio Baraldi and Laura Gavioli, 23–44. Amsterdam: John Benjamins.

———. Forthcoming. A genre-based approach to teaching dialogue interpreting. Special issue, *Interpreter and Translator Trainer* 8(2).

Tebble, Helen, and Di Hirsh. 1997. Sociolinguistic profiles of interpreting/translating students. In *Interpreting/translating education in the age of economic rationalism: Proceedings of the XVII Conference of the Interpreter Educators' Association of Australia (CITEAA)*, edited by Uldis Ozolins, 90–102. Melbourne: Centre for Research and Development in Interpreting and Translating, Deakin University.

Wadensjö, Cecilia. 1998. Community interpreting. In *Routledge encyclopaedia of translation studies*, edited by Mona Baker, 41–47. London: Routledge.

White, P. R. R. 1999. *An introductory tour through appraisal theory*. Accessed annually 1999–2012 from http://www.grammatics.com/appraisal/overview/Frame.htm.

———. n.d. *Appraisal homepage*. Accessed annually 2001–2012 from http://www.grammatics.com.appraisal.

Willis, Cameron, L. 2001. Linguistic features of rapport: An investigation into consultant physicians' linguistic use of rapport. Unpublished BA(Hons) thesis. Deakin University.

## Appendix A

## Conference Papers for the Medical Interpreting Project (1990–2012)

Notes: These papers are different from the workshops reported in Tebble 2003. Asterisks (*) indicate papers relevant to the training of physicians and other healthcare practitioners in how to work effectively with medical interpreters.

Hirsh, D. 2000, July. Interpreting interpersonal features in doctor-patient talk. Paper presented at the International Systemic Functional Congress, University of Melbourne, Melbourne.

Hirsh, D. 2001, July. Interpersonal features of interpreted medical consultations. Paper presented at the Applied Linguistics Association of Australia Annual Conference, University of Canberra, Canberra.

Tebble, H. 1990a, September. Towards a theory of interpreting. Paper presented at the Thirteenth Conference of the Interpreter and Translator Educators' Association of Australia, South Australian College of Advanced Education, Adelaide.

———. 1990b, November. Towards a theory of interpreting: Applications to consultations and interviews in the medical domain. Paper presented at the Victorian Central Health Interpreter Service Education Seminar, Melbourne.

———. 1991a, September. A prototypal model for community interpreting. Paper presented at the Second National Conference on Interpreting/Translating Research, Key Centre for Asian Languages and Studies, University of Queensland, Brisbane.

———. 1991b, November. An approach to teaching three-cornered situation interpreting. Paper presented at the Fourteenth Conference of the Interpreter and Translator Educators' Association of Australia, Royal Melbourne Institute of Technology, Melbourne.

———. 1992a, August. A discourse model for teaching dialogue interpreting. Paper presented at the International Conference on Discourse of the Professions, Uppsala University, Uppsala, Sweden.

———. 1992b, November. A discourse model for dialogue interpreting. Paper presented at the First Practitioners' Seminar, Annual Conference of Australian Institute of Interpreters and Translators, Melbourne.

———. 1993a, July. Some considerations of tenor in dialogue interpreting. Paper presented at the Twentieth International Systemic Functional Linguistics Conference, University of Victoria, Victoria, British Columbia.

———. 1993b, September. Testing the scale of certainty in medical consultations. Paper presented at the Annual Conference of the Australian Linguistic Society, University of Adelaide, Adelaide.

———. 1993c, September. Living with language: The classroom–community nexus for interpreting and medical students. Paper presented at the Applied Linguistics Association of Australia Annual Congress, University of Adelaide, Adelaide.*

———. 1994, August. Dialogue interpreting and discourse analysis. Paper presented at the International Conference on Recent Research in Interpreting, Turku, Finland.

———. 1995a, June. Research into tenor in medical interpreting. Paper presented at Critical Link 1: First International Conference on Community Interpreting in Medical, Legal, and Welfare Settings. Orillia, Ontario, Canada.

———. 1995b, September. A case study of tenor in medical interpreting. Paper presented at the Australian Systemic Functional Linguistics Conference, University of Melbourne, Melbourne.

———. 1996a, July. Investigating tenor in medical interpreting. Paper presented at the International Systemic Functional Conference, University of Technology, Sydney.

———. 1996b, February. A discourse-based approach to community interpreter education. Paper presented at the XIVth World Congress of the Fédération Internationale des Traducteurs (FIT), Melbourne.

———. 1996c, February. Interpreting as discourse. Paper presented at the International Seminar on Research in Interpreting and Translating, Deakin University, Melbourne.

———. 1997a, July. Communication in practice: Medical interpreting. Paper presented at the annual conference, Australian and New Zealand Communication Association, La Trobe University, Melbourne.

———. 1997b, July. Working with interpreters. Paper presented at the Department of Obstetrics and Gynaecology, Monash University, Melbourne.*

———. 1998a, July. Getting the model right for a theory of medical interpreting. Paper presented at the Twenty-Fifth International Systemic Functional Linguistics Conference, University of Wales, Cardiff, UK.

———. 1998b, July. The tenor of consultant physicians: Implications for medical interpreting. Paper presented at the Tenth Euro-International Systemic Functional Workshop, University of Liverpool, UK.*

———. 1998c, September. Medical interpreting. Pilot video presented at the Grand Round, Monash Medical Centre, Melbourne.*

————. 1998d, September. Exploring the interpersonal metafunction in interpreted medical consultations. Paper presented at the Department of Psychological Medicine, Monash Medical Centre, Melbourne.*

————. 1998e. Interpreting in palliative care. Paper presented at McCulloch House, Monash Medical Centre, Melbourne.*

————. 1998f, November. Medical interpreting. Book and video presented at the Victorian Trans-cultural Mental Health Seminar for Regional Liaison Officers, St Vincent's Hospital, Melbourne.*

————. 1999a, June. Report on Deakin/industry fellowship. Paper presented at the Deakin Centre for Academic Development, Deakin University Waterfront Campus, Geelong, Australia.

————. 1999b, October. The training of newly graduated doctors to work with interpreters. Paper presented at the National Conference of the Interpreter and Translator Educators' Association of Australia, Royal Melbourne Institute of Technology, Melbourne.*

————. 2000a, May. Interpreting for the depressed patient. Paper presented at the Georgetown University Round Table for Languages and Linguistics, Washington, DC.*

————. 2000b, March. The role of interpreters in communicating traumatic material: A linguistic perspective. Paper presented at the 3rd World Conference for the International Society for Traumatic Stress Studies, Melbourne.*

————. 2001a, May. Training doctors to work effectively with interpreters. Paper presented at Critical Link 3, Third International Conference on Community Interpreting, University of Quebec at Montreal, Canada.*

————. 2001b, November. Discourse analytical techniques applied to medical interpreting. Paper presented at the International Association of Applied Linguistics' Scientific Commission on Discourse, Discourse on Discourses: The language of work and education, University of Technology, Sydney.*

————. 2002, July. Briefing the interpreter. Paper presented at the Applied Linguistics Association of Australia, Annual Congress, Macquarie University, Sydney.

————. 2004a, May. Discourse analysis: Its relevance to ethical performance in medical interpreting. Paper presented at the Critical Link 4, International Conference on Community Interpreting, Stockholm University, Sweden.

————. 2004b, October. Interpreting the interpersonal. Paper presented at the AUSIT/ASLIA National Conference, Melbourne.

————. 2005, September. Interpreting the generic and the interpersonal. Paper presented at the International Conference on Translation, Solo, Java, Indonesia.

————. 2007a, February. Communicating with patients who do not speak your language. Paper presented at the Intercultural Communication in Health Professional Education Symposium, University of Melbourne, Melbourne.*

————. 2007b, April. What can interpreters learn from discourse studies? Paper presented at the Critical Link 5, International Conference on Community Interpreting, Sydney.

————. 2008a, July. Using SFL to understand and practise dialogue interpreting. Paper presented at the Thirty-Fifth International Systemic Functional Linguistics Conference, Macquarie University, Sydney.

————. 2008b, July. Using SFL to understand and practise dialogue interpreting. Workshop presented at the Thirty-fifth International Systemic Functional Linguistics Conference, Macquarie University, Sydney.

————. 2008c, September. Applying discourse theories to the education of interpreters. Paper presented at the National Interpreting and Translation Research Symposium, University of Western Sydney, Bankstown, Sydney.

————. 2009a, July. When medical ethics and ethnic values conflict who comes off best? Paper presented at the Third Conference, International Association for Translation and Intercultural Studies, Monash University, Caulfield, Melbourne.

————. 2009b, October. Some applications of systemic functional linguistics to interpreting. Paper presented at the International Conference on Systemic Functional Linguistics and Its Contribution to Translation Studies, Solo, Indonesia.

————. 2009c, November. An interpreted snippet of conversation about the soup pot. Paper presented at the Fifth Symposium on Discourse Analysis, Monash University, Clayton, Melbourne.

————. 2010a, July. Appraisal analysis and empathy. Paper presented at the Thirty-Seventh International Conference of Systemic Functional Linguistics, University of British Columbia, Vancouver, Canada.

————. 2010b, July. Interpreting empathy in medical consultations. Paper presented at the Critical Link 6, International Conference on Community Interpreting, Aston University, Birmingham, UK.*

————. 2010c, August. Using systemic functional linguistics to understand medical interpreting. Paper presented at the Hong Kong Polytechnic University, Hong Kong.

————. 2010d, November. An approach to studying empathy in a bilingual medical consultation. Paper presented at the Sixth Symposium on Discourse Analysis, Faculty of Arts, Monash University, Clayton, Melbourne.

————. 2011, March. Healthcare communication: Really how much care? Paper presented at the International Symposium on Healthcare Communication: Research and Training in an International Perspective, Hong Kong Polytechnic University, Hong Kong.*

————. 2012, November. Research methods for studying medical interpreting—Making use of SFL. Paper presented at the Eighth Symposium on Discourse Analysis, Faculty of Arts, Monash University, Clayton, Melbourne.

# APPENDIX B

Abbreviations and transcription conventions are as follows:

| | | | |
|---|---|---|---|
| Ack: | Acknowledgment | K1 | Primary knower |
| Ans: | Answer | K2 | Secondary knower |
| DIÓ: | Stressed syllable | P | Patient |
| Dr | Doctor | R | Responding |
| Elicit | Eliciting | ↑ | Rising intonation |
| Fu | Follow up | (( )) | Additional to speech |
| SFL | Systemic functional linguistics | | |

The source of the extract is identified in a code in brackets at the end of the extract. The medical practitioners in this project prefer to be described as physicians. The word *doctor* and its abbreviation "Dr" are used for the transcription. The abbreviation "P" is used only for *patient* and not for *physician*.

COMMENTARY

## Researching What Works: Helen Tebble's Applied Linguistic Approach to Interpreter Education

*Ian Mason*

THE LARGE-SCALE research project described in Helen Tebble's chapter has considerable significance for interpreter education for a number of reasons, each of which merits further consideration.

The first and foremost of these reasons is the availability of descriptive empirical research findings *as an input* to curriculum design, rather than as a confirmatory adjunct. From the outset in the mid-20th century, spoken language interpreter education in Europe drew largely on the acquired experience of pioneer (conference) interpreters, who became trainers during the early years of the first university-level interpreter schools and who were influential in the professionalization of interpreting via the establishment of international associations and codes of practice for interpreters. We owe an enormous debt of gratitude to these prestigious figures, who ensured that interpreting was taken seriously and that the profession earned respect. As a consequence, though, the precepts of proper practice and the tenets of interpreter training were mostly laid down in the absence of any methodical investigation of what seasoned interpreters actually do, how they make their decisions, and the consequences of their decisions. In short, prescription preceded description. Since those times much progress has been made (for example, in Canada and Australia) in working with the profession to arrive at workable codes of practice. Nevertheless, some areas of uncertainty still remain.

An illustration of this is the requirement for scrupulous accuracy, included in most codes of practice. Helen Tebble cites one such injunction, that of AUSIT: The interpreter shall "provide accurate renditions of the source utterance or text in the target language. Accurate is defined for this purpose as optimal and complete ..." (this volume, 59).

Susan Berk-Seligson's (1990) masterly exposition of the difficulties English-to-Spanish court interpreters face in seeking to translate English passive constructions would already cast some doubt on the practicality of this rule. However, there is a further point, well recognized in the field of pragmatics but not always admitted in interpreter education: "everything that is said" is only part of what gets communicated in any real encounter.

Helen Tebble's insistence on the importance of the *interpersonal* function in medical consultations brings out a dimension of communication that may be overlooked in approaches that focus purely on words: nonverbal communication (including gaze, gesture, facial expression, proxemics), implicature and inference, politeness, and so on. Direction of gaze has been shown to be a crucial element in the coordination of turn taking, one of the face-to-face interpreter's main tasks (cf. Wadensjö 1998). In the case of sign language interpreting, gaze is an integral part of the signing medium, but, in the case of spoken language interpreting, do interpreter education courses address the interactional function in detail? Beyond a general injunction from interpreters to primary participants to "look at each other and not at the interpreter" (as reported by Bot 2005, 132) or to interpreters to "maintain eye contact with the [client] if culturally appropriate" (Thompson 1987), we have not—at least until recently (see Davitti 2012, Mason 2012)—undertaken detailed description of gaze behavior in interpreter-mediated exchanges. Tebble's corpus of actual medical consultations affords the opportunity to do so. Moreover, she points out the advantages of this for interpreter training: Seeing how eye gaze works (and sometimes does not work) in practice is far more valuable for students than general advice simply to look at the client. Indeed, the fact that it is often the doctor and the patient, rather than the interpreter, who initiate a pattern of gaze that is detrimental to direct communication (Tebble 1998) needs to be witnessed and documented to be understood. Based on such empirical findings, coping strategies and teaching approaches can be developed.

Gaze and eye contact are just one set of features attended to in Tebble's applied linguistic perspective. Among other nonverbal features that she singles out as revealing "nuances of attitude" are emotive responses (such as laughter, illustrated in figure 3 and mentioned again later). Interpreter training surely has to address the whole area of emotive response. Should the interpreter "replay" the response (that is, reproduce the nonverbal aspects such as intonation, smiles, or frowns; cf. Wadensjö 1998, 247) or simply ignore it? We should note here that AUSIT also requires interpreters to convey nonverbal cues—see Tebble's earlier work (2012, 32). What are the risks of each of these options? How do clients react to any (mediated or unmediated) laughter that, to them, does not appear motivated? How is the interpreter to react to displays of distress, including anger and tears? Such situations, commonplace in professional practice, are not always given prominence in the curriculum.

Above all, it is Tebble's report of the use of *Appraisal* Analysis (Martin and White 2005), not as an a priori theoretical construct but more as an instrument of description of observed behavior, which enhances the learning of trainee interpreters and offers them ways to modulate their response (their translation) to the *affect* of the speaker rather than just to "what is said." Engagement and positive feedback (both verbal and nonverbal) by doctors are essential features of patient-centered care; their handling by interpreters requires awareness and sensitivity. Here is an area where there are many false friends, in the sense that what is intended as supportive comment in one culture may seem intrusive or disparaging, for example, if translated literally into another. Operating across languages and cultures, the interpreter who focuses on words alone may easily misrepresent (underplay or overplay) the affective attitude of a speaker, with potentially serious consequences for the way the consultation develops.

The pragmatics of politeness are particularly important in intercultural encounters, once again an area that is much better appreciated when seen as it happens than as an element of interpreting theory. Tebble's focus on the management of *rapport* (cf. Spencer-Oatey 2008) is an essential ingredient in training and a pointer to the future of medical interpreter training. Indeed, a relevant question for the trainer is, To what extent is the management of rapport embedded in the statements of assessment criteria we use for testing trainees' skills and aptitudes? The research reported by Tebble convincingly demonstrates the importance of rapport in real medical consultations; this importance now needs to be followed up in pedagogy, assessment, accreditation, and ultimately in codes of professional practice.

We come now to the main thrust of the research: the investigation of *genre* in medical consultations. For some, this topic may seem to be a relapse into formalism and linguistic theory for its own sake. It is far from that. Let us once again approach this from a practical perspective. It some-times happens that an interpreter notices that some point which she has just translated (say, from a patient) does not appear to be taken up by the other participant (say, a doctor), not noticed, perhaps, or assumed to be of minor importance. The interpreter may be able to rectify this loss by bringing the point back into focus but can only do so while it remains relevant to the current stage of the consultation. Detailed awareness of the structure of the consultation genre, down to the level of the individual move, provides interpreters with a kind of map, a means of orientation that allows them, at any juncture, to know: What stage(s) have we completed? What are we doing now? Where are we going next? It moreover assists them in adjusting their translations to the current purpose and stage of the exchange. The value of such awareness and hence its importance in train-ing programs is surely not controversial. Any specialized program would be enhanced by inclusion of generic structure analysis of the encounter (as in fig. 2 of Tebble's chapter). The asylum interview, the judicial hearing, police questioning, social security interviews, all of these genres are amenable to a structural analysis of this kind.

Finally, this chapter points to an area of concern that deserves greater prominence in interpreter education. It is the issue of *power*, not dealt with to any great extent by Tebble here but latent in much of what she has to say. Section 3 deals with the role of "knower." Knowledge is power; under-standing of who knows what in any exchange provides an insight not just into the institutional investiture of power in one party to the exchange but also into the essential negotiability of power. The "primary knower" (K1) and the "secondary knower" (K2) are not immutable roles ascribed from the outset. Tebble observes that the roles of K1 and K2 can change accord-ing to the type of move that the interlocutors use. In interpreter-mediated medical exchanges, each participant is a "knower": the doctor of advanced medical knowledge, the patient of his or her own symptoms and life his-tory, and the interpreter of two languages and cultures and the dynamics of communication. In the dynamics of the three-way interpreter-mediated exchange, participants can recognize and defer to each other's knowledge or, conversely, they can deny, overlook, or ignore it (for example, a judge who overrules an interpreter, an interpreter who omits something another party says, perhaps because it is deemed irrelevant, a client who bypasses the interpreter by communicating directly in the language of the other party). Moreover, participants do not embark on an exchange on an equal footing. An asylum seeker, for example, may have a valid story to tell but, as amply documented by Barsky (1994) and Maryns (2008) among others, they may not have access to the discourses that are recognized by the authorities in the host country. As an example, note the discrepancy between official discourse and the language of everyday experience in the following exchange attested by Barsky:

— You are claiming refugee status on the basis of race, religion, nationality, membership in a particular social group or political opinion. What is pertinent here to these categories?
— Because we are not allowed to dress in short dresses. They all say "cover your body well. And your face."
— Yes, but the question is about persecution on the basis of one of the five categories.
— When we go out, if we don't cover ourselves, people stare at us.
— Is that all?
— And they throw stones at us …

(Barsky 1994, 184)

In such cases, the interpreter may—or may not—exercise agency in order to ensure that a powerless voice is heard. Taken together with Angelelli's (2004) groundbreaking study of medical interpreting, in which issues of power and control feature prominently, Helen Tebble's research offers ample evidence of the interpreter's room for maneuver. Frank and informed discussion of the extent of interpreters' agency in particular genres and settings, and of the ethics of interpreter intervention, must surely feature in the interpreter education curriculum of the future.

In this review, we have singled out some significant research-driven analytical concepts that can enhance interpreter education. I believe that they show the value of the descriptive research of Helen Tebble and her colleagues as an input into training. More than anything else, it is the methodological approach of this kind of research that is valuable for designers of interpreter education programs. Rather than simply introducing specialized vocabulary and topic areas and dealing with interpreting techniques in the abstract, training can be effective by showing what happens in real events, revealing the interpreter's and others' moves and the consequences of those moves. Instead of a direction of study from, say, systemic functional linguistics via appraisal theory and the grammar of modality to prescription of appropriate interpreter behavior, we can use all these research insights in an approach to curriculum design that starts from discovery of how interpreters and others actually do their job (in terms of managing rapport, genre and appraisal), then considers the effectiveness or ineffectiveness of particular behaviors, before integrating these insights into interpreter training for patient care.

## References

Angelelli, C. 2004. *Medical interpreting and cross-cultural communication.* Cambridge: Cambridge University Press.

Barsky, R. 1994. *Constructing a productive other: Discourse theory and the convention refugee hearing.* Amsterdam: John Benjamins.

Berk-Seligson, S. 1990. *The bilingual courtroom: Court interpreters in the judicial process.* Chicago: University of Chicago Press.

Bot, H. 2005. *Dialogue interpreting in mental health.* Amsterdam: Rodopi.

Davitti, E. 2012. Dialogue interpreting as intercultural mediation: Integrating talk and gaze in the analysis of parent–teacher meetings. Unpublished PhD thesis. University of Manchester, UK.

Martin, J. R., and P. R. R. White. 2005. *The language of evaluation: Appraisal in English.* Basingstoke, UK: Palgrave Macmillan.

Maryns, K. 2006. *The asylum speaker: Language in the Belgian asylum procedure.* Manchester, UK: St. Jerome.

Mason, I. 2012. Gaze, positioning, and identity in interpreter-mediated dialogues. In *Coordinating participation in dialogue interpreting,* edited by C. Baraldi and L. Gavioli, 177–99. Amsterdam: John Benjamins.

Spencer-Oatey, H., ed. 2008. *Culturally speaking: Culture, communication, and politeness theory.* New York: Continuum.

Tebble, H. 1998. *Medical interpreting.* Geelong, Australia: Deakin University and Language Australia.

———. 2012. Interpreting or interfering? In *Coordinating participation in dialogue interpreting,* edited by C. Baraldi and L. Gavioli, 23–44. Amsterdam: John Benjamins.

Thompson, W. 1987. *Counselling with interpreters: Sexual assault interviews.* Sydney: New South Wales Department of Health, Health Media and Education Centre.

Wadensjö, C. 1998. *Interpreting as interaction.* London: Longman.

COMMENTARY

# A Converted Interpreting Trainer's Response
## *Ester S. M. Leung*

TEBBLE'S PUBLICATIONS are prolific yet have a clear focus on the application of linguistic theories to the education and training of community interpreters, particularly interpreters working in medical settings. This chapter is no exception to her overall principle and general approach to the study, and it serves as a step-by-step guide "for prospective PhD students and postdoctoral scholars of community interpreting" (this volume, 42). Using her Medical Interpreting Project, which was conducted at Deakin University and Monash University, together with a regional network of hospitals in Melbourne, she illustrates how the project was developed and conducted from the conception, ethics application, recruitment of research staff members, and data collection process through the analysis and application of the research results to the eventual design of the medical interpreting training courses.

The Medical Interpreting Project is "substantial," as Tebble describes it, in terms of its scale and resources. The fact that Tebble managed to video and audiotape the authentic interpreting events themselves is impressive, and the fact that the recordings are done by professional film crews and technicians makes the study invaluable. Effort and resources in such scale really are difficult to achieve in today's economized academic environment.

Studies in community interpreting have always been closer to the field of linguistics rather than translation studies because of the spoken nature of the interpreting activity itself. Most interpreting studies have a strong preference for using the perspectives and approaches of discourse analysis in analyzing the collected data, for example, in the exemplary works of Hale (2007), Angelelli (2004), Wadensjö (1998), Tebble (1996, 1999, 2004, 2008), Roy (2000), and Metzger, Collins, Dively, and Shaw (2003) with specific reference to sign language interpreting. Tebble's works often are distinguished from the others by her very practical orientation on how the research findings should be applied.

Among all other linguistic approaches, Tebble favors the systemic functional linguistics (SFL) approach of Halliday and Hasan (1985) and Halliday (1994), which argues that language is "metafunctionally" organized and has three semantic components: ideational, interpersonal, and textual (Halliday1994). Tebble has matched these three components to the different genre stages of interpreter-mediated medical consultations that she identified in her earlier work in 1999 and emphasized that rather than just rendering the ideational (factual) content, interpreters should also pay attention to the interpersonal components of the utterances in which the medical professional and patient may build up a rapport and trust.

From my own experience of working with ethnic minorities language interpreters in Hong Kong, the advantages of using an SFL approach in the analysis of the data as well as the training of the medical interpreters is prominent. SFL allows greater flexibility and generality to describe different languages by using different linguistic systems than the traditional grammarian approach, which takes individual grammatical items individually and which may not be available in all languages. A clear explanation of the different genre stages of the medical encounter will help interpreter trainees focus on the most significant function of every social stage involved and, hence, the most important information they can expect to be rendered.

Similar to the interpreting practices that Angelelli (2004) identified in her study in the United States, it is observed that ethnic minority interpreters in Hong Kong do assert their understanding and influence on the medical consultation process. They are found to have explained, advocated, and highlighted information that they deemed important for the patients. For example, the following is an excerpt from one of the interpreted communications recorded for my own study in Hong Kong. The patient is an Urdu speaker whose utterances were interpreted into English for the Chinese doctor in a public hospital. The interpreter is female. The consultation has entered into the "resolution/exposition" stage according to the "generic structure of interpreted medical consultation" (Tebble 1999).

01:D(octor): basically the check-up is normal. If you want to have further check-up we can arrange another scan. But I think if you would not like another you can just observe.

02:P(atient): yes of course.

03:I(nterpreter): observe now? It's up to her?

04:P:*toh haan iske ilaaj kaiskepaas koi nai hai … mere koa isajaa nedega?*

(Then, he does not have any treatment for it…will he let me go in this condition?)

05:I: *toh aap kya chahti hain?*

(Then what do you want?)

06:P: *nai main to ilaaj karn achahti hoon … kyun, kya masla hai mera andarka?*

(No, I want to have treatment for this. Why, what is problem inside me?)

07:I: She says that she wants to have treatment because she feels pain you have to do something for her

I have used this example in the training of the medical interpreter trainees in Hong Kong to demonstrate the possible impact that this rendering of interpretation may have on the communication process of the medical consultation. Rather than using the traditional grammar approach, I used the concept of "theme" and "rheme" of SFL to describe the changes of the rhemes of the interpreter's turns 03 and 07; and her introduction of a new theme in turn 07 ("because she feels pain" … "you have to do something for her"). By doing so she was advocating the doctor should take further action or give additional treatment to the patient. Also, the interpreter is using the third person to interpret rather than first person as most of the code of practices would have prescribed and, subsequently, used mostly reported speech in her interpretation throughout the communication process. The doctor has no way to find out whether the utterance is of the patient or the interpreter. The "textual" liaison word "so" used in turn 04 makes her utterance sound like a challenge to the patient as well. My interpreter trainees found discussion of this kind of example particularly useful and easy to grasp, and it helped them to be more aware of the impact that they may have on the communication process.

Tebble's linguistic approach and findings are significant and relevant to study that involves different language backgrounds similar to mine, in which different ethnic minority languages such as Urdu, Punjabi, Hindi, Tagalog, and Thai are involved. Her proposition of using the systemic functional linguistics grammar approach is especially useful in allowing me to develop training material that is not language specific for the medical interpreters of different language and cultural backgrounds. Also, "the generic structure of the interpreted medical consultation" can be used to show interpreter trainees what to focus on and, hence, how to take notes—one of the most important skills for interpreters—for this kind of medical consultation.

Perhaps, what can be further developed from Tebble's study is a detailed description of the evaluative criteria for the medical interpreter's performance, which is greatly needed in the development of training material and accreditation of medical interpreters. To be of use the criteria should, like Tebble's work, be based on authentic data, analyzed and organized systematically, whether using the SFL grammar approach or any other linguistic model.

## References

Angelelli, Claudia. 2004. *Medical interpreting and cross-cultural communication*. New York: Cambridge University Press.

Hale, Sandra. 2007. *Community interpreting*. Basingstoke, UK: Palgrave Macmillan.

Halliday, Michael. 1994. *An introduction to functional grammar*, 2nd ed. London: Edward Arnold.

Halliday, Michael, and Ruqaiya, Hasan. 1985. *Language, context, and text: Aspects of language in a social-semiotic perspective*. Geelong, Australia: Deakin University.

Metzger, Melanie, Steven Collins, Valerie Dively, and Risa Shaw, eds. 2003. *From topic boundaries to omission: New research on interpretation*. Washington, DC: Gallaudet University Press.

Roy, Cynthia. 2000. *Interpreting as a discourse process*. Oxford: Oxford University Press.

Tebble, Helen. 1996. A discourse-based approach to community interpreter education. In *New horizons: Proceedings of the XIVth World Congress of the Fédération Internationale des Traducteurs (FIT)*, Vol. 1, 385–94. Melbourne: Australian Institute of Interpreters and Translators.

———. 1999. The tenor of consultant physicians: Implications for medical interpreting. *Translator* 5 (2): 179–200.

———. 2004. Research into tenor in medical interpreting. In *Collected papers from* Interpreting Research. Tokyo: JAIS.

———. 2008. Using systemic functional linguistics to understand and practise dialogue interpreting. In *Proceedings of the 35th International Systemic Functional Conference (ISFC): Voices around the world*, edited by Canzhong Wu, Christian M. I. M. Matthiessen, and Maria Herke, 146–51. Sydney: Macquarie University.

Wadensjö, Cecilia. 1998. *Interpreting as interaction*. London: Longman.

TERRY JANZEN

# The Impact of Linguistic Theory on Interpretation Research Methodology

## Abstract

The interpretation researcher's view of language—her linguistic theory—crucially impacts each key element of the research: the research process itself, the researcher's view and interpretation of the data, and research findings. In this chapter Terry Janzen examines why the interpretation researcher needs both a well-developed and useful theory of linguistic structure and a theory of interpretation and suggests how these might work together as tools to get the most out of interpretation research. Basic to this discussion is that a theory of language must underlie assumptions about language, even if that theory is not consciously or overtly explicated, because assumptions will be there regardless and will impact the interpretation researcher's work profoundly. In addition to this, the interpreting educator is equally impacted by her understanding of linguistic structure and the nature of communication, which permeates her discussion of the interpretation process with her students, and which is thus imparted to each new generation of interpreting practitioners.

IN THIS chapter we explore how the interpretation researcher's theory of language and theory of interpretation impact the research process and, in particular, how the researcher views and interprets the data. In the past it has sometimes been thought that linguistic theory has little to offer the field of interpretation (e.g., Seleskovitch 1976), which may have been the case regarding more structuralist views of language; however in recent years advances on several fronts in linguistic research are proving to be both complementary and informative to the study of interpretation.

87

Studies of dialogue and discourse analysis, for example, have gained importance in both linguistic and interpretation research (e.g., Napier 2002,
2004; Roy 2000; Wadensjö 1998). The information that linguists are learning about how speakers and signers structure their discourse from naturally
occurring language samples is now shaping modern linguistic theory, and
this has clear application to interpretation research. Most important, the
cognitive linguistic view of language and communication that Wilcox and
Shaffer (2005) take, building on the work of Langacker (1991, 2000) and
others (e.g., Reddy 1979, 1993; Sperber and Wilson 1995; Turner 1991), is
directly applicable to interpretation research in terms of how this theory
explains language structure and language interaction, along with additional
cognitive elements that are assumed to be part of our interaction processes,
such as subjectivity, contextualization, and ultimately, *inter*subjectivity.

The interpretation researcher's view of language—her linguistic
theory—crucially impacts her view of the data and thus impacts research
findings. We examine why the interpretation researcher needs a well-
developed and useful theory both of linguistic structure and of interpretation and suggest how these might work together as tools to get the most
out of interpretation research methods.

In what follows we look first at the interpreter's, the interpretation researcher's, and the interpreter educator's theories of language, treating
interpretation fundamentally as a linguistic pursuit and therefore concep-
tualizing interpretation research equally as a linguistic pursuit. In the section entitled "The interpreter researcher's theory of language" we examine
some of the ways that linguists have understood the form and function
of language and how this influences both the interpretation researcher
and the interpreting educator. In the next section, "Shaping a theory of
interpretation: The impact of linguistic theory" we look at what some of
the impacts of interpretation researchers' views on language and language
theories have been as they undertake to explain elements of interpretation,
and in the final section we draw some conclusions and point out some important implications for interpreting educators. Basic to this discussion
is that a theory of language must underlie assumptions about language,
even if that theory is not consciously or overtly explicated, because assumptions are there regardless and profoundly impact the interpretation
researcher's work.

## The Interpreter Researcher's Theory of Language

The premise of this chapter is that the interpretation researcher's assumptions about—or theory of—language underlie both her theory of interpretation and her understanding of interpretation data in her research. Some researchers may argue that they are unconcerned with linguistic theory, as Seleskovitch has in the past (1976), but I suggest that such a view is essentially untenable, because even if a researcher claims agnosticism in this regard, she cannot undertake research on a linguistic subject without considering the nature of the material she is studying and what lies behind its use.

## An Uneasy Relationship

Seleskovitch's objection to linguistic theory may have been a reaction to linguistic structuralism and the rise of the formalist, Chomskian approach in the 1970s. Interpretation, she says, "involves only the oral processing of an oral message, [which] is in most cases successful in transcending the linguistic aspects of the message. This is why the theory of interpretation is not concerned with descriptive or comparative linguistics but with speech performance" (Seleskovitch 1976, 95). The object of linguistic study at that time was primarily the written sentence, the meaning of which (if meaning was considered at all) was apparent because of the individual meanings contributed to the whole by each word, whereas context meant nothing because it could not be measured. In Seleskovitch's way of thinking, the meanings that the interpreter needs to contend with are not the dictionary definitions of words, which transcend individual, contextualized usages; rather, speakers have one particular meaning in mind when a word is chosen in contextualized discourse. She offers this advice: "A word of warning to the student interpreter who may fall into the trap of linguistics, failing to realize that the science of linguistics is essentially devoted to the study of language and not to the application of language to communication" (Seleskovitch 1976, 102). Indeed, if the goal of linguistics is to define and refine a theory of underlying structure as universal grammar that encompasses all language(s), then this pursuit might be of little use to interpreters (although, as the discussion in what follows of the Language Acquisition

Device (LAD) illustrates, there may be facets of a formalist theory that do impact interpreters' approach to and understanding of language competence and their potential to achieve it as bilinguals).

## Cognitive and Contextualist Theories

Since the 1970s new branches of theoretical linguistics have surfaced that, as Linell (1997) suggests, do impact the interpreter's tasks, which are functionalist, social-interactionalist, and contextualist in nature. These theories are anchored in spoken and, more recently, signed discourse that take interaction as primary and written text as peripheral and thus are more explanatory when applied to interpretation theory. To these I would add that in recent years functionalist linguistic theory has become increasingly usage based (e.g., Bybee and Hopper 2001; Hopper 1998) and, coupled with the understanding that interpretation as communication is not different from any discourse as communication (e.g., Wilcox and Shaffer 2005), this suggests that theories of linguistics and interpretation can converge in extremely productive ways. Interpretation researchers such as Tabakowska (2000) and Wilcox and Shaffer (2005) have also espoused a cognitive–linguistic view of interpretation as communication activity, which may also prove to be productive, given that the cognitivist agenda begins with conceptualization, and from there attempts to understand meaning relationships, along with how speakers and signers assemble linguistic units to reflect their intentions. This approach is a cogent way of describing what interpreters do, as what all communicators do, and serves to resolve the "black box" conundrum at the core of many early interpretation theories of meaning transfer.

In some cases, the assumptions (or hypotheses, if you will) that a linguistic theory makes about language have clear and direct implications for what the researcher expects.

In a formalist, Universal Grammar (UG) account of linguistic structure and language acquisition, for example, an LAD is posited (Chomsky 1965), by which the language learner sets parameters in her developing grammar based on input evidence. The problem in our approach to second language (L2) learners is that once parameters are set, we may wonder whether a language with different parameter settings can be learned at all. The difficulty that adults typically experience learning an L2 is well documented, and its effect on individuals striving to become interpreters can be profound. In some UG-based views, the problem may be insurmountable. Sharwood Smith (2000) suggests that the L2 learner may be thus resistant to L2 grammatical elements because her L1 parameters, once set, block the input data of, or the "evidence" found in, L2 utterances that the learner encounters, and nothing can be done about it. "If corrective feedback (negative evidence) and input flooding will not help, then you may be stuck for good however rich or impoverished your particular version of the L2 happens to be" (Sharwood Smith 2000, 38).

Parameter setting in this sense may not be particularly problematic if, as Seleskovitch (1978) requires, the interpreter comes to the task with superior competence in her two working languages. She would have to have mastered the two languages relatively early in life, which is highly problematic in the field of signed language interpreting because the overwhelming majority of these interpreters have learned a signed language such as American Sign Language (ASL) as adults. This presents at least two problems for interpretation researchers. First, if the notion of message equivalence is in any way part of the research question, how does the researcher determine that her subjects display linguistic competence? Second—a question with profound implications for much research on signed language interpretation—how complete is our knowledge of the grammar of any signed language, including ASL? Linguists have been building this knowledge, but at present there are still numerous gaps in what we do know, and we might expect that interpreters have been attempting to learn the "rules" of grammar for their respective signed language based on what they are told by linguists (that is, in the grammars they read). This idea is discussed in more detail later in this chapter, but for the moment, as two brief examples we might consider our limited understanding of the role that "depiction" plays in signed language discourse and grammar (e.g., Dudis 2004a, 2004b), as well as the ways that simultaneous constructions are used (Vermeerbergen, Leeson, and Crasborn 2007), which is considered typological for signed language structure.[1] Slobin (2006)

---

1. However, see Kendon (2011) on "multimodal" constructions where speakers' gestures may be considered as structural elements in their utterances. Kendon concludes that such simultaneity may not be exclusive to signed languages.

claims that linguistic researchers have frequently misrepresented the grammars of signed languages by virtue of approaching these languages from an ethnocentric starting point based on their knowledge of, and linguistic expectations of, some of the best-known spoken languages in the world, such as English, French, and German, with the result that grammatical descriptions of signed languages look a great deal like those of these spoken languages. He posits instead that signed languages typologically pattern like many less-known spoken languages. Once again, I stress the point that interpreters are the beneficiaries of linguistic knowledge; what interpreters believe about grammatical structure impacts their language usage, and furthermore, interpretation researchers are not differently privileged in this regard. Thus, researchers' grammaticality judgments in interpreters' target texts and message equivalency measures are based both on the interpreter-as-subject's linguistic competencies and the researcher's understanding of grammaticality.

A cognitive–linguistic view on second language learning, however, may provide some insights to the cross-linguistic demands of interpretation, which means that in this theory meaning is dependent on conceptualization and conceptualization differs from person to person, which thus necessitates the notion of construal (Achard 2008). Tyler (2008) also evokes a cognitive–linguistic view on second language instruction, suggesting that, for example, in teaching modal verb usage to second language learners, imparting an understanding of the conceptualization of events is key to the learner grasping the function and meaning of modal verbs in both their first and second languages. As Janzen and Shaffer (2013) show, modals are a highly subjective linguistic category that when used in an interpreted text may reflect either the source speaker's stance or the interpreter's view of the situation. Although it is clear that this view might assist the interpretation researcher, the impact of understanding the functional aspects of the linguistic category of modals carries through to interpreter educators as well. If they are aware of the subjective weight of modals and the cognitive underpinnings of their usage in discourse, they are better able to hear and see what their students are doing and engage them in discussion regarding their own use of modals in, and across, their working languages.

# The Functions of Linguistics and Their Value to Interpretation Research

This section is not intended as a description of major linguistic theories in an attempt to evaluate their worth as applied to interpretation theories but rather looks broadly at what linguistics sets out to do. In this sense, we may consider the compatibility of the goals of linguistics with those of interpretation theories. Because interpreting is a strikingly complex linguistic activity, interpretation researchers cannot likely work without involving at least some aspects of linguistic theory, whether or not it is their explicit agenda, and in the following sections we examine how this is so.

## Universal Grammar

A primary goal of linguistics, at least since the latter half of the 20th century, has been to devise and refine a theory of language structure. A main tenet of this "formalist" program has been that grammar is innate and universal, some version of which must be discovered and mastered by the young language learner that corresponds to the particular language spoken in the child's immediate environment. Universal Grammar is a theory of "languages and the expressions they generate" (Chomsky 1995, 167) that attempts to formulate the principles underlying language structure that are part of the child's innate language faculty such that it explains how the speaker can generate an infinite number of sentences from a relatively small, finite set of building blocks. Arguably, this linguistic agenda motivated Seleskovitch's stance that linguistics has limited application to interpretation, if any at all. In generativist, universalist theory, semantics has not traditionally played a major role, and Seleskovitch's position was that semantics, although decidedly a semantics situated in a current discourse context, was key, while form was unimportant and dismissible (Seleskovitch 1978).

## The Relationship Between Form and Meaning

Most linguistic theory at the very least acknowledges some relationship between form and meaning, and a number of theories consider the form/meaning connection to be primary, for example, Bybee's (1985) approach to the study of morphology and the role of diagrammatic iconicity in syntactic structures in Haiman (1985) and Simone (1995). This linguistic agenda goes well beyond the lexical level, although word meaning has understandably received a great deal of attention (e.g., Cruse 1986; Evans 2009). With advances in linguistics that extend into the areas of conversation, contextualization, and pragmatics, meaning has been investigated in terms of discourse features (Blakemore 2002) and of constructions themselves. In a theoretical area referred to as Construction Grammar, Goldberg (1995, 1998) has shown that meaning is evident not only from lexical elements but also from construction features. For example Goldberg (1998) demonstrates that transfer is apparent in Subject–Verb–Object–Object$_2$ constructions in English, so that the sentence *Pat baked Chris a cake* includes the element of transfer (the cake went from Pat to Chris) even though the meaning of transfer is associated with none of the words in the sentence.

Meaning is at the core of much theorizing in interpretation studies, although the relationship between the interpreter and meaning has not always been explicit. Wilcox and Shaffer (2005), whose theory is dealt with in more detail later in this chapter, outline a number of conduit models of interpretation put forward by signed language interpretation theorists in which meaning is somehow extracted from the source text, often said to be separable from, and thus void of any sort of linguistic form whatsoever and analyzed by the interpreter in this nonlinguistic way. This premise itself takes its cue from linguistics, which has attempted to show that the referent of (i.e., the meaning of) an entity is the same no matter what the linguistic shape that names the entity is like. The thing named by the English word *cat* is the same thing as a *chat* or *Katze* or *gatto* or 고양이. Thus linguistic form is understood to be arbitrary, and this is taken to mean, for interpreters, that meaning is independent from form. Note that Seleskovitch (1978, 9) advocates the "immediate and deliberate discarding" of source text form and Colonomos (1992) identifies a "formless message" at the center of her model. On the other hand, Janzen (2005b) suggests that meaning may not be quite so separable from its linguistic pairing but that this is not as problematic as it has been made out to be. This is a contextualist stance in which meaning is only apparent (constructed, actually) from available cues, that is, from contextualized words and constructions, features of the source speaker and the overall situation, and all of these elements must be thoroughly mined before they are let go as the interpreter then turns to a new set of formal (linguistic) elements with which to build a target message with a meaning of its own. Thus the interpreter will deal with two meanings, not one, and her best hope is that they are as congruent as possible. This process is cogently dealt with in the cognitive model of Wilcox and Shaffer (2005), who regard meaning not in a formalist sense, to be found in the words, but constructed within each individual communication event participant. It might be true that the source speaker is a meaning-maker, but so is the interpreter, and so is the target text recipient, and no one ever has direct access to another's meaning. Meaning can in no way be transferred down the line.

Here the application to interpreting instruction is clear: How the interpreter educator talks about meaning "transfer" influences how students of interpretation apprehend the text, work to understand meaning, and recognize their own role in the process. Approaches such as "meaning is there to be discovered" and "meaning is inherent in the word/phrase" distance the interpreting student from the text, whereas a co-constructed understanding of meaning draws the student into the process of exegesis explicitly. Granted, this cognitively oriented theoretical approach demands a more rigorous examination of subjectivity and objectivity on the part of the interpreter, but the outcome is bound to be a more realistic, and ideally more cognizant, view of how a target text can be constructed and of the interpreter's responsibility to that text.

## Descriptive and Comparative Linguistics

A longstanding objective of linguistics has been to piece together the grammars of individual languages, a branch of linguistics often referred to as descriptive linguistics. There are several purposes in doing this. First, it is a way to document languages, and second, describing the grammars of languages reveals much about the human capacity for language. Signed language interpreters in particular are the beneficiaries of this kind of linguistic endeavor whether they are aware of it or not. Without the acknowledgment that signed languages are true languages, and without descriptions of their grammars that show that they are far from versions of the spoken languages of the surrounding communities as was evident in the early works of Tervoort (1953) for Sign Language of the Netherlands (NGT) and Stokoe (1960) and his colleagues (Stokoe, Casterline, and Croneberg 1965) for ASL, for example, interpreters would have not progressed in the way they have as professional bilingual mediators. And because we still know so little about the grammars of these languages, this continues to be of concern for interpreters, the researchers who study them, and for interpreter educators. The more that linguists learn about signed language grammars, the better interpretation researchers are able to undertake message and text analysis, and examine equivalency issues in interpreters' work.

A further effect of descriptive linguistics is that once a body of knowledge begins to build across languages, linguists can conduct typological studies, that is, they can examine similarities and differences across a wide spectrum of languages to see how cross-linguistic patterns of language use are evident. It has been tempting to think of all signed languages as being of one type, particularly because of similarities in articulation structure and use of a large three-dimensional space, for example, but as more and more signed language grammars are investigated, typologists are showing that there are profound differences in structure (Wilkinson 2009; Zeshan 2005) well beyond the more obvious and well-noted differences in lexicon (Klima and Bellugi 1979).

Seleskovitch's objection to descriptive and comparative linguistics, besides that these have historically been based on written language, was more than likely because her expectation of interpreters was that they came to the task fully competent in their working languages and because she and the interpreters she speaks to are conference interpreters, meaning that they would typically be working with major languages and not lesser-known and poorly described ones. These expectations, however, may not hold for both spoken and signed language interpreters working with lesser-studied languages, who are more likely to work in community and educational settings, whose language training can be quite variable, and who work with languages that are not fully described, and in some respects have grammatical descriptions that are in fact controversial. Working interpreters are not usually, and do not need to be, linguists conducting linguistic research, although signed language interpretation researchers and theorists often are linguists as well. Even if they are not, linguistic theory goes hand in hand with what they do.

## Variationist Studies

In the past several decades, variationist studies have begun to interest linguists, notably with Labov's work in the early 1970s (e.g., Labov 1972a,

1972b), under the branch of linguistics called sociolinguistics. Along a functionalist vein, variation in language use is expected, motivated, and not considered peripheral to a core, rule-governed grammar, and a language theory must account for this variation along with more stable aspects of linguistic structure. This being said, functional linguists in principle understand language as not very stable but instead, because of usage-oriented factors, both lexicon and grammar are constantly in flux (Bybee 2001; Haspelmath 2004; Janzen 2012). A (functionalist) emergentist view is that grammar is not stable whatsoever but is always and continually emergent (Hopper 1998). This has implications for interpretation researchers for several reasons. First, language change across populations of users and over time will critically affect data that is gathered by the researcher. Second, how interpreters, many of whom are L2 learners, understand variation factors and linguistic phenomena will directly impact their work, and these factors must be taken into account when researchers examine interpreted texts.

Thus, variationist works such as those by Lucas, Bayley, and Valli (2001), van Herreweghe and Vermeerbergen (2004), Perniss, Pfau, and Steinbach (2007), and also Leeson (2005b), who describes contributing factors to variation in the exceptional case of Irish Sign Language, have important implications for signed language interpreters and researchers. They establish that interpreters unavoidably encounter variation in their work, and they need a model of language structure that encompasses this and can explain it. Both Leeson (2005b) and Malcolm (2005) examine the interpreter's response to features of variation in signers' discourse based on an underlying variationist model of language.

## Conversation Analysis

A relatively new approach to understanding language use and structure is conversation analysis. In this approach, natural conversation is recorded and transcribed in an effort to understand how people use language in natural environments. The general premise is that casual conversation, a major source of routinized linguistic expression (Scheibman 2002), "is concerned with the joint construction of social reality" (Eggins and Slade 1997, 6). This approach is particularly amenable to interpretation research if we consider that interpreted discourse is primarily dialogic, located in social settings, and that the interpreter is a social and conversational participant—albeit with a particular role that other participants do not share—in the social and linguistic exchange. Studies such as Wadensjö (1998) on Swedish–Russian interpreters and Roy (2000) on ASL–English interpreters are examples of research that implements a conversation analysis approach in which a detailed examination of the stream of linguistic utterances is conducted to discover how the discourse is managed by the interpreter.

## Corpus Studies

The recent availability of computers, and thus computational linguistics, has brought about a new approach to linguistic analysis, broadly referred to as "corpus linguistics." Corpus linguistics refers to the "computerized retrieval, and subsequent analysis, of linguistic elements and structures from corpora" (Gries 2008, 411), where a corpus is a "machine-readable collection of (spoken or written) texts that were produced in a natural communicative setting, and the collection of these texts is compiled with the intention (i) to be representative and balanced with respect to a particular linguistic variety or register or genre and (ii) to be analyzed linguistically" (2008, 411). The advantage to corpus studies is that large amounts of natural language data can be mined for actual usage patterns across speakers, such that grammatical generalizations are based on usage rather than introspection or elicited responses from individual speakers. Thus corpus, usage-based analyses of grammar are thought to more accurately reflect the state of grammar for a language across many users at a given time.

In recent years interpretation and translation researchers have embraced a corpus approach to their studies (e.g., Baker 1995; Becker 2011; Williams 2009, Winters 2009; and others), although at times the "corpus" consists only of single or few texts (e.g., Winters 2009) as opposed to a sizable collection of texts (e.g., Wadensjö 1998), even though in Wadensjö's (1998) study, she does not identify the number of speakers or interpreters nor the size of the corpus. Winters (2009) analyzes only two translations of *The Beautiful and Damned* by F. Scott Fitzgerald. In Williams (2009) the original texts and translations of research articles amounts to almost 500,000 words, still relatively small compared to typical linguistic corpora, which frequently number in the several millions. Thus there is generally something of a difference between linguists' notion of corpora, which can include the discourse of hundreds of speakers, and at least some of the work of interpreters and translators. Nonetheless, as interpreters and translators build theories on actual usage, there is a greater chance that they can show what takes place in the interpreting process, which is of great interest to cognitive linguistics and cognitively oriented interpreting theorists. For interpreting educators, this invites evaluation of actual practices and adoption of what works, and later re-evaluation, with their students, of what may not work and thus what may lead to better practice. However, as Kenny (1998) points out, the bottom-up approach that corpus studies reflect may lead to numerous new insights into translation studies, which have to date tended to be top-down approaches where theorists have sought data as evidence to support more abstract hypotheses on translation and interpretation.

## Conceptualization and Language Structure

Finally, cognitive linguistics deals with the relationship between cognition and linguistic expression. In his "rough guide" Geeraerts (2006) distinguishes between cognitive linguistics generally and the more formalized theory of Cognitive Linguistics, given that many theories of language are cognitive in some sense—after all, it is the human mind where language knowledge resides—but the Cognitive Linguistics approach (let us call it a collection of theories) is very specific about what it addresses and how. Drawing on the editorial statement of the first issue of the journal *Cognitive Linguistics* in 1990, Geeraerts states that "this approach sees language 'as an instrument for organizing, processing, and conveying information'—as something primarily semantic" (2006, 3). He follows with four essential tenets of Cognitive Linguistics: (1) that linguistic meaning is perspectival, that is, it is a subjective (as opposed to objective) way of viewing the world that depends crucially on construal; (2) that linguistic meaning is dynamic and flexible; (3) that linguistic meaning is encyclopedic and nonautonomous, in that it is not distinct from other cognitive functions and capacities; and (4) that linguistic meaning is based on usage and experience, in other words that linguistic expressions, no matter what language we speak or sign, fall out from our experience of the world (Geeraerts, 2006, 4–6). Of this Geeraerts says that "the experience of language is an experience of actual language use, not of words like you would find them in a dictionary or sentence patterns like you would find them in a grammar" (Geeraerts, 2006, 6).

In the discussion that follows, we look in more detail at Wilcox and Shaffer's (2005) view of how the interpreter, and thus researcher, must understand meaning within a cognitive perspective, and Janzen and Shaffer's (2008) contextualist view of co-constructed, intersubjectively motivated meaning. Here suffice it to say that this approach might appeal to interpreters and interpretation researchers because it is about what interpreters actively do in a very real sense. Thus it may be a fruitful theory by which to understand and explain more about the interpreting process.

## Shaping a Theory of Interpretation: The Impact of Linguistic Theory

Interpretation is by nature a linguistic enterprise. While it is the case that aspects of interpretation can come under the research microscope that do not depend much on the analysis of linguistic material, such as demographics, the majority of research involves some aspect of linguistic expression. Consider Tabakowska's forceful statement regarding the nature of the interpreter's source text (ST) and target text (TT): "Creating the ST and the TT are two linguistic processes. Therefore, an appeal to a theory of language is a necessary prerequisite *for all explanation* of such processes" (Tabakowska 2000, 84, italics added).

Here we look at some of the ways that linguistic theories can impact researchers' approaches to their research design and the data they collect and analyze. As has been suggested, it is not possible for an interpretation researcher to *not* have her work informed by a theory of language. To proceed from an agnostic position, by which I mean along the lines of Dawkins (2006), as a refusal to commit to one way of thinking or another (Dawkins 2006, 47, calls this the "Permanent Agnosticism in Principle"), because she will still be guided by what she thinks that language is, whether or not this is consciously acknowledged or articulated.

In the mid-1960s ASL–English interpreters' knowledge of ASL structure was just beginning to unfold, thanks in large part to William Stokoe and his colleagues (Stokoe 1960; Stokoe, Casterline, and Croneberg 1965) and the work in his language laboratory. At the same time, the Registry of Interpreters for the Deaf in the United States set out a code of ethics (Quigley and Youngs 1965) that includes the following as principle 8:

> In the case of legal interpreting, the interpreter shall inform the court when the level of literacy of the deaf person involved is such that literal interpretation is not possible and the interpreter is having to grossly paraphrase and restate both what is said to the deaf person and what he is saying to the court. (Quigley and Youngs 1965, 10)

As well, the second part of principle 9 states:

> Those who understand manual communication may be assisted by means of translating (rendering the original presentation verbatim), or interpreting (paraphrasing, defining, explaining, or making known the will of the speaker without regard to the original language used). (Quigley and Youngs 1965, 10)

These statements are as specific as the code gets regarding language usage. In retrospect, it seems that at the time interpreters were cognizant of differences between English-like signing (translating; verbatim) and something else (grossly paraphrasing; making known the will of the speaker without regard to the original language used—which would be English), but their wording does not suggest that they were able to analyze the process in terms of two languages with differing grammar structures. Still, we can say that they were in fact guided by a theory of language, based on what they knew about linguistic structure at the time.

Clearly, we have learned a great deal since then. As the field of linguistics continued to put forward evidence that signed languages were true languages and began building a body of knowledge about signed language structure, interpreters eagerly took this knowledge and applied it to their own field. Popular volumes such as Baker and Cokely (1980) for ASL are evidence that growth in linguistic and cultural knowledge was quite rapid and widespread. The benefits of such work, perhaps as "how-to" manuals for signed language interpreters, has been far-reaching both in training and in interpreters' own linguistic knowledge building, but they are neither complete descriptions of the grammars of the signed language nor have they stood up over time. Linguistic research has continued to uncover grammatical principles, and as of late, usage principles that have changed our knowledge of grammar. As two examples, let us briefly consider the internal structure of signs and the role of topic constituents.

Stokoe et al.'s (1965) dictionary was groundbreaking in its assertion that all signs in ASL have distinguishable parts from several categories each with a finite number of members: handshapes, locations in space and on the body, and movements. Rather than unanalyzable wholes, each sign could be understood as composed of a discrete combination of simultaneously articulated parts, thus demonstrating duality of patterning (Hocket 1960) as a necessary design feature of human language structure. This phonetic arrangement has since been challenged by phonologists who have recognized more complexity in sign forms. Liddell and Johnson (1989), Brentari (1998), and others have shown that signs can be analyzed along temporal lines as well. That is, not all aspects of the sign occur exactly simultaneously. Brentari's model in particular contrasts features of signs that remain static temporally through the articulation of the sign while others change (are prosodic), including movement from one location to another or a change in handshape aperture. This has resulted in a very different view of sign structure and a whole new set of constraint proposals.

A second example of change in our view of grammatical structure has to do with topic phrases and topic marking in ASL. In the work of Baker and Cokely (1980) and Valli and Lucas (1992), topic-comment structured clauses are treated as a possible sentence type along with declaratives, interrogatives, imperatives, and others. Commonly an example is given such as [HOMEWORK]-TOP I DETEST "As for homework, I detest it" (adapted from Valli and Lucas 1992, 282) with the function of topic marking (or "topicalization," which can indicate a theory-dependent notion of movement from one slot in the clause structure to another) to make some information such as a subject or object more prominent. Janzen (1998, 1999) shows, however, that topics serve as grounding information from which to view the information found in the latter part of the clause or sentence (the "comment") and are not the focus of the utterance but often background information, and further, that topic marking serves to mark topic shift rather than topic maintenance. Besides this, it was demonstrated that objects as topic-marked phrases were very rare, most likely because the verb and its object together frequently consist of new or focused information, and thus it is typically incongruent with the role of topic marking.

Understanding that our linguistic knowledge base has changed drastically and continues to do so affects the language-related research of interpretation researchers and theorists and, eventually, when interpreting educators access this research, it impacts the way that practitioners approach their work. Granted, the fact that this body of knowledge is still growing (earlier it was stated that a problem for researchers who depend on linguistic analyses is our yet incomplete linguistic descriptions of signed languages) means that interpretation researchers cannot do less than keep abreast of new linguistic work. The two fields are too closely related to expect otherwise.

## Is Meaning in the Words?

If we take meaning as primary in interpreters' work, what do they think it is, where do they go looking for it, and what do they do once they think they've located it? Seleskovitch (1978) talks about determining the sense of a message and discarding the words, for example, and Colonomos (1992) has suggested that meaning must be extracted from the source text as a "formless message." Clearly, in these statements, the interpretation theorist has theorized that form and meaning can be disconnected. Yet, even though it has been taken that meaning is extractable, many views on language consider it a given that meaning is found in the words that a speaker or signer uses. Wilcox and Shaffer (2005) claim that this is the essence of a conduit model of language. Linell (1997) likewise contrasts two models of human communication: a transfer (conduit) model and a social-interactionist model.

Wilcox and Shaffer claim that in much of signed language interpretation theorists' work to date, meaning is treated as transferable: It is found within the words of the source text, even if the surrounding context is fully acknowledged, can be extracted (and should be), and then is reformulated in target text terms. Linell suggests that this is in line with formalism, that "language provides us with signs with fixed meanings, and the proper use of this code will guarantee shared understanding" (Linell 1997, 52). This conduit view of meaning is that it is fixed, and the listener or watcher—including the interpreter—must discover it. Wilcox and Shaffer suggest, then, that as long as this view of language and of meaning persists, interpreters will not be able to truly move away from a conduit model of the task.

There are at least two additional effects of this theoretical view. First, because it is assumed that language is an adequate mechanism for the accurate transmission of meaning, and thus transfer of meaning occurs similarly in an interpretation context, complete understanding among interlocutors is expected and usually accomplished, barring outside interference. Second, stemming from this is the assumption that given sufficient preparation (e.g., linguistic, cultural, and technique training) interpreters can transmit equivalent source to target messages. In practice, this can break down for a host of reasons, and to find out why and how to correct this, researchers engage in error analyses such as that found in Cokely (1992). Of the process Cokely (1992, 73; where sL = source language; tL = target language) says:

> For an interpretation to be considered accurate or appropriate, the meaning of the source language message must be determined by the interpreter and conveyed in such a way that meaning is intelligible in the target language. The very nature of the interpreting process makes it possible to determine accuracy or appropriateness by comparing the interpreted tL text with the source language text it is supposed to convey. Comparison and analysis of both sL and tL texts make it possible to determine the extent to which interpreted text tokens adhere to or deviate from the meaning of their sL text counterparts.

Each deviation from the meaning of the source text, then, is enumerated by Cokely (1992) as a "miscue" in the form of omissions, additions, substitutions, etc. Linell (1997) contends that exercises such as this decontextualize equivalency, and further, they perpetuate the view that meaning can be discovered and transferred and that deviation from an objectively ideal transfer can be quantified.

In a cognitive-theoretical view of language, expressions serve as clues to meaning, but a person's meaning is never directly accessible. The best we can hope for, Wilcox and Shaffer (2005) say, is that we make inferences based on the evidence that is set out, that is, the words and constructions the speaker chooses, and assemble a meaning ourselves. In this sense, understanding is always provisional and only partly shared (see also Linell 1997). Wilcox and Shaffer suggest that we might get further with understanding the task of communication—and the interpreter's task is equally one of communication—if we expect inexactness, and then try to figure out, or analyze, what goes right. Two additional tenets important to this approach to language are that meaning is actually co-constructed (Linell 1997; Wilcox and Shaffer 2005; Janzen and Shaffer 2008) between discourse participants, and that meaning is always locally contextualized (Janzen and Shaffer 2013). Linell goes so far as to say that meaning and contexts emerge together. I take this to mean that, as meaning is negotiated and co-constructed in the situational context, the discourse, which is a shared affirmation of co-constructed meaning, is built in parallel with a contextual domain throughout the event. We might think that the "context" of a communication event constitutes the external, situational factors that are present, but which are perhaps benign. However, as the discourse participants' knowledge bases change because of the negotiation of meaning over a period of time, this profoundly influences the context, such that the context as a whole at the beginning of the event is not the same context that is apparent by the end of the event.

Thus a contextualist view of language takes into account this dynamicity; the interpretation researcher under this view considers how meaning emerges in the contextualized discourse, and because the interpreter is by definition a communicator, she must equally be aware of how she contributes to and is affected by the communication partnership (see Shaffer, this volume). Again, a cognitive linguistics approach assumes that the process of interpretation is fundamentally no different than the process of speaking or of signing, that is, of using language to communicate (Tabakowska 2000; Wilcox and Shaffer 2005). The applicability of a cognitivist theory of language to translation studies, according to Tabakowska (2000, 86) is this:

> Both deal with equivalence and nonequivalence of images, and the cognitivist model incorporates precisely those aspects of language that have always frustrated language-oriented translation theorists: the inherent subjectivity of meaning, the omnipresence of the unpredictable "human factor", the non-dichotomy of meaning and form, the illusive and elusive charm of the Sapir-Whorf hypothesis, the ubiquity of metaphor, the mystery of "false friends", the vague status of synonymy and homonymy.

It is not that "error analyses" cannot be conducted, but the beginning point must be different. For example, in Wadensjö's (1998, 2002 [1993]) study of Swedish–Russian interpreters in medical and police interviews, she makes note of various types of target text renditions the interpreters offer that are representative (or not) of source text utterances. She finds that frequently the interpreters could not be said to have the goal of uttering a rendition that is intended as an equivalency to a piece of source text, but instead the goal is a pragmatically driven, fully contextualized version of the original. In other words the interpreter represents the source speakers and their goals through a series of strategized renditions-as-utterances, with as much potential to sway the discourse and the contexts that emerge for all participants as do the primary participants in the interchange.

Perhaps here a caution is in order: I am not suggesting that the interpreter is unconstrained in her choices or her behavior; perhaps the task is made even more difficult by loosening the conduit reins. However, as Wilcox and Shaffer (2005) and Janzen and Korpiniski (2005) point out, the interpreter must go all the further in assuming responsibility for her own decisions not just in terms of behaviors appropriate to the work but in her language choices as well. To do this demands a clear understanding of how communication works, what communicators do, and how the interpreter's participation in the event can actually, *in very real terms*, affect every aspect of the event and each participant's impression of it. This is a very different way of conceiving of the limits of her role.

In a study of Australian Sign Language–English interpreters' participation in communication events, Napier (2002, 2004) examines the occurrence of omissions in interpreted texts. Although she found a high ratio of omissions that were unconscious or unintended, or were evident because the interpreter appeared to have no other strategy with which to deal with a problem, a significant number of omissions were purposefully chosen. In a conduit-model-based error analysis, any such omission would be problematic, but Napier entertains the possibility that some omissions are deliberate, strategic, and, most crucially, successful. Napier (2002, 172) concludes:

> The concept of omissions being used by interpreters as a conscious linguistic coping strategy has been one of the main threads throughout the book. It has been determined that in order to effectively work as linguistic and cultural mediators using an interactive model of interpreting, interpreters employ the use of conscious strategic

omissions in deciding what information is translatable and relevant to each language and culture.

It is clear from this passage that Napier's theory of linguistic structure, in this case a participant-driven contextualist view, is behind her view of her data, and her findings are instructive in this light. Because meaning is constructed in the mind of the message recipient, the interpreter's target text must also be understood as constructed, not transferred directly.

Gile (1995) outlines numerous strategies available to the interpreter when the task presents problems. It is not my intent here to list and address the plethora of issues faced by interpreters, except to acknowledge, as every interpreter experiences, that linguistic problems are many and for good reasons. Gile's perspective is that the interpreter must deal with problems in terms of the goals of maximizing information recovery, minimizing interference, and maximizing the impact of the communication (Gile 1995, 201–203). Among the many tactics he lists is that of strategic omission, suggesting that omission may at times be a calculated, prudent choice on the part of the interpreter that does not detract from meaning recovery and instead serves to enhance the overall target text and message.

Leeson (2005a) demonstrates that signed language interpreters are no different from spoken language interpreters in this regard, as does the work of Napier. Janzen (2005a) suggests that both meaning and linguistic form are resources the interpreter must use when constructing a target text, but her strategies in grappling with the source and composing the target message will inevitably contribute to how the target text, and thus the target message, is shaped. These views suggest, even if not overtly, that message meaning and linguistic form are closely tied, which exemplifies the notion that one's linguistic theory underlies her approach, her understanding of the data, and ultimately her findings.

## Further Issues in Dealing With Data

Without question, there are many issues to contend with, and a clear vision of the roles that language structure, meaning, and contextual elements play in human interaction in the mind of the researcher who deals with linguistically oriented data, whether or not mediated by interpretation, is imperative.

## Linguistic Egocentrism

Slobin (2006) points out the danger of narrowly comparative linguistic research that overascribes category features of one language to another. For
Slobin, if your model of language includes categories of nouns, verbs, and
adjectives of a certain type and with certain features, and if your syntax requires certain elements exemplified by languages such as English, you are
apt to find them in the new language you are studying whether or not they
are actually there. This problem is exacerbated by "glossing," that is, because signed languages typically do not have either written forms or standard transcriptions of phonetic forms, when notating data English words
(along with other necessary diacritics) are used as glosses to represent the
signs. The problem is that if the chosen gloss has particular attributes in its
categorization in English, there is a temptation to transfer these attributes
to the sign that is labeled by the glossed word. Slobin suggests that because
both ASL word categorization and its grammar differ greatly from English,
English words in fact do a terrible job at representing ASL, but that we do
not always see this because the English words in the gloss seem to suffice.

## Factoring in Linguistic Competence

Another issue has to do with limited subject populations and language
fluency levels. Metzger's (1999) study on interpreters' neutrality has far-
reaching implications, suggesting that because interpreters speak for the
primary participants, they have the potential to "frame the task in ways
that impact the nature of an interaction" (Metzger 1999, 49). This greatly
understates the facts. Under the cognitivist and contextualist frameworks
outlined previously, the interpreter by virtue of even being there impacts
the nature of the interaction regardless of whether she or the primary participants are cognizant of it.

   One aspect of linguistic structure that Metzger investigates is the use of
pronouns by her study's discourse participants and interpreters. She finds
that for both the student interpreter who is interpreting in a mock medical interview and a professional interpreter in an actual medical interview,
pronouns do not consistently match those used by the primary participants
(e.g., substituting a second-person pronoun for a third-person pronoun
when the doctor is referring to the patient). The topic is complicated and
Metzger discusses the many issues surrounding frames and footings (after

Goffman 1981) but does not address the potential discrepancies between her two interpreter subjects nor their understanding of what they should do with the pronouns they encounter in the source texts. How do English speakers and ASL signers frame their utterances with respect to conventions of pronoun use? How do we learn about the differences that are apparent? Does the fact that a conversation is mediated by interpretation, as opposed to one that is not so mediated, change the parameters of language use? Stratiy (2005) suggests that it does, that pronominal reference to a particular person is different in ASL when that person is present than when they are absent. Metzger evokes the ASL discourse convention of shifted reference when the signer stands in for a third-person referent and therefore can use a first-person pronoun to indicate that third-person referent. However, when the interpreter uses a first-person pronoun because the present English-speaking participant said "I," this goes against the conventions of ASL conversational form. The point here is that when the researcher approaches her linguistic data, both her own theory of language and the competencies and practices of her subjects must be considered.

## The Relation Between Linguistic Form and Discourse Strategies

It can sometimes be tempting to be prescriptive in the application of linguistic knowledge in the interpreting context. As mentioned earlier the linguistic competencies of the interpreter are an important consideration when drawing conclusions from the data, but perhaps even more critically, the researcher's understanding of what is linguistic (i.e., required by the grammar) and what is "extralinguistic" (i.e., determined by discourse pragmatics) will greatly impact her findings. Gile (1995) states clearly that when formulating the target text, the interpreter must be grammatical (he refers to this as Linguistically Induced Information (LII); Gile 1995, 61), but the question that obviously follows is, what is required by the grammar? Lawrence (1995) and Humphrey and Alcorn (2001) claim that ASL "expansions" are required elements (and, ostensibly, "compressions" [Finton and Smith 2004] for English) because without them an ASL signer could not understand a speaker's intended meaning. Janzen and Shaffer (2008) argue, however, that very little of what Lawrence and Humphrey and Alcorn claim can truly be relegated to required grammatical structure and that they are confusing grammatical use with interpreter strategies

based on the discourse principles of shared experience and contextualization. Lawrence bases her claims on the erroneous concepts of "high-" and
"low-context language," purportedly taken from Edward T. Hall (1976 and
elsewhere), but Hall never talks about high and low context in terms of
language. His model is of high- and low-context *cultures*, which he stresses
form a continuum, and in which *communication* is affected to varying degrees depending on the situation and intent. This is squarely within the
domain of pragmatics, for which the conversationalist, whether an English
speaker, ASL signer, or user of any other language, will inevitably have a
long list of potential linguistic expressions from which to choose to suit her
particular discourse need dependent on her subjective and "intersubjective"
(Janzen and Shaffer 2008) perceptions of the contextualized participants.

## *Misunderstanding the Function of Linguistic and Discourse Items*

Once again I stress that we can essentially go only with what we know—
our linguistic understanding of signed language structure and function is
far from complete but is continuing to build. It is always good science to be
skeptical, to allow for yet another question as Dawkins (2006) cautions. For
interpretation researchers, I suggest, especially because interpreting is an
activity that is so subjective in nature, that this cautionary note is not a negative one: It drives our research on. As but one small, but very telling example,
consider the recent revealing work on depiction in signed language discourse
(Dudis 2004a, 2004b). Depiction is a linguistic strategy in which the signer
takes on features of the referent being described and in effect demonstrates
their actions. It is thought that many such depictions have regularized into
so-called "depicting verbs" (Liddell 2003), roughly "classifier-type" verbs
(although note that classifiers in signed languages have as of late come under descriptive scrutiny—see Schembri 2003). Students of signed language
have frequently been encouraged to use depiction (not necessarily under
that label) in their signed discourse because it somehow enhances the clarity
of their signing. This includes interpreters, who have thus learned that their
discourse is much more ASL-like if it includes a liberal amount of depiction
usage. Perhaps there is an unintended effect in interpretation. Stratiy (2005)
argues that depiction implies first-hand knowledge: How could an interpreter depict the actions of someone unless she had witnessed it herself? As a
Deaf target text recipient, Stratiy claims that when an interpreter depicts an

action taken from the English speaker's source text, the depicted elements are implied to have taken place, and yet the interpreter *was not there*. In addition, depiction is only possible by choosing a subjective perspective on the event, which further implicates the interpreter. Stratiy goes so far as to suggest that by doing this, the interpreter invites mistrust. Clearly, if this is the case, interpreters need to reassess what they understand about elements such as depiction and what its place might be in the interpreted context, and interpreter educators would do well to know the issues and to be able to guide students toward informed choices. As Tabakowska (2000, 95) notes, "seemingly local decisions often have global consequences."

## Shaping a Theory of Interpretation Through Research Methodologies

It has been argued that because interpretation is so pointedly a linguistic task, the interpretation researcher cannot approach her object of study without a deep-seated understanding of the role of linguistic form and corresponding meaning in discourse. Wilcox and Shaffer (2005) stress that interpretation is itself communication and that the interpreter operates under the same communication parameters as any human communicator. However, the requirements of the interpreter-as-communicator are compounded by the dual nature of the role: the interpreter is both listener/watcher and text creator.

The position of meaning in communication, that it cannot be accessed directly but must be constructed by the recipient, additionally affects the researcher. We talk about the "text" and the "message", but like the discourse communicator and the interpreter-as-communicator, the researcher also has no access to meaning—no access to the message. All she can do is observe the available clues and draw inferences about what the message might be. In other words, especially in research dealing with equivalencies, or message representation or appropriate use of linguistic expression, the researcher is in the same boat as her subject. That said, the benefits of situating interpretation research in modern linguistic theories and methodologies are beginning to be apparent, and in fact they may be symbiotic. Along with cognitivist and contextualist views in linguistics as compatible with the aims of interpreters and interpretation researchers, the linguistic and discourse activity of interpretation would seem to be an appropriate arena to examine language usage in an online task that tests the boundaries of cognitive functions (remembering that in the cognitive framework, language use is not seen as isolated from cognition generally). Taylor Torsello, Gallina, Sidiropoulou, Taylor, Tebble, and Vuorikoski (1997, 168) suggest that "interpreters and people working on interpretation, then, have every right to demand the linguistics they need; but they must also be willing to accept the challenge of offering a laboratory for experimentation and for the development of that linguistic theory."

A pertinent question might be whether all interpretation researchers need also to be linguists. The answer is no, although many are. Interpretation research draws from numerous fields: anthropology and cultural studies, psychology, sociology, ethics and philosophy, kinesics, and physiology, to name a few. Interpretation researchers cannot but help involving these fields too as the direction of their research dictates. However, the fact remains that central to their work is linguistic activity and, even if not expressly intended, interpretation researchers do contribute to the field of linguistics in a vastly important way.

A further, equally pertinent question is whether interpreter educators need to be linguists. Here as well the answer is no, although some are and do contribute to our linguistic knowledge of interpreters' working languages and to the theories of language that underlie principles of use. Most important, however, is that interpreter educators have some current knowledge of linguistics, such that their interactions with student interpreters are grounded in usable theory that in turn gives students the tools for insightful analysis of their texts and their work in general. As has been explicated previously, every interpreter, whether researcher, practitioner, or interpreter educator, must have a theory of language, explicit or not, based on which they make assumptions about what interpretation is like: How we come to believe we understand meaning, how meaning is expressed, how we search for clues to meaning when it is unclear, and what we believe we can impart to our target audience for their understanding.

Ultimately, the efforts of interpretation research allow us to frame and reframe our understanding of what interpretation is and what interpreters do. Our knowledge of the task has been shaped in no small part by our knowledge of human language. We are moving well beyond simplistic conduit-model notions of language into the realm of contextualized, socially oriented, intersubjective models. Informed methodologies in interpretation research do much to support these endeavors.

# References

Achard, Michel. 2008. Teaching construal: Cognitive pedagogical grammar. In *Handbook of cognitive linguistics and second language acquisition,* edited by Peter Robinson and Nick C. Ellis, 432–55. New York and London: Routledge.

Baker, Charlotte, and Dennis Cokely. 1980. *American Sign Language: A teacher's resource text on grammar and culture.* Silver Spring, MD: T.J. Publishers.

Baker, Mona. 1995. Corpora in translation studies: An overview and some suggestions for future research. *Target* 7 (2): 223–43.

Becker, Viktor. 2011. When and why do translators add connectives? *Target* 23 (1): 26–47.

Blakemore, Diane. 2002. *Relevance and linguistic meaning: The semantics and pragmatics of discourse markers.* Cambridge: Cambridge University Press.

Brentari, Diane. 1998. *A prosodic model of sign language phonology.* Cambridge, MA: MIT Press.

Bybee, Joan L. 1985. *Morphology: A study of the relation between meaning and form.* Amsterdam: John Benjamins.

———. 2001. *Phonology and language use.* Cambridge: Cambridge University Press.

Bybee, Joan, and Paul J. Hopper, eds. 2001. *Frequency and the emergence of linguistic structure.* Amsterdam: John Benjamins.

Chomsky, Noam. 1965. *Aspects of the theory of syntax.* Cambridge, MA: MIT Press.

———. 1995. *The minimalist program.* Cambridge, MA: MIT Press.

Cokely, Dennis. 1992. *Interpretation: A sociolinguistic model.* Burtonsville, MD: Linstok Press.

Colonomos, Betty. 1992. Processes in interpreting and transliterating: Making them work for you. Workshop handout, Front Range Community College, Westminster, Colorado.

Cruse, D. A. 1986. *Lexical semantics.* Cambridge: Cambridge University Press.

Dawkins, Richard. 2006. *The God delusion.* Boston, MA: Houghton Mifflin.

Dudis, Paul G. 2004a. Depiction of events in ASL: Conceptual integration of temporal components. Doctoral dissertation, University of California at Berkeley.

———. 2004b. Body partitioning and real-space blends. *Cognitive Linguistics* 15 (2): 223–38.

Eggins, Suzanne, and Diana Slade. 1997. *Analysing casual conversation.* London: Cassell.

Evans, Vyvyan. 2009. *How words mean: Lexical concepts, cognitive models, and meaning construction.* Oxford: Oxford University Press.

Finton, Lynn, and Richard Smith. 2004. The natives are restless: Using compression strategies to deliver linguistically appropriate ASL to English interpretation. In *CIT: Still shining after 25 years, Proceedings of the 15th National Convention, Conference of Interpreter Trainers,* edited by Elissa M. Maroney, 125–43. N.p.: Conference of Interpreter Trainers.

Geeraerts, Dirk. 2006. Introduction: A rough guide to cognitive linguistics. In *Cognitive linguistics: Basic readings,* edited by Dirk Geeraerts, 1-28. Berlin: Mouton de Gruyter.

Gile, Daniel. 1995. *Basic concepts and models for interpreter and translator training.* Amsterdam: John Benjamins.

Goffman, Erving. 1981. *Forms of talk.* Philadelphia: University of Philadelphia Press.

Goldberg, Adele E. 1995. *Constructions: A construction grammar approach to argument structure.* Chicago: University of Chicago Press.

———. 1998. Patterns of experience in patterns of language. In *The new psychology of language: Cognitive and functional approaches to language structure,* edited by. Michael Tomasello, 203–19. Mahwah, NJ: Lawrence Erlbaum.

Greis, Stefan Th. 2008. Corpus-based methods in analyses of second language acquisition data. In *Handbook of cognitive linguistics and second language acquisition,* edited by Peter Robinson and Nick C. Ellis, 406–31. New York: Routledge.

Haiman, John, ed. 1985. *Iconicity in syntax.* Amsterdam: John Benjamins.

Hall, Edward T. 1976. *Beyond culture.* Garden City, NY: Anchor Press/ Doubleday.

Haspelmath, Martin. 2004. On directionality in language change with particular reference to grammaticalization. In *Up and down the cline: The nature of grammaticalization,* edited by Olga Fischer, Muriel Norde, and Harry Perridon, 17–44. Amsterdam: John Benjamins.

Hocket, Charles. 1960. The origin of speech. *Scientific American* 203:88–96.

Hopper, Paul J. 1998. Emergent grammar. In *The new psychology of language: Cognitive and functional approaches to language structure,* edited by Michael Tomasello, 155–75. Mahwah, NJ: Lawrence Erlbaum.

Humphrey, Jan H., and Bob J. Alcorn. 2001. *So you want to be an interpreter? An introduction to sign language interpreting.* 3rd ed. Amarillo, TX: H & H.

Janzen, Terry. 1998. Topicality in ASL: Information ordering, constituent structure, and the function of topic marking. Doctoral dissertation, University of New Mexico, Albuquerque.

―――. 1999. The grammaticization of topics in American Sign Language. *Studies in Language* 23 (2): 271–306.

―――. 2005a. Introduction to the theory and practice of signed language interpreting. In *Topics in signed language interpreting: Theory and practice*, edited by Terry Janzen, 3–24. Amsterdam: John Benjamins.

―――. 2005b. Interpretation and language use: ASL and English. In *Topics in signed language interpreting: Theory and practice*, edited by Terry Janzen, 69–105. Amsterdam: John Benjamins.

―――. 2012. Lexicalization and grammaticalization. In *Handbook on sign languages* edited by Markus Steinbach, Roland Pfau, and Bencie Woll, 816–41. Berlin: Mouton de Gruyter.

Janzen, Terry, and Barbara Shaffer. 2008. Intersubjectivity in interpreted interactions: The interpreter's role in co-constructing meaning. In *The shared mind: Perspectives on intersubjectivity*, edited by Jordan Zlatev, Timothy Racine, Chris Sinha, and Esa Itkonen, 333–55. Amsterdam: John Benjamins.

―――. 2013. The interpreter's stance in intersubjective discourse. In *Sign language research, uses, and practices*, edited by Laurence Meurant, Aurélie Sinte, Myriam Vermeerbergen, and Mieke Van Herreweghe, 63–84. Berlin: Mouton de Gruyter.

Janzen, Terry, and Donna Korpiniski. 2005. Ethics and professionalism in interpreting. In *Topics in signed language interpretation: Theory and practice*, edited by Terry Janzen, 165–99. Amsterdam: John Benjamins.

Kendon, Adam. 2011. Gesture first or speech first in language origins? In *Deaf around the world: The impact of language*, edited by Gaurav Mathur and Donna Jo Napoli, 251–67. Oxford: Oxford University Press.

Kenny, Dorothy. 1998. Corpora in translation studies. In *Routledge encyclopedia of translation studies*, edited by Mona Baker, 50–53. London: Routledge.

Klima, Edward S., and Ursula Bellugi. 1979. *The signs of language*. Cambridge MA: Harvard University Press.

Labov, William. 1972a. *Sociolinguistic patterns*. Philadelphia: University of Philadelphia Press.

―――. 1972b. *Language in the inner city*. Philadelphia: University of Philadelphia Press.

Langacker, Ronald W. 1991. *Concept, image, and symbol: The cognitive basis of grammar*. Berlin: Mouton de Gruyter.

―――. 2000. *Grammar and conceptualization*. Berlin: Mouton de Gruyter.

Lawrence, Shelly. 1995. Interpreter discourse: English to ASL expansions. In *Mapping our course: A collaborative venture, Proceedings of the tenth national convention, Conference of Interpreter Trainers*, edited by Elizabeth A. Winston, 205–14. N.p.: Conference of Interpreter Trainers.

Leeson, Lorraine. 2005a. Making the effort in simultaneous interpreting: Some considerations for signed language interpreters. In *Topics in signed language interpretation: Theory and practice*, edited by Terry Janzen, 51–68. Amsterdam: John Benjamins.

———. 2005b. Vying with variation: Interpreting language contact, gender variation, and gender difference. In *Topics in signed language interpretation: Theory and practice*, edited by Terry Janzen, 251–92. Amsterdam: John Benjamins.

Liddell, Scott K. 2003. *Grammar, gesture, and meaning in American Sign Language*. Cambridge: Cambridge University Press.

Liddell, Scott K., and Robert E. Johnson. 1989. American Sign Language: The phonological base. *Sign Language Studies* 64: 195–277.

Linell, Per. 1997. Interpreting as communication. In *Conference interpreting: Current trends in research*, edited by Yves Gambier, Daniel Gile, and Christopher Taylor, 49–67. Amsterdam: John Benjamins.

Lucas, Ceil, Robert Bayley, and Clayton Valli, eds. 2001. *Sociolinguistic variation in American Sign Language*. Washington, DC: Gallaudet University Press.

Malcolm, Karen. 2005. Contact sign, transliteration, and interpretation in Canada. In *Topics in signed language interpretation: Theory and practice*, edited by Terry Janzen, 107–33. Amsterdam: John Benjamins.

Metzger, Melanie. 1999. *Sign language interpreting: Deconstructing the myth of neutrality*. Washington, DC: Gallaudet University Press.

Napier, Jemina. 2002. *Sign language interpreting: Linguistic coping strategies*. Coleford, UK: Douglas McLean.

———. 2004. Interpreting omissions: A new perspective. *Interpreting* 6 (2): 117–42.

Perniss, Pamela M., Roland Pfau, and Markus Steinbach, eds. 2007. *Visible variation: Comparative studies on sign language structure*. Berlin: Mouton de Gruyter.

Quigley, Stephen P., and Joseph P. Youngs. 1965. *Interpreting for Deaf people*. Washington, DC: U.S. Department of Health, Education, and Welfare.

Reddy, Michael. 1979. The conduit metaphor: A case of frame conflict in our language about language. In *Metaphor and thought*, edited by Andrew Ortony, 284–324. Cambridge: Cambridge University Press.

Reddy, Michael. 1993. The conduit metaphor: A case of frame conflict in our language about language. In *Metaphor and thought* edited by Andrew Ortony, 164–201. 2nd ed. Cambridge: Cambridge University Press.

Roy, Cynthia B. 2000. *Interpreting as a discourse process.* New York: Oxford University Press.

Scheibman, Joanne. 2002. *Point of view and grammar: Structural patterns of subjectivity in American conversation.* Amsterdam: John Benjamins.

Schembri, Adam. 2003. Rethinking "classifiers" in signed languages. In *Perspectives on classifier constructions in sign languages*, edited by Karen Emmorey, 3–34. Mahwah, NJ: Lawrence Erlbaum.

Seleskovitch, Danica. 1976. Interpretation, A psychological approach to translation. In *Translation: Applications and esearch*, edited by Richard W. Brislin, 92–116. New York: Gardner.

———. 1978. *Interpreting for international conferences.* Washington, DC: Pen and Booth.

Sharwood Smith, Michael. 2000. Attentional mechanisms and the language acquisition device: Reflections on communication and developmental processes. In *Language processing and simultaneous interpreting: Interdisciplinary perspectives*, edited by Birgitta Englund Dimitrova and Kenneth Hyltenstam, 25–44. Amsterdam: John Benjamins.

Simone, Raffaele, ed. 1995. *Iconicity in language.* Amsterdam: John Benjamins.

Slobin, Dan I. 2006. Issues of linguistic typology in the study of sign language development of Deaf children. In *Advances in the sign language development of deaf children*, edited by Brenda Schick, Marc Marschark, and Patricia Elizabeth Spencer, 20–45. Oxford: Oxford University Press.

Sperber, Dan, and Deirdre Wilson. 1995. *Relevance: Communication and cognition.* 2nd ed. Oxford, UK: Blackwell.

Stokoe, William C. 1960. *Sign language structure: An outline of the visual communication systems of the American deaf.* Studies in linguistics, Occasional Papers 8. Buffalo, NY: University of Buffalo.

Stokoe, William C., Dorothy C. Casterline, and Carl G. Croneberg. 1965. *A dictionary of American Sign Language on linguistic principles.* Washington, DC: Gallaudet College Press.

Stratiy, Angela. 2005. Best practices in interpreting: A Deaf community perspective. In *Topics in signed language interpreting: Theory and practice*, edited by Terry Janzen, 231–50. Amsterdam: John Benjamins.

Tabakowska, Elżbieta. 2000. Is (cognitive) linguistics of any use for (literary) translation? In *Tapping and mapping the processes of translation and interpreting: Outlooks on empirical research*, edited by Sonja Tirkkonen-Condit and Riitta Jääskeläinen, 83–95. Amsterdam: John Benjamins.

Taylor Torsello, Carol, Sandra Gallina, Maria Sidiropoulou, Christopher Taylor, Helen Tebble, and A. R. Vuorikoski. 1997. Linguistics, discourse analysis and interpretation. In *Conference interpreting: Current trends in research*, edited by Yves Gambier, Daniel Gile, and Christopher Taylor, 167–86. Amsterdam: John Benjamins.

Tervoort, Bernard T. 1953. *Structurele Analyze van Visueel Taalgebruik binnen een Groep Dove Kinderen* [Structural analysis of visual language use within a group of deaf children]. Amsterdam: North-Holland.

Turner, Mark. 1991. *Reading minds: The study of English in the age of cognitive science*. Princeton, NJ: Princeton University Press.

Tyler, Andrea. 2008. Cognitive linguistics and second language instruction. In *Handbook of cognitive linguistics and second language acquisition*, edited by Peter Robinson and Nick C. Ellis, 456–88. London: Routledge.

Valli, Clayton, and Ceil Lucas. 1992. *Linguistics of American Sign Language*. Washington, DC: Gallaudet University Press.

van Herreweghe, Mieke, and Myriam Vermeerbergen, eds. 2004. *To the lexicon and beyond: Sociolinguistics in European Deaf communities*. Washington, DC: Gallaudet University Press.

Vermeerbergen, Myriam, Lorraine Leeson, and Onno Crasborn, eds. 2007. *Simultaneity in signed languages: Form and function*. Amsterdam: John Benjamins.

Wadensjö, Cecilia. 1998. *Interpreting as interaction*. London: Longman.

———. 2002 [1993]. The double role of a dialogue interpreter. In *The interpreting studies reader* edited by Franz Pöchhacker and Miriam Shlesinger, 355–370. London: Routledge.

Wilcox, Sherman, and Barbara Shaffer. 2005. Towards a cognitive model of interpreting. In *Topics in signed language interpreting: Theory and practice* edited by Terry Janzen, 27–50. Amsterdam: John Benjamins.

Wilkinson, Erin. 2009. Typology of signed languages: Differentiation through kinship terminology. Doctoral dissertation, University of New Mexico.

Williams, Ian A. 2009. A corpus-based study of Spanish translations of the verb "report" in biomedical research articles. *Meta* 54 (1): 146–60.

Winters, Marion. 2009. Modal particles explained: How modal particles creep into translations and reveal translators' styles. *Target* 21 (1): 74–97.

Zeshan, Ulrike. 2005. Sign languages. In *World atlas of language structures*, edited by Martin Haspelmath, Matthew S. Dryer, David Gil, and Bernard Comrie, 558–67. Oxford: Oxford University Press.

# Making Language Theory Explicit
### David Quinto-Pozos

OFTEN I find myself at an event—such as an academic presentation—for which an interpreter is part of the communication that unfolds. In those situations, I tend to be curious about the strategies that the interpreter is employing, and I cannot avoid occasionally paying attention to how she is managing the task of communicating across languages and cultures. What I am not consciously considering, however, are the various theoretical approaches that underlie my informal assessment, even though those beliefs are the basis for the metrics that I am engaging.

Interpretations can be *evaluated*—examined to determine what may be successful and what may be lacking—through the lenses of various interpreting specialists who function as *evaluators*, such as the interpreter researcher, the interpreter educator, and the interpreter herself. In his chapter, Terry Janzen reminds the reader that the task of evaluating an interpretation is inherently tied to one's conceptualization of language and communication, including one's theories and models of language structure and processes of communication. In other words, the need to recognize that everyone has inherent beliefs about language and communication, whether or not those views have come about through formal study, is an important aspect of conducting an analysis because the professional's notions will impact how they evaluate an interpretation. Janzen claims that this is true for interpreting researchers and educators, and it is likely true for interpreter practitioners— even when they find themselves in the audience for an interpreted event.

Janzen also argues for evaluations and analyses that hold as primary the task of co-construction of meaning rather than the separation of form and meaning as has been argued in previous approaches to interpretation (e.g., Seleskovitch, 1979). This forces the interpreter evaluator to go beyond comparing the formal units (e.g., syntactic structures, words, morphemes) of the source and target languages to determine if an interpretation is successful; the co-construction of meaning must be contextualized, and that framing is an important part of the analysis, according to Janzen. The approach that Janzen advocates has the potential to lead the interpreting profession—research, teaching, and practice—into the future by encouraging professionals to carefully consider pragmatic and contextual factors for the evaluation of interpreter effectiveness. Because this approach also places substantial emphasis on the co-construction of meaning, there is an obvious need to carefully examine the roles of the various communicators who are involved in a situation.

Evaluation of an interpretation based on a contextualization approach has challenges. Participants' perceptions of co-construction of communication may not align, and each situation offers its own unique constellation of shared and unshared knowledge among the hearing and deaf people and interpreters who are participating in an event. There is no single formula for a successful interpretation; each situation will influence how an interpretation unfolds. That fact may be a primary reason for my curiosity at interpreted events; I am interested in how *that* particular interpreter is managing the interpretation within *that* particular setting (with specific participants, dynamics, and topics of communication). This means that interpreter researchers, educators, and practitioners must develop metrics for reliably evaluating interpretations that consider as primary the context and facts about shared and unshared knowledge among participants.

With respect to specific linguistic features of interpretation, Janzen's proposal to consider the role of context is in line with various works that examine common discourse strategies that are used in English and American Sign Language (ASL)—such as strategies that deaf people use when communicating with different groups of people (e.g., see Humphries and MacDougal 1999/2000; Quinto-Pozos and Mehta 2010; Quinto-Pozos and Reynolds 2012; Zimmer 1989). In short, a message is communicated in different ways to people across different situations, and this must be considered when evaluating interpretations.

With respect to the teaching of interpreting, Janzen's approach encourages the interpreter educator to consider the models and theories of language and communication to which they subscribe in order to make those explicit as part of the process of evaluating interpretations. Janzen suggests that linguistic theory has been conspicuously absent from the various models of interpretation that have been used for teaching interpreting, which has presumably had an effect on curricula development for interpreting programs over the years. What may be lacking is a solid grounding in theory of language and communication that would serve as a foundation for theories of interpretation; after all, interpretation is a process that strongly resembles the process of engaging in communication (Linell 2009 refers to this process of language in use as *languaging*).

Janzen notes that there are different theoretical approaches to language and communication analysis. Whereas this is true (especially with respect to differences between functionalist and so-called formalist approaches), it is also likely that proponents of any one framework would support some of the basic tenets of another theory because it is difficult to analyze communication without holding beliefs about the basic structure of language in addition to beliefs about the ways in which people interact using language. The act of framing interpreting research and teaching within particular theoretical approaches to language and communication allows us to test those theories, especially as they relate to the communicatively similar practice of interpreting. Interpreting research that finds its way to the interpreter training classroom is an ideal way to connect theory to practice; interpreting researchers must capitalize on this positioning and further the work of translational research.

One particular challenge for interpreter educators is that they must determine how to teach a skill that is very dependent on context. Students need to learn about techniques for co-constructing meaning based on one's assumptions or knowledge of how language and communication occurs within a particular constellation of people, topic(s), and so forth. This teaching philosophy differs notably from an approach that places primary pedagogical focus on the source language in an attempt to produce a so-called target language equivalent message. The lens must be widened to include other factors, and that widening involves explicit recognition of one's conceptualization, theories, and models of language and communication.

Encouraging interpreter researchers to consider their language and communication theories and models and make them explicit in the analysis creates a win–win scenario for the fields of signed language interpreting research and applied linguistics research; it allows language specialists from multiple disciplines (e.g., interpreters, translators, language instructors, interpreter educators, computational linguists who work on translation, etc.) to interact more through the literature. Spoken language interpreting and translating researchers could potentially benefit from discussion of signed language interpreters' work within explicit language and communication frameworks, and signed language interpreters have much to learn from approaches to translation and spoken language interpretation. As one example, spoken language interpreters might be curious about the role of prosody in an interpreted message and how that prosody can signal various features of the language and interpretation (e.g., see Nicodemus 2009). Interpreter evaluators might also be interested in the material made ostensive by speakers and interpreters—those choices that speakers and interpreters make about specific contexts and how they communicate (e.g., see Stone 2005, for an account of relevance theory and Deaf interpreter practices). Interpreter educators and their students could also benefit tremendously from highlighting relevant aspects of their beliefs about language and communication and how those beliefs influence their judgments of interpretations; that would provide these lifelong learners with frameworks for analyzing and improving upon examples of their work. In short, one way to learn from each other is for each of us to make explicit our theories of language and communication, as Janzen suggests.

Janzen is issuing a call to arms to interpreting specialists to make explicit their language and communication theory—whether it be in formal analyses such as those performed by interpreter researchers or informal assessments that interpreters are drawn to by their curiosity. What Janzen suggests requires more than using metalinguistic/metacommunicative abilities for analysis; interpreting specialists need to make explicit the models and theories of language and communication that are driving their analyses and claims. By making language theory explicit, an interpreter specialist may come closer to achieving *ne plus ultra* within their own work and within any work that they do for advancement of the field. The task is not an easy one, but it is a vital step in the interpreting profession's continued development.

# References

Humphries, T., and F. MacDougall. 1999/2000. "Chaining" and other links: Making connections between American Sign Language and English in two types of school settings. *Visual Anthropology Review* 15 (2): 84–94.

Linell, P. 2009. *Rethinking language, mind, and the world dialogically.* Charlotte, NC: Information Age.

Nicodemus, B. 2009. *Prosodic markers and utterance boundaries in American Sign Language interpretation.* Washington, DC: Gallaudet University Press.

Quinto-Pozos, D., and W. Reynolds. 2012. ASL discourse strategies: Chaining and connecting–explaining across audiences. *Sign Language Studies* 12 (2): 41–65.

Quinto-Pozos, D., and S. Mehta. 2010. Register variation in mimetic gestural complements to signed language. *Journal of Pragmatics* 42:557–84.

Stone, C. 2005. Toward a Deaf translation norm. PhD dissertation. University of Bristol, UK.

Seleskovitch, D. 1978. *Interpreting for international conferences.* Washington, DC: Pen and Booth.

Zimmer, J. 1989. Toward a description of register variation in American Sign Language. In *The sociolinguistics of the Deaf community*, edited by Ceil Lucas, 253–72. San Diego: Academic Press.

# COMMENTARY

# Shifting Paradigms
## *Lorraine Leeson*

TERRY JANZEN's chapter captures much about the gaps that exist in the linguistic to applied linguistic transfer space. As our knowledge develops with respect to how language works, it sometimes seems that the gap widens between what linguists know and how this knowledge is applied in teaching. This is equally true for researchers and practitioners in the field of interpreting, interpreting research, and interpreter education. At the same time, as Janzen explains, the relationships among linguistic theory, interpreting theory, interpreting research, and interpreter education are symbiotic and ones we cannot afford to ignore.

Janzen asks whether we need a "well-developed and useful theory of linguistic structure and a theory of interpretation" that frames both interpreting and interpreting research as fundamentally linguistic pursuits. He notes that while early formalist approaches to linguistics may have had little to offer interpreting theorists, more recent branches of theoretical linguistics, especially within a cognitive linguistics framework, have surfaced that impact the functionalist, social-interactionalist, and contextualist nature of the interpreter's task. These assist the interpreter researcher in attempting to account for successful interpreting in practice. They are all models that have found their way into some interpreter education programs and are slowly seeping into our broader research paradigm.

A case in point is cognitive linguistic–inspired analyses of interpreting (Wilcox and Shaffer 2005). Wilcox and Shaffer see interpretation as communication activity and see the interpreter as impacting the nature of the interaction regardless of whether the primary participants are cognizant of it, simply as a result of being there. This is, as Janzen notes, a long way from the conduit model of education that most interpreters have experienced. While conduit approaches suggest that meaning is conveyed in the linguistic form of the source language and can be unpackaged in some way by the interpreter and successfully transferred to the target language, Wilcox and Shaffer argue that this is not the way communication works. Like Janzen, they point out that interpreters do not gain access to meaning via form. Janzen tells us that "in a cognitive-theoretical view of language, expressions serve as clues to meaning, but a person's meaning is never directly accessible" (this volume, 104). This is a key principle that underpins Wilcox and Shaffer's argument that without extensive knowledge, interpreters simply cannot construct meaning (2005, 44). Further, we may need to rethink our understanding of context. Janzen suggests that "context" in communication events includes both the external situational factors present and awareness that the knowledge base of participants in any given event changes over time, in turn profoundly influencing the context. If we as interpreters assume a single static "context" rather than a pragmatically driven dynamic process, we are less likely to be as successful in our work as we could be.

Embracing this argument, we can say that a paradigmatic shift is required: If we are to benefit from such linguistics work, then we must reconsider how meaning is construed via the medium of language. We need to appreciate that meaning is not housed in form alone but that form follows function. More fundamentally, we must engage in examining what it really means for interpreting practice when we consider that we collectively co-construct meaning each time we speak or sign, or when we interpret in pragmatically dynamic communicative settings. Janzen's paper offers an excellent starting point to support the willing interpreter in dipping a toe into the waters of this growing swell of literature, an essential starting point.

This new way of understanding language and cognition has the potential to radically change how we talk about the relationship between language and culture, how we categorize knowledge and experience, and how these are packaged in different languages. The expectation of simple mappings between form and function often leads to clunky, prescriptive, and formulaic interpreted texts that consumers of interpreting services frequently comment on. However, what frames our analysis of such things? How do we get interpreters (students, novices, and experts) beyond our inherited beliefs?

As Janzen suggests, it has to start with those of us engaged in education and research. We have to acknowledge the symbiotic relationship between linguistics and interpreting research, and we have to keep abreast of the key findings. We also have a duty to embed such learning in our practices. This may mean sometimes radical rethinking of our field's prescribed truths about how we interpret, some of which Janzen addressed in his chapter.

Wilcox and Shaffer suggest that we engage in "success analysis" (2005, 45) and problematize interpreting as successful communication, which in turn should open up pathways to understand more about how the interpreting process works. This, they suggest, will bring us further than our current model, which focuses only on failure to communicate.

Another linguistically driven approach that has exponentially driven forward our understanding of signed languages in recent years is corpus sign linguistics. Significant corpora now exist for Auslan, British Sign Language, Sign Language of the Netherlands, French Sign Language, Swedish Sign Language, Flemish Sign Language, German Sign Language, and Irish Sign Language. From a linguistic analysis perspective, corpora offer new possibilities for testing linguistic hypotheses, but corpora also have the potential to change the face of interpreter/translator education. Sinclair (2004, 1) says that

> this cornucopia [i.e., the richness of corpus data] has not been welcomed with open arms, neither by the research community nor the language teaching profession. It has been kept waiting in the wings, and only in the last few years has any serious attention been paid to it by those who consider themselves to be applied linguists. For a quarter of a century, corpus evidence was ignored, spurned and talked out of relevance, until its importance became just too obvious for it to be kept out in the cold.

While a growing number of corpus projects on signed languages that make use of ELAN, a software program developed by the Max Planx Institute, Nijmegan, have emerged in recent years, Leeson (2008) reports that these have not yet generally been harnessed for purposes other than linguistic analysis, with the early exception of the Signs of Ireland corpus (Leeson and Saeed 2012). Leeson outlines some of the ways that the corpus is used in interpreter education, including providing a baseline for exploring collocational norms for Irish Sign Language (ISL) for looking at the distribution of discourse features as well as features such as metaphor and idiomatic expression. When working from a spoken to a signed language, student translators can check a signed language corpus to check whether collocations that they think are possible are used by Deaf signers. This offers students a mechanism for actively considering how their notion of how ISL works compares with how a range of signers talk about similar topics or, from a grammatical function perspective, how aspects of language structure are used by Deaf signers. Following Sinclair, we should embrace the increasing availability of signed language corpus data and analyses of same as a cornucopia for the field of sign language interpreting research, practice, and education.

The crucial point emerging from Janzen's chapter is that if we, as interpreters, ignore the profusion of evidence presented to us from the linguistics field, we risk a significant disservice to the communities which we serve. For interpreter educators to ignore such evidence fundamentally risks holding back our field. We have a duty of care to be exacting in our work and to understand more fully the nature of communication, the pragmatics that drive certain structures, and the semantics embedded within certain linguistic choices. We have a duty of care to the interpreting students we educate to give them a research-led education. We have a duty of care to the Deaf and hearing communities we work with to develop our competence as best we can over time. This demands continuous engagement with the literature given that, as Janzen says, linguistic activity is central to the work of interpreters and "interpretation researchers ... contribute to the field of linguistics in a vastly important way" (this volume, 112).

## References

Leeson, L. 2008. Quantum leap: Leveraging the signs of Ireland digital corpus in Irish Sign Language/English interpreter training. *Sign Language Translator and Interpreter* 2 (2): 149–76.

Leeson, L., and J. Saeed (2012). *Irish Sign Language*. Edinburgh: Edinburgh University Press.

Sinclair, J. 2004. *How to use corpora in language teaching*. Amsterdam: John Benjamins.

Wilcox, S., and B. Shaffer 2005. Towards a cognitive model of interpreting. In *Topics in signed language interpreting*, edited by T. D. Janzen, 27–50. Amsterdam: John Benjamins.

BARBARA SHAFFER

# Evolution of Theory, Evolution of Role: How Interpreting Theory Shapes Interpreter Role

By your metaphors so shall you be known.

—Raymond D. Fogelson

## Abstract

Regardless of the languages being considered, it has often been said that: "you can't interpret what you don't understand." Of course, such a statement necessarily refers to *meaning*, but the beliefs we hold about *how* we understand are also of importance. Our beliefs about things such as words, sentences, discourse, prosody, human interaction, and culture shape what we believe about meaning, which in turn influences the way we approach the interpretation task and how we educate future interpreters. In this chapter we explore the notion of meaning and how our understanding of it shapes our conception of our professional role as American Sign Language (ASL) / English interpreters.

ASL/ENGLISH interpreting is a young profession, despite the long history of volunteer interpreting services. I simply mean that it has not been considered a profession for long and has been the subject of academic inquiry for only a short time. If we agree that the 1964 meeting in Muncie, Indiana, represents one of the earliest professional gatherings on the subject, then the field of interpreting is a scant 48 years old at the time of this writing. Yet, in that roughly half a century, we have seen tremendous growth and have done much careful work with the goal of better understanding the task we approach daily. We have made great strides in improving the

128

service we offer. Our thoughtful discussions have done much to prepare future interpreters.

One issue that has followed us through the decades, however, is the notion of interpreter role. In the following sections, the role of the ASL/English interpreter is considered within the context of the intellectual discussions that guided us. The theme I suggest is as follows: Our misconceptions about language and specifically our discomfort with mistaken beliefs about the nature of meaning and the concept of *the message* have directly and indirectly (albeit often tacitly) spurred the ever-evolving view of our professional role. Our changing views of our role also then become part of interpreter education program curricula.

Metaphors are often used to understand theories and models. We use metaphors unconsciously and consciously throughout our day. Metaphors help us understand our world and communicate with others. They shape how we think (Lakoff and Johnson 1980), and the metaphors we create influence how we understand the very thing we created the metaphor to describe. In the case of interpreting, we first created metaphors of our professional role that described us as passively conveying information, not influencing the communicative event. That metaphor pervades the literature on both interpreter role and message analysis. The metaphor, rather than simply a means for describing our role, began to shape our role *and* our work.

As a young undergraduate student I remember being faced (in Psychology 101) with the quote: "Ontogeny recapitulates phylogeny." Quite frankly, as a phrase it had me stumped. I understood each of the words, more or less, but could not make sense of the sentence. I grappled with its meaning. This theory, that the embryonic development of an individual organism (its ontogeny) follows the same path as the evolutionary history of the species (phylogeny), has since been discredited. However, as a somewhat ironic sidebar of sorts, it is fitting here. One can consider the interpreting field not just in terms of its history but also in terms of the development of the individual interpreter, because, of course, each of us has an ever-evolving understanding of the message and our role. Each interpreter's evolving conceptualization of role probably resembles the field's transformation, whether the interpreter is formally educated, certified, and well read in the works of her field or not.

# Early Conceptualizations of Role and Language

In this section I review some of our early discussions of the interpreter's role, summarize the literature on meaning and the message in ASL/English interpreting, and link both with linguistic theories of the time. For comparison, the more prominent contemporary theories of interpreting found in the spoken language literature will also be mentioned, as they were heavily influenced by linguistic theories of the time. ASL/English interpreters were also influenced by popular linguistic thinking.

The 1965 book *Interpreting for Deaf People* is arguably one of the first materials published by our fledgling field. Quigley and his colleagues were charting new territory.[1] *Interpreting for Deaf People* was published just one year after (and as a direct result of) the historic meeting in Muncie, Indiana. This was the same year that PL 89-333 was passed, marking the beginning of payment for ASL/English interpreters in vocational rehabilitation and identifying interpreters as a "service" provided to vocational rehabilitation clients. This was also just five years after William Stokoe (1960) published the groundbreaking *Sign Language Structure: An Outline of the Visual Communication Systems of the American Deaf*, in which he proposed that the communication of deaf Americans could be considered using the same linguistic tools as spoken or written languages. In fact, though Stokoe cautions in his preface that he is not a linguist, nor the right person to determine whether ASL is a language, he refers to it from the opening paragraphs forward as such and analyzes it using linguistic principles. This was the first time someone had published such an opinion regarding what we now call ASL.[2] In 1965, the same year the Quigley book was published, Stokoe (along with Carl Croneberg and Dorothy Casterline) published *A Dictionary of American Sign Language on Linguistic Principles*. In 1971 the Linguistic Research Laboratory was established at Gallaudet College. My point is simple: The profession of ASL/English interpreting in the United

---

1. While often referred to as "Quigley and Youngs (1965)," the Library of Congress entry for *Interpreting for Deaf People* lists only Stephen Quigley as the cited author and Joseph Youngs as the co-chairman of the committee. Therefore, the book is referred to here as Quigley (1965). It is also important to remember that *Interpreting for Deaf People* was a committee effort.

2. It must be mentioned that Ben Tervoot had come to the same conclusions in 1953 regarding the use of sign communication in the Netherlands.

States was born *alongside* the field of ASL language linguistics. It goes without saying that at this time there were no college-level interpreter preparation programs for the dissemination of new information.

With or without that historical contextualization, it is clear when reading *Interpreting for Deaf People* that little was known about ASL. The concepts of "interpreting" and "translating" were also new to most of us, and though borrowed from larger fields, such terms were often used quite differently. For example, Quigley (1965, 1) notes in the definitions section that

> It is important that the difference between interpreting and translating be clearly understood. In translating, the thoughts and words of the speaker are presented verbatim. In interpreting, the interpreter may depart from the exact words of the speaker to paraphrase, define, and explain what the speaker is saying. Interpreting requires adjustment of the presentation to the intellectual level of the audience and their ability to understand English. The interpreter needs to be aware of the differences in the use of interpreting and translating. When translating, the interpreter is recognizing that the deaf person is a highly literate individual who prefers to have his thoughts and those of hearing persons expressed verbatim. Translating is not commonly used as highly literate deaf people frequently do not need the services of an interpreter unless they are in situations where misunderstanding might arise which could result in financial or personal loss.... For many deaf people, it is necessary to paraphrase, define, and explain a speaker's words in terms and concepts which they can understand. This is interpreting.

Although this sort of definition might surprise us now, given where we currently are as a field, it is important to remember that many early interpreters were also teachers, church members, social service providers, and, very often, family members and friends. No formal training was available for those who wished to become interpreters, and "best practices" were based on the experiences of volunteers who had learned by interacting with and being guided by the deaf community.

To help frame this quote further, at the time the philosophy was that there was one way to communicate with and for literate deaf people, called "above average" deaf signers (the description of which resembles what is now referred to as transliterating) and a distinctly different way to communicate with and for "low-verbal deaf persons" (Quigley 1965, 37). With respect to the latter, Quigley and his colleagues assert that when "in interpreting for low-verbal deaf persons, the interpreter paraphrases, rephrases, defines, simplifies, and attempts to give the literal sense or conceptual essence of idiomatic expressions.… The use of analogy, parallelism, and examples are helpful in this type of interpreting" (39). For the "above average" deaf signer, by contrast, fingerspelling was an option when there was no ASL "equivalent" for an English word. As Janzen and Shaffer (2008, 12) note, the effect of this approach was that such translations were often taught to interpreting students as the only way to sign these items. Novice interpreters and students spent many hours memorizing these signed "paraphrases" for use in their interpretation.

Because at the time interpreters were just becoming aware of the notion of ASL as a language with syntax, morphology, and word formation principles, most of the strategies given in *Interpreting for Deaf People* were for specific lexical items. A novice interpreter, upon seeing translations for words such as *cataract* (Quigley 1965, 72) as THIN WHITE INSIDE EYE, COVER PART USE TO SEE, SLOWLY GET WORSE, CAN'T SEE, MUST REMOVE might be left feeling that the lexicon of ASL was impoverished. They may also have assumed that the paraphrases provided were the correct way to interpret something. In other words, interpreters may have believed that such paraphrases were formulaic and obligatory when interpreting for a "low-verbal" deaf person.

I turn now to beliefs about the interpreter's role in the early days of the profession. Most of us are aware of the origins of the profession. We know that interpreting began as "favor," "duty," or "the right thing to do." We recall being told of the "helper model" of interpreting. Early descriptions of our role, which were documented soon after establishment of the American Registry of Interpreters for the Deaf (RID), eschewed the helper model, perhaps in a concerted effort to establish professionalism, boundaries, and best practices. From those early meetings in 1964 and 1965 "machine" and "conduit" models of interpreting were born. Quigley (1965, 52) refers to this directly: "part of the interpreter's training and experience should include some self-discipline so that the interpreter always makes a strong effort to remain detached, neutral, and as completely impersonal and objective as possible." The first code of ethics for professional signed language / spoken language interpreters also reflects a conduit metaphor.

Solow (1981, ix) describes the conduit model in much the same way many of us still consider it. She says:

> The sign language interpreter acts as a communication link between people, serving only in that capacity. An analogy is in the use of the telephone—the telephone is a link between people that does not exert a personal influence on either. It does, however, influence the ease of communication and speed of the process. If the interpreter can strive to maintain that parallel positive function without losing vital human attributes, then the interpreter renders a professional service.

The implication here is clear: We are simply a means for two (or more) people who do not share a common language to communicate with each other. If we do our jobs well, we add nothing to the exchange other than helping to make it possible.

From our origins a scant 15 years earlier, ASL/English interpreting had transitioned from favor to skilled profession, from helper to conduit. The conduit metaphor was likely a necessary phase in our development given our origins and our roots in deaf education, religion, and the social services. Conduit and machine models reflected our active desire to minimize our role and allow our deaf consumers autonomy. Early interpreting texts focused on our lack of participation, and as the 1965 text illustrates, early works suggested interpreting was a formulaic activity and could be taught as such (Janzen and Shaffer 2008). With conduit/machine models of interpreting, the emphasis is on the role of the interpreter, not on interpreting as a communicative, intersubjective interaction. Implicit here is the idea that the message is not a subject warranting much consideration.

Perhaps more striking, however, is how modern textbooks and scholarly articles describe our early models. Humphrey and Alcorn (2001), for example, claim that: "when looking at the work of an interpreter functioning from this philosophical frame, you would see a 'verbatim' transmission of words/signs. Interpreters focused on volume, being sure to sign every word spoken and speak every word produced" (8.1). Clearly, this represents a reconceptualization of how the conduit model was first described and understood by working interpreters, since even as early as Quigley's work in 1965 there was an understanding that interpreters must make decisions about the structure of the target text. "Conduit-era" interpreters were never exclusively transliterators. Yet, it seems that this is how they are remembered (at least by some). Do our metaphors for our work have such influence on us that they *shape* how we retrospectively consider our work?

As Wilcox and Shaffer (2005) noted, our conceptualization of our role shifted often as the field matured. With time and experience we started to more fully understand that the linguistic choices we made had impacts. We began to consider the notion of "the message." Yet, our understanding of the importance of the source language, paralinguistic factors, context, and extralinguistic variables such as the relationships among the discourse participants was still lacking. Our research on meaning was still fraught with conduit metaphors, and that research made its way into interpreter education programs.

Wilcox and Shaffer (2005), in reviewing earlier models, summarized how a conduit metaphor of meaning remained (despite the shift in our professional role) with several telling quotes. For example, Stewart, Schein, and Cartwright (1998) summarized Ingram's 1974 "semiotic model" state as follows:

> A message is first coded for transmission—a process called encoding. The code may be English, ASL, or nonlanguages such as gestures, facial expressions, or grunts. The message is then transmitted over a channel (e.g., speech or writing). When received, it is decoded (i.e., put into a form accessible to the receiver). Any signal that interferes with trans- mission of the message is labeled noise…. These are concepts familiar to engineers who develop and analyze communication systems. (45–46)

The "message" as it is referred to here is ostensibly understood to be more akin to some notion of an "utterance" than to what Seleskovitch (1978) and others (discussed later in this chapter) refer. The message in Ingram's model is encoded, transmitted, and then decoded. Inherent to such an understanding of how communication works is the idea that mean- ing is contained within utterances. An interpreter's task is to uncover the meaning and then repack it in the target language with an emphasis on "equivalence" [but see Seleskovitch (1976), who claims that "equivalence" is the goal of translators but not necessarily a feasible goal for interpreters].[3]

---

3. Seleskovitch makes the distinction in part due to the ephemeral nature of speech. It is of note, though, that translators and interpreters very often share the same working languages, which leads to overlap and opportunities for analysis of written texts by interpreters, that is, unless one of the working languages is a signed language.

Form here is understood to be important only inasmuch as it is needed to comprehend the message. Beyond that, the interpreter's goal is to discard (to rid herself of) the form.[4] Humphrey and Alcorn continue this metaphor:

> Communicators must construct messages in a grammatically correct way in order to make sense. However, after the meaning being conveyed has been extracted from a sentence and understood by the listener, the specific grammatical structure no longer serves any purpose. This is because grammar is not needed to retain the information carried in an utterance. While interpreters must be fluent in their grammatical use of both languages they work in, *they work predominantly in the pragmatic realm to uncover the meaning of the message and the purpose intended by the sender.* [...] Thus, it is critical for interpreters to understand how messages are constructed in order to extract meaning from the utterances they are expected to interpret. (2001, 1.8–9; italics theirs)

We seem to spend much time considering what to do with the message but not much time considering the message.

In the earlier days of the field such beliefs about interpreting were not unique to ASL/English interpreters, of course, nor were they even limited to interpreters. Popular theoretical linguistic theories of meaning likely had a profound influence on both spoken/spoken language interpreting *and* on spoken/signed language interpreting.

Generative theories of linguistics, most notably those of Noam Chomsky and his protégés, radically changed how linguists considered semantic and pragmatic meaning and ultimately influenced the work of interpreters as well. In generative linguistic theories, researchers worked from the belief that grammar was fully explicit. It was conceived of as a finite set of rules that could be applied to *generate* all those and only those sentences that are grammatical in a given language. Generative grammatical theories led to the use of terms such as *deep structure* and *surface structure* and the idea that "meaning" could be accounted for in a given sentence by understanding the deep structure of the utterance. Not much more was considered with respect to meaning, and as Croft and Cruse (2004, 1) described it, "semantic phenomena are assigned to the 'periphery.'"

---

4. One has to wonder if ASL/English interpreters were even more concerned with the discarding of linguistic form due to worries of language mixing and language 1 (L1) interference.

Without going further, suffice it to say that linguistic theories popular in the 1960s and 1970s did little to help the working interpreter analyze the message. Seleskovitch (1976, 102) seems to be saying as much when she states:

> A word of warning to the student interpreter who may fall into the trap of linguistics, failing to realize that the science of linguistics is essentially devoted to the study of language and not to the application of language to communication.

Ostensibly such a response is a reaction to generative linguistic theories of the time.

## ANALYZING "THE MESSAGE"

Translation studies and interpreting studies describe "the message" in different ways. Both descriptions are helpful to us in our work, however. For example, Eugene Nida, a well-known biblical translator and researcher who popularized an approach to translation that focuses on formal and dynamic (functional) equivalence, spent much time studying text (message) analysis. Regarding dynamic equivalence he states, "The role of the translator is to facilitate the transfer of message, meaning and cultural elements from one language into another and create an equivalent response from the receivers. The message in the source language is embedded a cultural context and has to be transferred to the target language" (1964, 13) and further that it is "the total meaning or content of a discourse; the concepts and feelings which the author intends the reader to understand and perceive" (Nida and Taber 1969, 205).

Seleskovitch, a conference interpreter, contrasts translation with interpretation similarly. Interpretation, she asserts, "focuses on the ideas expressed in live utterances rather than on language itself; it strictly ignores all attempts at finding linguistic equivalents ... and concentrates on finding the appropriate wording to convey a given meaning at a given point in time and in a given context, whatever that wording (i.e., the formulation used by the interpreter) or the original wording may mean under different circumstances" (1976, 93). In her view one component of the message is the dynamic, real-time interaction among context, the communicators, and the actual utterances themselves. Interpreting involves the identification of relevant concepts. Especially important to her view is that original and target language wordings may correspond only in their temporary meaning in a given speech performance "without necessarily constituting equivalent language units capable of reuse in different circumstances" (1976, 92).

Hatim and Mason (1990) suggest that translators (and presumably interpreters) are charged with conveying the same message to the target audience that is intended for the source text audience. However, as Janzen and Korpiniski (2005, 184) remind us, "the overall knowledge base, cultural perspective, and contextual expectations the target audience have may differ greatly from that of the source language audience." Meaning, they say, is inferred. Hatim and Mason, they suggest, tell us that "meaning equivalence is only drawn through the assumptions the audience can make about what the speaker must mean, that is, by inferring the meaning" (2005, 184). Finally, equivalence (as Hatim and Mason describe it) is a more approachable ideal if the interpreter has adequate linguistic skills and understanding of cultural norms.

In an essay on consecutive and simultaneous interpreting, Russell (2005, 145) describes what she calls a meaning-based model of interpreting. In it, she describes some of the components of the source language message:

1. Syntactic knowledge
2. Semantic knowledge
3. Associated knowledge and background experience
4. Cultural awareness
5. Contextual knowledge

When analyzing the source language message the interpreter must process information at lexical, phrasal, sentential, and discourse levels. Russell adds, "This could include identifying register and style features such as the use of politeness markers, and structural items such as syntactic forms needed to convey particular question or answer styles, say in a courtroom setting" (2005, 145).

This discussion makes it clear that to many of us "message" and "utterance" are not equivalent concepts. It also highlights the interactive nature of discourse (and of interpreted discourse). Meaning does not exist within words, phrases, and utterances (Roy 2000; Wilcox and Shaffer 2005; Janzen and Shaffer 2008). Meaning is dynamically co-constructed by discourse participants in a specific context. Discourse participants engage in continual online assessments of each other's knowledge stores and construct their messages accordingly. As Janzen and Shaffer (2008) stress, interpreters are full discourse participants who must also co-construct meaning.

Interpreters must continually make online assessments of their addressee's (as well as their own) comprehension and make necessary adjustments referred to here and elsewhere in the literature (by Gile [1995] and others, for example) as contextualization. In much of the ASL/English interpreting research, the closest correlates to contextualization are the so-called "expansion techniques" first popularized by Lawrence (1995) and further elaborated on by Humphrey and Alcorn (2001) and others. However, as Janzen and Shaffer (2008) point out, the "techniques" Lawrence attempts to claim to be unique features of ASL are in fact pan-language strategies. As with the Quigley text (1965), they are typically discussed as being formulaic and even conceived of as being an obligatory component of ASL grammar. Expansion techniques as commonly discussed within the "bilingual/bicultural mediator" framework, and contextualization as a discourse (and interpreting) strategy are discussed in the remaining sections of the chapter.

## CURRENT POPULAR INTERPRETING THEORIES

Interpreting theories come and go; this much is clear. Each new theory represents our then-current understanding of our task and role. Current popular theories represent a dramatic departure from early models that asked us to be mindful to not influence the communication event. We know now that our very presence has an impact on the situation and that the linguistic and extralinguistic decisions we make are of great importance. In fact, we now seem to be embracing our active role. This is most clearly seen in the so-called "bilingual/bicultural mediator" model and the discussions of the interpreter as an "ally." I return to the notion of interpreter as "ally" later.

While most familiar to most of us in the context of ASL/English interpreting, the "bilingual/bicultural" model was actually discussed early on by Etilvia Arjona (a spoken language interpreter) and later referenced for ASL interpreting by Roy (1993) and others. Arjona (1978, 36) claimed that language and culture were inseparable and, as such, "the translation process is considered as taking place within a situational/cultural context that is, in itself, an integral part of the process and that must be considered in order to bridge, in a meaningful manner, this gap that separates both sender and receptor audiences." Humphrey and Alcorn (2001, 8.10) understood this to mean that the interpreter's task is to perform "cultural and linguistic mediation while accomplishing speaker goal and maintaining dynamic equivalence." As Stewart, Schein, and Cartwright describe it:

> Adherents of the bilingual–bicultural approach believe that interpreters should explain the cultural implications of an utterance when this is deemed essential to its understanding, and hence should practice cultural mediation. If a participant from Great Britain says, "Look under the bonnet," the direction means "Open the car's hood." Should interpreters interpose a brief explanation of the differences between British and American automotive terms? Or should they interpret the expression as "Look under the hood."? Opinions vary. (2004, 112)

While it is unclear what Stewart, Schein, and Cartwright themselves believe, the implications of brief cultural explanations are clear: The interpreter is making online decisions that the communication participants cannot understand each other, even with the use of an interpreter, unless the interpreter explains things she believes are unfamiliar to the other discourse participants.

Although on the surface this description seems to be akin to what Arjona proposes, it clearly represents a much more involved, active, and empowered role for the interpreter. Stewart, Schein, and Cartwright (2004), in introducing the bilingual–bicultural mediator (which they refer to as "bi-bi") model, acknowledge that at times such an approach appears not far removed from a helper model when they state:

> Though not advocating a complete return to the helper role, Bi-Bi does not accept interpreters as conduits or mediators in all situations. Bi-Bi proponents argue that an interpreter on assignment with a terminally ill deaf person may in fact assume the role of an "ally" for that person. In effect, Bi-Bi allows interpreters the latitude to define their precise role on a situation-by-situation-basis. (2004, 36)

Of the same hypothetical situation, they go on to note:

> Except for the helper aspect, other sign language interpreting models
> would probably not allow for such cultural mediation on the part of
> the interpreter. The Bi-Bi model carries with it the danger of being
> viewed as parentalistic, because cultural mediation will ensue when,
> in the judgment of the interpreter the deaf and hearing people will
> not understand something. (2004, 37)

Conceivably the reader is meant to understand that some of the concepts
introduced and discussed by medical and paramedical professionals may be
unfamiliar to a deaf patient or his or her family. While it is possible that
some aspects of death and dying may be understood differently by different
cultures, without additional context from the authors it is unclear from this
quotation what *cultural* mediation they are referring to.

In contrast Triandis (1976), a spoken language interpreter/translator, in
an essay on minimizing translation, describes the importance of culture to
translation thusly:

> In any translation one has to face the problem of the extent to which
> what he has to translate is culture-specific (emic) or universal (etic).
> It is easy to see that etic concepts such as fire, moon, and sun pro-
> duce fewer translation difficulties than to emic concepts, such as the
> Greek concept of *philotimo* or the Anglo-American concept of *fair-*
> *ness*. (1976, 229; italics in original)

Clearly, here Triandis is talking about the difficulties interpreters and
translators face when the lexical item in the source language is culturally
bound and culturally defined. From his description, it seems quite clear
what "cultural mediation" might mean to our work. It becomes clearer why
Triandis, Nida, and others struggled with the goal of "dynamic equivalence." Culturally specific words must be translated into the target language (and culture) where no such cultural referent perhaps exists. Triandis
suggests that one way to define a culturally specific (emic) concept is in
terms of "etic" attributes. As he puts it, "If we relate our emic concepts
to this framework we will be able to achieve equivalence, by measuring
what is unique (emic) in terms of a common yardstick (etic dimensions)"
(1976, 231). Triandis, Nida, and others acknowledge that culture is more
deeply embedded in language and experience than mere lexical items, but
the study of such gives us a starting point from which to work.

Simon (1995) gives several clear examples of the importance of understanding the source culture in translation and interpretation. She states (1995, 45) that "to understand the words 'snow' or 'high school' or 'Holy Ghost' and translate them adequately, you must understand the culture from which they emerge and the cultures to which they are destined."

Applying this approach to ASL/English interpreting proves more challenging than it would appear on first glance. Humphrey and Alcorn (2001, 8.11–8.12) state that the bilingual–bicultural interpreter interprets both "explicitly stated ideas and information that is conveyed implicitly" if needed. This, they say, requires linguistic and cultural expansions and reductions. Interpreters, in this view, make their decisions with one of three perceived necessities in mind: linguistic need, cultural need, or difference in experiential frame. A "difference in experiential frame" is described by Humphrey and Alcorn as the varied life experiences of deaf people that interpreters face and the necessity of providing "experientially specific information so the recipient can have a schema allowing information to be successfully conveyed and understood" (2001, 8.13).

The example they use to illustrate this involves a Canadian speaker and an American consumer. The Canadian refers to removing his shoes in a house. "A bilingual–bicultural interpretation would require briefly providing the information that it is customary to remove the shoes when entering someone's home. Without doing that, the audience might misunderstand or miss the point of the illustration being given" (2001, 8.14). They caution that one has to be mindful not to slip into "helper" mode of adding or deleting information to help or protect one's client. It would seem judicious to also seriously consider the parameters of each type of adjustment. Why, for example, is the concept of Canadians removing their shoes considered a difference in experiential frame rather than a cultural expansion?

It is clear that as our role as ASL/English interpreters evolves, we need to revisit the notion of culture and always consider carefully the reasons and motivations for and implications of the additions we make to interpreted texts. I say additions because as Leeson (2005) and Janzen and Shaffer (2008), among others, have reminded us, this type of adjustment or "contextualization" (see Gile 1995, for example), including those that makes the (assumed) implicit explicit are, in fact, additions to the source language text. Contextualization as a type of cultural mediation is discussed in the sections that follow. First, a short review of culture may help frame the remainder of the discussion.

## DEFINING CULTURE

Katan (1999, 16) notes that most people have a somewhat instinctual sense of what *culture* means to them and yet a definition of it has been "notoriously elusive and difficult." It seems that for many of us culture is a case of "you know it when you see it," but is that really accurate or adequate? Regardless, it is clear that a priori assumptions about the nature of culture are inadequate when one believes one's charge is to *mediate* cultural differences.

Perhaps one of the better known descriptions of culture is that of Edward B. Tylor. Culture, he states, is "that complex whole which includes knowledge, belief, art, morals, law, custom, and any other capabilities and habits acquired by man as a member of society" (Tylor 1924/1871, 1). The late Clifford Geertz, a symbolic and interpretative anthropologist, proposed a decidedly cognitive definition of culture that seems well suited to application in linguistics and interpreting: "[Culture is] an historically transmitted pattern of meanings embodied in symbols, a system of inherited conceptions expressed in symbolic forms by means of which men communicate, perpetuate, and develop their knowledge about and attitudes toward life" (Geertz 1973, 89).

Schnieder (1976, 204) frames it more richly:

Culture is, by definition here, a system of symbols and meanings. Culture contrasts with norms in that norms are oriented to patterns for action, whereas culture constitutes a body of definitions, premises, statements, postulates, presumptions, propositions, and perceptions about the nature of the universe and man's place in it. Where norms tell the actor how to play a scene, culture tells the actor how the scene is set and what it all means. Where norms tell the actor how to behave in the presence of ghosts, gods, and human beings, culture tells the actors what ghosts, gods, and human beings are and what they are all about.... The world at large, nature, the facts of life, whatever they may be, are always part of man's perception of them as that perception is formulated through his culture. The world at large is not, indeed it cannot be, independent of the way in which his culture formulates his vision of what he is seeing.... Reality is itself constructed by the beliefs, understandings, and comprehensions entailed in cultural meanings.

Of significance in Schneider's definition is the juxtaposition of culture and norms and the assertion that it is norms that tell us how to behave whereas culture tells us how to make sense of things. Such a distinction seems imperative for our work.

## CULTURAL MEDIATION AND ADJUSTMENT

To this point, we have discussed some aspects of meaning and the concept of the message and we have reviewed several frameworks for understanding culture, but we have not yet explored the remainder of the task of a "bilingual/bicultural mediator": that of the mediator. In her 1999 book, *Reading Between the Signs: Intercultural Communication for Sign Language Interpreters*, Anna Mindess explores the idea of the interpreter as mediator explicitly. She notes:

> It is interesting that our profession, for at least the past ten years, has been using the term *bicultural mediator* to describe what we do without much inquiry into the mediator half of the term. By examining the duties of professional mediators, we will see if this is really an appropriate title for us. (1999, 153)

Though she concludes that "cultural mediator" would be a good and appropriate role for ASL/English interpreters, she does not believe interpreters currently function entirely as such. She draws several parallels between interpreters and mediators (such as adhering to tenets of neutrality and confidentiality). We diverge, she states, from mediators when it comes to the nature of our involvement. Mediators are not expected to be inconspicuous in their work. Perhaps most important, while interpreters are restricted with respect to their influence on a given situation, the understood, explicit goal of the mediator is actively to influence the situation and work toward agreement among the parties. She concludes that "the bicultural mediator model of sign language interpreting is more wishful thinking than a description of reality. It would be wonderful if we could help each side appreciate the other's reality, ... [and] encourage the participants to look beyond their immediate wants to their long-term interests" (2001, 155).

Mindess goes on to note that it would be nearly impossible to truly function as a mediator (or perhaps more accurately a "cultural broker") while simultaneously interpreting the message accurately, but she does stand firm in her belief that we must mediate as much as is necessary to *"impart each speaker's true intention, making adjustments for differences in communicative style in situations where our failure to do so would result in a misunderstanding of the real meaning of the statement"* (1999, 182; italics in the original). Mindess is describing something that, while sharing some of the attributes of a bicultural mediator, is also descriptive of an "ally" as well. Discussions of interpreter-as-ally abound in the literature. Early calls for interpreters to be allies of the deaf community focused on decision making and stressed that decisions regarding interpreting should made within the social and political culture surrounding deaf and hard of hearing adults. In other words, it was a call for interpreters to be allies at a macro level, by actively and respectfully supporting the goals deaf communities have for themselves. "Ally," then, is not a model of interpreting. It does not help us better analyze the message, nor does it aide us in functioning in our day-to-day role. In fact, believing that "ally" is a model of our role may further complicate our decision-making processes.

Regardless of our training, how we understand our role, or how much we have consciously analyzed our work, most of us are at least somewhat aware that discourse participants (including ourselves) have unique cultural experiences and rhetorical traditions and that attention to these differences can influence an interpreter's linguistic choices. For interpreters, there are several areas that need further exploration if we are to wear the label of cultural mediator.

First, it is not always evident what the interpreter should do with cultural differences on the job. Should the interpreter compensate for differences as Mindess (1999) maintains, or facilitate an "exchange" of cultures that allows the interlocutors to experience each other's cultures? Simon (1995) discusses this concept for written translation work and suggests allowing the reader of a translated text to experience the cultural elements associated with the source language culture. Could the same be a goal for interpretation? In theory, the communication interactions between deaf and hearing people could be richer, more satisfying, and even somewhat educational if participants were allowed some insights into each other's cultural frame. Any time an interpreter decides to add context for the recipient of the interpreted text she runs the risk of bleaching the interaction of the source language culture. We hope that such decisions are made with great care and in collaboration with the other discourse participants. Second, it is often not obvious how specific cultural elements are reflected in linguistic constructions in ASL or in English. How does the interpreter know that a particular linguistic or grammatical choice fits the supposed cultural experience of the recipient? As we know, a given country's deaf community is varied with respect to familial (ethnic, religious) culture, educational background, and experience with a signed language. Put another way, an interpreter is often asked to consider culture when framing her discourse without clear targets.

Finally, if we are asked (or believe that our code of professional conduct requires us) to take such an active role, how does the interpreter juggle this against the belief that she must not alter the content of the message? How does she reconcile her understanding about her active role, against the power dynamics at play?

## CONTEXTUALIZATION IN INTERPRETATION

Janzen and Shaffer (2008) suggest that a good starting point for our decision making about our role is assessment of each unique communication situation. Decisions can then be made based on the specific deaf and hearing participants and their relationships with each other and the communicative event. They note:

> Contextualization is always present in discourse as a necessary means to make our interactions coherent, both within the immediate discourse context and over the course of time. Contextualizing, where the speaker decides "on-line" the extent to which she must contextualize, is an inherently intersubjective action, taking place regardless of which language is being used, because of the negotiated nature of discourse. Further, it occurs whether the discourse participants share the same language or are attempting to communicate across a language boundary with, say, an interpreter. (2008, 334)

Here the notions of "intersubjectivity" and "contextualization" interact. *Intersubjectivity*, for the purposes of this chapter, refers to how people co-construct meaning in a given situation, relying on their ability to assess the experiences, knowledge stores, and perspectives of others. Perhaps more subtly, intersubjectivity refers to the shared meanings constructed by people in their interactions with each other and used by us to help interpret the meaning of elements of our social and cultural lives.

Intersubjectivity refers to how we as communicators assess other's comprehension and adjust our interactions accordingly. Contextualization is one such adjustment. It is something we add to our discourse based on our assessment of our interlocutor's understanding (and potential for understanding). We choose our utterances with our best assessment of interlocutor's knowledge stores and perspectives in mind. If, for example, we believe a specific cultural referent, concept, or lexical item needs to be contextualized, we do so, keeping our communication as concise as is necessary and possible.

To illustrate: I am from the high desert Southwest. If conversing with a colleague or friend who lives in the same area I might (confident that I would be understood) state something like: "It's getting warm; I need to get the swamp cooler set up this weekend." I may even simply say, "I need to set up the swamp this weekend." If I were talking with a friend in, say, Ireland, I may *choose* to add more context, explaining that a swamp cooler is a small metal machine consisting of tubes that drip water over thin sheets of straw (or more recently, synthetic fiber) and a motor that then blows the water-cooled air into the house. Or I might *not* contextualize and may wait to see if my interlocutor indicates through some sort of visual or linguistic feedback that she knows (or does not know) that a swamp cooler is a hybrid humidifier and air conditioner. The point is this: As communication partners we negotiate the amount of context that is necessary.[5]

Interlocutors also modify their lexical choices based on their addressee. For example, I might refer to my summer trip as my "vacation" when talking to American friends or family and "holiday" when talking to Canadian or European friends. Or I may consciously choose (for some specific communicative purpose) to say "vacation" when conversing with a Canadian.

---

5. Note that because meaning is not contained in words and phrases, a phrase such as *swamp cooler* cannot be understood simply by combining swamp and cooler. A swamp cooler does not cool a swamp.

Regarding the previous example, depending on the discourse context, I may simply say: "I need to get my air conditioner ready for summer." In other words, I may decide to be imprecise. Linell (1995) describes the relationship between interlocutors as a "continuous, collective process, where interactors mutually check understandings. What is said and understood gets continually updated on a turn-by-turn basis; each contribution to a dialogue displays (or can display) some understanding or reaction to the prior contribution" (193).

When an interpreter is added to a discourse event, she also must become an intersubjective participant. Her decisions will necessarily have an impact on the communication situation because she too will be engaged in a constant online assessment and adjustment of her utterances. As Janzen and Shaffer (2008) caution, interpreters should carefully consider the contextualization they add and perhaps begin their interpretation by assuming the interactants have a shared understanding that will allow them to understand each others' utterances without the addition of context by the interpreter. Stratiy (2005) also suggests interpreters would do best to err on the side of assuming communication will be successful without added context from the interpreter. She goes on to say that to do otherwise, in other words to begin by unilaterally adding context, shows a lack of respect for consumers by assuming that people will *not* understand. Finally, Wadensjö says that there is a "tendency to underestimate the patient's ability to understand (which is sometimes considered patronizing)" (1998, 225).

Interpreters work in a variety of settings, typically with a variety of (hearing and deaf) consumers. Our work requires a challenging mix of professional (ethical and linguistic) decision making. It is laudable, then, that as a profession we are continually evaluating our role and work in an effort to be ever better.

The aim of this chapter was to offer a review of our history with an emphasis on the metaphors that follow (and perhaps even plague) us, with a view to the future. Our continued evolution will make it necessary for us to finally rid ourselves of the conduit metaphor of meaning through a careful and mindful exploration of discourse and meaning. When we have a more conscious grasp of message analysis we can view our decision-making processes more clearly. Contextualization will be added intersubjectively and in negotiation with the other discourse participants, rather than as an a priori default. Contextualization will be specific to the discourse situation. If we are able to finally consider the message from a linguistic and cultural perspective we may find that we need to revisit our description of our role once more.

## REFERENCES

Arjona, Etilvia. 1978. Intercultural communication and the training of interpreters at the Monterey Institute of Foreign Studies. In *Language interpretation and communication*, edited by David Gerver and H. Wallace Sinaiko, 35–44. New York: Plenum.

Croft, William, and D. Alan Cruse. 2004. *Cognitive linguistics*. Cambridge: Cambridge University Press.

Fogelson, Raymond D. 2001. David Schneider confronts componential analysis. In *The cultural analysis of kinship: The legacy of David M. Schneider*, edited by Richard Feinberg and Martin Ottenheimer, 33–45. Urbana: University of Illinois Press.

Geertz, Clifford. 1973. *The interpretation of cultures*. New York: Basic Books.

Gile, Daniel. 1995. *Basic concepts and models for interpreter and translator training*. Amsterdam: John Benjamins.

Hatim, B., and Mason, I. 1990. *Discourse and the translator*. London: Longman.

Humphrey, Jan H., and Bob J. Alcorn. 2001. *So you want to be an interpreter? An introduction to sign language interpreting*. 3rd ed. Amarillo, TX: H & H.

Ingram, Robert M. 1978. Sign language interpretation and general theories of language, interpretation, and communication. In *Language interpretation and communication*, edited by David Gerver and H. Wallace Sinaiko, 109–18. New York: Plenum.

Janzen, Terry, and Barbara Shaffer. 2008. Intersubjectivity in interpreted interactions: The interpreter's role in co-constructing meaning. In *The shared mind*, edited by Jordan Zlatev, Timothy P. Racine, Chris Sinha, and Esa Itkonen, 333–55. Amsterdam: John Benjamins.

Janzen, Terry, and Donna Korpiniski. 2005. Ethics and professionalism in interpreting. In *Topics in signed language interpreting*, edited by Terry Janzen, 165–99. Amsterdam: John Benjamins.

Katan, David. 1999. *Translating cultures: An introduction for translators, interpreters, and mediators*. Manchester, UK: St. Jerome.

Lakoff, George, and Mark Johnson. 1980. *Metaphors we live by*. Chicago: University of Chicago Press.

Lawrence, Shelly. 1995. Interpreter discourse: English to ASL expansions. In *Mapping our course: A collaborative venture: Proceedings of the Tenth National Convention, Conference of Interpreter Trainers*, edited by Elizabeth A. Winston, 205–14. Charlotte, NC: Conference of Interpreter Trainers.

Leeson, Lorraine. 2005. Making the effort in simultaneous interpreting: Some considerations for signed language interpreters. In *Topics in signed language interpretation: Theory and practice*, edited by Terry Janzen, 51–68. Amsterdam: John Benjamins.

Linell, Per. 1997. Interpreting as communication. In *Conference interpreting: Current trends in research*, edited by Y. Gambier, D. Gile, and C. Taylor, 49–67. Amsterdam: John Benjamins.

Mindess, Anna. 1999. *Reading between the signs: Intercultural communication for sign language interpreters*. Yarmouth, ME: Intercultural Press.

Nida, Eugene A. 1964. *Towards a science of translating*. Leiden, the Netherlands: E. J. Brill.

Nida, Eugene A., and C. R. Taber. 1969/1982. *The theory and practice of translation*. Leiden: E. J. Brill.

Quigley, Stephen P. 1965. *Interpreting for Deaf people*. Washington, DC: U.S. Department of Health, Education, and Welfare.

Roy, C. B. 2000. *Interpreting as a discourse process*. New York: Oxford University Press.

Roy, Cynthia. 1993. The problem with definitions, descriptions, and the role of metaphors of interpreters. *Journal of Interpretation* 6 (1): 127–54.

Russell, Debra. 2005. Consecutive and simultaneous interpreting. In *Topics in signed language interpreting*, edited by Terry Janzen, 135–64. Amsterdam: John Benjamins.

Seleskovitch, Danica. 1976. Interpretation: A psychological approach to translation. In *Translation: Applications and research*, edited by R. W. Brislin, 92–116. New York: Gardner.

———. 1978. *Interpreting for international conferences*. Washington, DC: Pen and Booth.

Schneider, David. 1976. Notes toward a theory of culture. In *Meaning in anthropology*, edited by Keith Basso and Henry Selby, 197–220. Albuquerque: University of New Mexico Press.

Simon, S. 1995. Delivering culture: The task of the translator. In *Future Trends in Translation*, 44–56. Manitoba, Canada: Presses Universitaires de Saint-Boniface.

Solow, Sharon Newmann. 1981. *Sign language interpreting: A basic resource book*. Silver Spring, MD: National Association of the Deaf.

Stratiy, A. 2005. Best practices in interpreting: A Deaf community perspective. In *Topics in signed language interpreting: Theory and practice*, edited by Terry Janzen, 231–50. Amsterdam: John Benjamins.

Stewart, David A., Jerome D. Schein, and Brenda E. Cartwright. 2004. *Sign language interpreting: Exploring its art and science*. Needham Heights, MA: Allyn & Bacon.

Stokoe, William C. 1960. *Sign language structure: An outline of the visual communication systems of the American deaf*. Studies in Linguistics: Occasional Paper 8. Buffalo, NY: University of Buffalo.

Stokoe, W. C., D. Casterline, and C. Cronenberg. 1965. *A dictionary of American Sign Language on linguistic principles*. Washington, DC: Gallaudet College Press.

Tervoort, Bernard T. 1953. *Structurele analyse van visueel taalgebruik binnen een groep dove kinderen*. Amsterdam: Noord-Hollandsche Uitgevers Maatschappij.

Triandis, Harry. 1976. Approaches toward minimizing translation. In *Translation: Applications and research*, edited by Richard Brislin, 229–43. New York: Gardner Press.

Tylor, Edward B. 1924. *Primitive culture*, 7th ed., 2 vols. New York: Brentano's.

Wadensjö, C. 1998. *Interpreting as interaction*. London: Longman.

Wilcox, S., and B. Shaffer. 2005. Towards a cognitive model of interpreting. In *Topics in signed language interpreting: Theory and practice*, edited by Terry Janzen, 27–50. Amsterdam: John Benjamins.

# Examining the Notion of Interpreter Role Through a Different Linguistic Lens

*Jemina Napier*

IN THIS chapter, Shaffer documents our understanding of interpreter role by analyzing how the metaphorical descriptions of interpreter role have evolved according to different linguistic theories. Essentially, Shaffer is challenging our understanding of role and the concept of mediation by introducing readers to a perspective that draws on a linguistic framework that differs from the traditional: cognitive linguistics (Evans and Green 2006). The consideration of interpreter role within a cognitive linguistic framework enables us to draw on a paradigm in our field that is largely untapped in the literature of signed language interpreting studies.

Many readers will be familiar with the historical shift in the discussion of interpreter role over time. Shaffer refers to Roy's seminal (1993) article that discusses the inadequacy of then-existing role metaphors in interpreting and acknowledges that earlier discussions were typically linked to sociological considerations of the status of Deaf people and the subsequent empowerment of Deaf people. The paradigm shift of the interpreter role from helper to conduit to bilingual–bicultural ally was well documented during the 1990s (e.g., McIntire and Sanderson 1995; Pollitt 1997), and the role of signed language interpreters in the United States has been analyzed from a "systems approach" by comparing the transition of perceptions of interpreter role in line with new legislation and different iterations of the code of ethics (Swabey and Mickelson 2008).

The predominant reason for the paradigm shift was likely directly in relation to the recognition of the status of signed languages as real languages,

---

I greatly appreciate Cynthia Roy for planting the seed of the ideas that support the discussion in this commentary.

151

as documented by Shaffer, but it was not articulated in that way. The focus historically has been on the status of Deaf people rather than any linguistic theories, but Shaffer suggests that the changing understanding of interpreter role can be attributed to a shift in adoption of linguistic theories in relation to discussions of signed language interpreting.

Shaffer outlines the shift from psycholinguistic perceptions of how the message is rendered by interpreters (e.g., Ingram, 1978) to a sociolinguistic understanding of the interpreter as a co-participant in interaction and co-constructor of the message (e.g., Metzger 1995; Roy 2000a). She also refers to the linguistic framework of intercultural communication (Mindess 2006) and how Mindess refers to the need for interpreters to consider cultural aspects of how a message is understood. The term *intercultural communication* has been described in three different ways by Piller (2011), who uses the terms *cross-cultural communication, intercultural communication,* and *interdiscourse communication.* While cross-cultural communication inspects distinct aspects of cultural groups comparatively, intercultural communication assumes and investigates the different communicative features among different cultural groups in interaction with each other. On the other hand, interdiscourse communication puts aside the existence of cultural groups and examines different aspects of communicative practices in discourse under diverse circumstances. In general, intercultural communication investigates aspects of cultural differences between and within distinct groups, which is an ideal paradigm for the consideration of signed language interpreting. This idea of cultural variability has been discussed in relation to signed language interpreters by Page (1993), but apart from the works of Mindess and Page, the framework of intercultural communication is largely ignored in the signed language interpreting studies literature, and thus discussions of interpreter role have not benefitted from consideration of this sociolinguistic theory.

One particular construct that Shaffer refers to is the notion of interpreters as cultural mediators as opposed to linguistic mediators, which confirms the fact that discussion of role can be aligned with linguistic theories. Pöchhacker (2008) and Napier (2012) have recently discussed whether interpreting should be considered as a form of mediation. Pöchhacker defines the difference between two types of mediation: (1) intervening between conflicting parties or viewpoints (legal) and (2) the activity of an intermediate to transmit something (interpreting). Pöchhacker states that there are four different terms typically used to describe interpreter mediation: (i) linguistic mediation, (ii) cultural mediation, (iii) interlingual mediation, and (iv) intercultural mediation. Wadensjö (1998) has also classified two types of mediation: translation as mediation ("talk as text"—mediation between languages and cultures) and interpersonal mediation ("talk as activity"—interpreting enables communication between persons or groups who do not speak the same language). Rather than adopting only one form of role, as suggested in earlier writings (helper, conduit, etc.), Wadensjö suggests that the interpreter actually has a double role (2002).

The term *interpreter mediation* became more popular in the interpreting studies literature after it was recognized that interpreters do have a role in facilitating communication from a sociolinguistic perspective, but Pöchhacker (2008) notes the potential conflict between the concepts of mediation in a contractual sense and in a communicative sense. The contractual notion of mediation relies on the neutrality of the mediator to broker an agreement (often legal), whereas the communicative notion of mediation relies on the participation of the interpreter to coordinate and relay talk. The conduit role of an interpreter aligns itself well to the contractual notion of mediation, but the inherent requirements of the interpreter's role (i.e., to participate and co-construct the message) means that it is not always viable. In her survey of legal personnel and court interpreters in Australia, for example, Lee (2009) found that legal personnel strongly objected to use of the term *mediation* as they felt it was not within the interpreter's role (as they perceived the term from a legal/contractual standpoint). Pöchhacker (2008, 14) states: "Every interpreter is a mediator (between languages and cultures), but not every mediator is an interpreter."

Therefore, perhaps we should not throw out the baby with the bathwater? Pollitt (2000) used this phrase to describe the pendulum swing from the conduit to the interactive model of the interpreter role and argued that although we had embraced change in relation to this paradigm shift, it was still sometimes appropriate to function as a conduit and adopt a more literal interpreting approach (see also Napier 2002). The same could be said for the notion of interpreter-mediated communication: We have embraced this paradigm shift and wholeheartedly accepted the sociolinguistic explanation of the interpreter's role. But where is the line to be drawn? There is a need for more interpreting research to investigate the interactions between our role and notions of mediation: *Do* we mediate? *How* do we mediate? *When* do we mediate? *Why* do we mediate? *Should* we mediate? (Napier 2012). Should we be talking about role in terms of interpreter-mediated communication or interpret-*ed* communication/ interaction? Or as per Shaffer's suggestion, perhaps we should consider the interpreter's role in terms of contextualization?

In her chapter, Shaffer draws on cognitive linguistics as a framework (Evans and Green 2006). There is an emerging body of sign linguistic research in this area (see for example, Leeson and Saeed 2012; Wilcox and Morford 2007), but until Shaffer's discussions, there has been little application in signed language interpreting research (see also Wilcox and Shaffer 2005). Cognitive linguists see language as being all about meaning (as opposed to seeing language as a system of formal rules). In cognitive linguistic terms, there are four general principles that apply to linguistic meaning: (i) it is perspectival, (ii) it is dynamic and flexible, (iii) it is encyclopedic and nonautonomous, and (iv) it is based on usage and experience. Leeson (2010) advocates for the analysis of the message in signed language interpreting from a cognitive linguistic point of view, in order to consider meaning above the lexical level and pay attention to how meanings change depending on the context and how dynamic use of language operates to demonstrate new concepts. She asserts that language use in real life is always contextualized and therefore the study of interpreting should be contextualized. Shaffer also refers to contextualization in interpreting, in terms of how interpreters "don" their role.

Shaffer's understanding of the role of the interpreter through a cognitive linguistic lens is an important consideration for interpreter practitioners, educators, and researchers. Essentially, the sociolinguists (Metzger 1995; Roy 2000a; Wadensjö 1998) and the cognitive linguists are talking about the same thing, but using different linguistic constructs. For example, the notion of contextualization could also be likened to Giles, Coupland, and Coupland's (1991) communicative accommodation theory, which is situated within the linguistic subdiscipline of pragmatics.

Shaffer's discussion of role in relation to linguistic theories is indicative of the current thinking in our field and the fact that our understanding of role is an evolving paradigm. It is important to examine the interpreter's role through different lenses, and this cognitive linguistic account of the interpreter role can complement other newer accounts of the interpreter role that are also drawing on other linguistic theories. For example, Robert Lee has evolved his earlier discussion of interpreter role (see Lee 1997) in collaboration with Peter Llewellyn-Jones, where they are developing the concept of the interpreter's "role space" (Lee and Llewellyn-Jones 2011), by drawing on sociolinguistic and pragmatic theories (e.g., Giles et al. 1991; Goffman 1981). Rather than "donning" a role, Llewellyn-Jones and Lee (2012) suggest that interpreters "enact" their role and align and converge with participants in different ways. That enactment essentially is the contextualization that Shaffer refers to.

Deeper exploration of interpreter role in relation to different linguistic theories, as suggested by Shaffer, could provide more evidence to challenge notions of interpreter neutrality (as per Metzger 1995), and lead to much needed refinements of the model of signed language interpreting, and community interpreting more broadly (Turner 2007). Critical discussion of the interpreter role through different linguistic lenses will enable us to problematize the notions of interpreter as active participant, interpreting as mediation, and the complexity of the interpreter's role in any language pair.

Along with the paradigm shift in our understanding of the interpreter role, there has been a transition in the way we educate interpreters. We now teach interpreting students about discourse, about managing (not just facilitating) communication (Roy 2000b), and about context-based ethical decision-making (Dean and Pollard 2011). We teach them how to critically reflect on language, culture, interpersonal communication, and their own practice. We need to continue the dialogue between researchers and practitioners (as recommended by Shlesinger 2009), and also consider what researchers and educators can learn from one another. To provide a holistic view of interpreter role, discussing the work of Shaffer and others can enable interpreting students to make informed choices about their work. We have a responsibility, however, to educate not only interpreting students but also practitioners, who may have undergone training when different linguistic theories and interpreter models were in fashion. It is also essential that we educate our clients and our consumers on the evidence-based shifts taking place in the way we represent our role as interpreters.

Leeson, Wurm, and Vermeerbergen (2011) note that there are three dimensions to the emerging signed language interpreting research field that can be applied to our discussions and investigations of interpreter role: (1) we have *zero-generation research*, which includes descriptive and prescriptive works (earlier descriptions of role); (2) we have evidence from *first-generation research* that provide theoretical considerations and analyses (this is where we are now—analyses of role through different linguistic lenses); and (3) we need *second-generation research* that investigates what students and professionals do with the knowledge gleaned from first-generation research (i.e., how they actually enact their roles in practice in comparison with what they have learned). I look forward to seeing more research in this area.

## REFERENCES

Dean, Robyn, and Robert Q. Pollard. 2011. Context-based ethical reasoning in interpreting: A demand control schema perspective. *Interpreter and Translator Trainer* 5:156–82.

Evans, Vyvyan, and Melanie Green. 2006. *Cognitive linguistics: An introduction*. Mahwah, NJ: Erlbaum.

Giles, Howard, Nikolas Coupland, and Justine Coupland. 1991. Accommodation theory: Communication, context, and consequence. In *Contexts of accommodation*, edited by Howard Giles, Nikolas Coupland, and Justine Coupland, 1–68. Cambridge: Cambridge University Press.

Goffman, Erving. 1990. *The presentation of self in everyday life*. London: Penguin.

Ingram, Robert M. 1978. Sign language interpretation and general theories of language, interpretation, and communication. In *Language, interpretation, and communication*, edited by David Gerver and H. Wallace Sinaiko, 109–18. New York: Plenum.

Lee, Jieun. 2009. Conflicting views on court interpreting examined through surveys of legal professionals and court interpreters. *Interpreting* 11:35–56.

Lee, Robert. 1997. Roles, models, and world views: A view from the states. *Deaf Worlds* 13:40–44.

Lee, Robert, and Peter Llewellyn-Jones. 2011. Re-visiting role: Arguing for a multi-dimensional analysis of interpreter behavior. Paper presented to the Supporting Deaf People Online Conference, February.

Leeson, Lorraine. 2010. Puzzled? What IS that signer doing (and HOW am I supposed to interpret it)? Keynote presentation to the Annual Conference of the Australian Sign Language Interpreters Association, Brisbane, August 27–29.

Leeson, Lorraine, and John I. Saeed. 2012. *Irish Sign Language: A cognitive linguistic account*. New York: Columbia University Press.

Leeson, Lorraine, Svenja Wurm, and Myriam Vermeerbergen. 2011. "Hey Presto!" Preparation, practice, and performance in the world of signed language interpreting and translating. In *Signed language interpreting: Preparation, practice, and performance*, edited by Lorraine Leeson, Svenja Wurm, and Myriam Vermeerbergen, 2–11. Manchester, UK: St. Jerome.

Llewellyn-Jones, Peter, and Robert Lee. 2012. Getting to the core of role: Defining the role space of interpreters. Paper presented to the Conference of Interpreter Trainers, Charlotte, NC, October 17–20.

McIntire, Marina, and Gary Sanderson. 1995. Who's in charge here? Perceptions of empowerment and role in the interpreting setting. *Journal of Interpretation* 7 (1): 99–113.

Mindess, Anna. 2006. *Reading between the signs: Intercultural communication for sign language interpreters*, 2nd ed. Yarmouth, ME: Intercultural Press.

Napier, Jemina. 2002. *Sign language interpreting: Linguistic coping strategies*. Coleford, UK: Douglas McLean.

———. 2012. Research and best practices in community interpreting: To mediate or not to mediate? Paper presented at the Webinar, MARIE Center and University of Alberta, April.

Page, Jo Ann. 1993. In the sandwich or on the side? Cultural variability and the interpreter's role. *Journal of Interpretation* 6:107–26.

Piller, Ingrid. 2011. *Intercultural communication: A critical introduction*. Edinburgh, UK: Edinburgh University Press.

Pöchhacker, Franz. 2008. Interpreting as mediation. In *Crossing borders in community interpreting: Definitions and dilemmas*, edited by Carmen Valero-Garcés and Anne Martin, 9–26. Philadelphia: John Benjamins.

Pollitt, Kyra. 1997. The state we're in: Some thoughts on professionalisation, professionalism, and practice among the UK's sign language interpreters. *Deaf Worlds* 13:21–26.

———. 2000. On babies, bathwater, and approaches to interpreting. *Deaf Worlds* 16:60–64.

Roy, Cynthia. 1993. The problem with definitions, descriptions and the role metaphors of interpreters. *Journal of Interpretation* 6:127–154.

———. 2000a. *Interpreting as a discourse process*. Oxford: Oxford University Press.

———. 2000b. Training interpreters: Past, present and future. In *Innovative practices for teaching sign language interpreters*, edited by Cynthia Roy, 1–14. Washington, DC: Gallaudet University Press.

Shlesinger, Miriam. 2009. Crossing the divide: What researchers and practitioners can learn from one another. *International Journal of Translation and Interpreting Research* 1:1–14.

Swabey, Laurie, and Paula G. Mickelson. 2008. Role definition: A perspective on 40 years of professionalism in sign language interpreting. In *Crossing borders in community interpreting*, edited by Carmen Valero-Garcés and Anne Martin, 51–80. Amsterdam: John Benjamins.

Turner, Graham H. 2007. Professionalisation of interpreting with the community: Refining the model. In *The Critical Link 4: Professionalisation of interpreting in the community*, edited by Cecilia Wadensjö, Birgita E. Dimitrova, and Anna-Lena Nilsson, 181–92. Philadelphia: John Benjamins.

Wadensjö, Cecilia. 1998. *Interpreting as interaction*. London: Longman.

———. 2002. The double role of a dialogue interpreter. In *The interpreting studies reader*, edited by Franz Pöchhacker and Miriam Shlesinger, 354–71. London: Routledge.

Wilcox, Sherman, and Barbara Shaffer. 2005. Towards a cognitive model of interpreting. In *Topics in signed language interpreting*, edited by Terry Janzen, 27–50. Amsterdam: John Benjamins.

Wilcox, Sherman, and Jill Morford. 2007. Empirical methods in signed language research. In *Methods in cognitive linguistics*, edited by Maria Gonzalez-Marquez, Irene Mittelberg, Seana Coulson, and Michael J. Spivey, 171–200. Amsterdam: John Benjamins.

# COMMENTARY

# Our History and Ideas We Best Not Forget
*Christopher Stone*

IN AN ever-changing world, it is important that we, as interpreters and interpreter educators, reflect on how we situate ourselves in different circumstances and contexts. Interpreters have been doing this for centuries (the earliest evidence of sign language interpreting appears to be from the 17th century, as described in Miles 2000, 123) but this has gained greater collective attention in the past 50 years as sign language interpreters have moved into providing professional services. In this commentary, I show the evolving understanding of our role and the different lenses that have been applied to our work.

These lenses are important for interpreting students to acknowledge and consider because they give students the reflective tools to work as professionals in the 21st century. Interpreters need to be able to negotiate their place and space within interactions and explain their professional decisions to all parties involved. Professionals now examine not manifested behaviors but rather the motivations behind those behaviors. Our students need to be mindful of this and educated appropriately.

As demonstrated by Barbara Shaffer in her chapter, although aspects of our work have been emphasized differently by various interpreter trainers and scholars, much of the groundwork was laid out by Quigley (1965). Careful reading of original texts gives us a clearer understanding of how our profession has evolved, ensuring our students have information that supports both the development of their understanding and the development of our profession.

## HOW RESEARCH ENABLES US TO BETTER
## UNDERSTAND PEOPLE AND COMMUNICATION

As interpreter educators we need to pay attention to research on the nature of communication; human communication is rooted in our capacity to use language and understand each other in different situations. As technology (e.g., high-definition video, electroencephalography [EEG], functional magnetic resonance imaging [fMRI], etc.) moves forward we are better able to explore how information processing occurs (Moser-Mercer 2000/2001) and how individuals achieve mutual understanding (Clark and Krych 2004). This communication is potentially made more complex when working with the Deaf community, whose members display varying levels of bilingualism and whose desire to access English and sign language within a single event may require going beyond the simple notions of transliteration and interpretation, as discussed in Shaffer's chapter.

Shaffer begins to explore the types of decisions interpreting students need to be bold enough to make. The "additions" that we make vis-à-vis the explicit propositions in the source language necessitate that our students understand how to ensure we as interpreters are "present" in our renderings (Stolze 2004) and how to render at an inference level that takes into account audience design (Bell 1984).

We need to encourage our students to consider the decisions an interpreter must make to ensure successful interpreter-mediated interactions and to meet the (possibly competing) goals of the participants for that interaction. Relevance theory (Sperber and Wilson 1995) gives us greater insight into how ostensive communication occurs, and it enables us to consider inference as part of human communication and the role of language within it.

Within this theoretical framework, contextual assumptions (including culture) give us an approach that takes into account the knowledge of participants, their cultural practices, and the information available to those participants within their cognitive environment. These cognitive environments can include information made manifest within the environment, language, and co-language gestures, as well as knowledge made relevant both within the unfolding interactions and from any previous interactions.

Our job as educators is to support our students' understanding of this complex interplay between different factors within the participants' cognitive environments, as informed by research. Shaffer gives us insights into this from a variety of interpreting and translation scholars' work, and this discussion helps shed light on the issue for students. The discussion could go further by drawing upon relevance theory as applied to translation and interpreting (Sequeiros 2002; Stone 2009) and even the field of lexical pragmatics (Wilson and Carston 2007) to explore the notion that even "lexical interpretation typically involves the construction of an ad hoc concept or occasion-specific sense, based on interaction among encoded concepts, contextual information and pragmatic expectations or principles" (Wilson and Carston 2007, 2).

## WHERE WE GO FROM HERE

We need to begin to have sophisticated discussions over the many aspects of contextual assumptions that interpreters bring to bear in any single situation and to provide formative feedback to our students that build upon their developing skills and understandings of the multiple roles interpreters may enact (Baker 2006).

As Wadensjö (1998) highlighted, interpreting can be broken into two separate tasks, the translation and the coordination of interaction. This necessarily requires us to think of talk both as text (as inspired by the field of translation) and as activity (as inspired by evolving understandings of human communication motivated by linguistics, psycholinguistics, and the psychology of language). This approach often confuses our students as they grapple with becoming professionally fluent (Grosjean 1997) in two or more languages, while trying to conceive of the "interpreter-in-context" (Wadensjö 2004, 106).

Shaffer neatly draws our attention to the contradictions in different approaches to message analysis, different understandings of culture, and different terminology applied to the role interpreters may take in different situations and client groups. Schaffer also draws upon her own development as an interpreter, astutely identifying that with experience one's approach to the job changes, in light of that experience, with an ever-increasing understanding of spoken "text" as "activity" (Wadensjö 1998).

Initially interpreters often concern themselves with the task of translation and understand the notion of message in a narrow sense. This narrow understanding enables students to better control their development and feel that they are making progress. With great experience in the field, the notion of message begins to incorporate not only the translation task but also the coordination of an interaction and the ostensive communication made manifest in the shared cognitive environment. If we are mindful of this developmental pathway of our students, we are better able to ensure our graduates have a sophisticated understanding of being an interpreter in the 21st century and the demands any given situation may place upon them.

## Conclusion

Shaffer enables us to revisit our history as a profession and reminds us that our students' learning trajectories have been somewhat similar. The challenge she requires of us is to move beyond notions of speech as text with its accompanying (unhelpful) metaphors toward interpreting as an intersubjective communicative activity. Furthermore, research in fields other than translation and interpretation (such as human communication, pragmatics, and relevance theory) further enable us to understand the types of decisions we as humans (interpreters and our service users alike) make within these interlingual interactions.

## References

Baker, Mona. 2006. Contextualization in translator- and interpreter-mediated events. *Journal of Pragmatics* 38:321–37.

Bell, Allan. 1984. Language style as audience design. *Language in Society* 13 (2): 145–204.

Clark, Herbert H., and Meredyth A. Krych. 2004. Speaking while monitoring addressees for understanding. *Journal of Memory and Language* 50:62–81.

Grosjean, François. 1997. The bilingual individual. *Interpreting* 2:163–87.

Miles, Michael. 2000. Signing in the Seraglio: Mutes, dwarfs, and jestures at the Ottoman Court 1500–1700. *Disability and Society*, 15 (1): 115–34.

Moser-Mercer, Barbara. 2000/01. Simultaneous interpreting cognitive potentials and limitations. *Interpreting* 5 (2): 83–94.

Sperber, Dan, and Deirdre Wilson. 1995. *Relevance: Communication and cognition*. Oxford: Blackwell.

Sequeiros, Xosé R. 2002. Interlingual pragmatic enrichment in translation. *Journal of Prgamatics* 34:1069–89.

Stolze, Radegundis. 2004. Creating "presence" in translation. In *Claims, changes, and challenges in translation studies: Selected contributions from the EST Congress*, edited by G. Hansen, K. Malmkjaer, and D. Gile, 39–50. Amsterdam: John Benjamins.

Stone, Christopher. 2009. *Toward a Deaf translation norm*. Washington, DC: Gallaudet University Press.

Quigley, Stephen P. 1965. *Interpreting for Deaf people*. Washington, DC: U.S. Department of Health, Education, and Welfare.

Wadensjö, Cecilia. 1998. *Interpreting as interaction*. London: Longman.

———. 2004. Dialogue interpreting: A monologising practice in the dialogically organised world. *Target* 16 (1): 105–24.

Wilson, Deidre, and Robyn Carston. 2007. *A unitary approach to lexical pragmatics: Relevance, inference, and ad hoc concepts*. Accessed on February 10, 2013, from http://www.phon.ucl.ac.uk/home/robyn/pdf/Wilson-Carston-Unitary-Approach-2007.pdf.

ELIZABETH A. WINSTON

# Infusing Evidence into Interpreting Education: An Idea Whose Time Has Come

## ABSTRACT

In this chapter Elizabeth A. Winston explores the pressing need for, the rich potential of, and the challenges associated with infusing effective evidence-based teaching practices into sign language interpreting education. As a first step, criteria need to be delineated for evaluating evidence and review processes must be established for identifying evidence-based practices in interpreter education. Once identified, interpreter educators and sign language researchers need to join forces to ensure that these practices are incorporated widely into interpreter education. Winston argues for a comprehensive and principled approach to interpreting education that is founded on the principles of effective evidence-based practices.

THE INFUSION of evidence-based practices into interpreter education is both needed and long overdue. Evidence, developed by and collected from research that evaluates the impact and effectiveness of educational practices, should be a basic factor in decisions about curriculum, assessment, choice of resources, materials, and strategies. Communities across the world have pressing needs for qualified interpreters, regardless of language combinations. In the case of sign language interpreter education, we also face an ever-increasing distance from our roots in the Deaf community (Cokely 2005; Monikowski and Peterson 2005). Moreover, we recognize that current preparation practices are not satisfying the demand for qualified interpreters (NCIEC 2007–2010). It is essential that educational practices be firmly grounded in evidence to most efficiently prepare qualified, successful

164

interpreters. Evidence-based teaching approaches need to replace seat-of-the-pants practices, which are often based in little more than folklore.

Infusion of evidence-based practices into any field presupposes that such practices have been identified and are available. In a field as young as sign language interpreter education, that is not yet the case. Indeed, this early in our history, *evidence* may need to be defined more broadly than it is in experimental sciences, such as chemistry or physics. It is useful to look to other service professions[1] to understand their approaches to evidence-based practice, definitions of evidence, types of acceptable evidence, and relative strengths of various types. With such definitions and criteria in hand, it will be possible to gather all of our known practices, evaluate the evidence that demonstrates their impact, and determine their effectiveness in interpreter education. This will only be possible if educators and researchers collaborate to ensure that practices are solidly grounded in research and that they satisfy the needs of interpreting educators.

The fragmented pieces of knowledge, theories, approaches, strategies, and practices that exist today overwhelm educators in sheer number and variety. At first glance they appear to be scattered in all directions, with few discernible patterns or shapes to provide a sense of logic to them. Collecting and evaluating each practice to determine if it is based on evidence is a first step. Understanding where each fits into the puzzle that is interpreter education, and which pieces are missing, is the next step. Ensuring that they are accessible to any who needs them is the final goal. It is incumbent upon us to take stock of what exists so that we gain perspective about the scope of the challenge to infuse evidence-based practices into interpreter education.

## EXISTING PRACTICES

Before exploring ways to infuse evidence into interpreter education practices, it is critical to review the existing body of knowledge and identify what already exists to help in this endeavor. By examining related fields, such as language acquisition, assessment, adult education, and spoken language translation and interpretation, we can broaden our horizons and

---

1. Although many people currently refer to interpreting as a "practice profession," I use the descriptor "service profession" to reflect the purpose of our practice.

expand the possibility of finding evidence-based practices already in existence. In fact, there are many resources that currently exist within sign language interpretation. Like pieces of an unfinished puzzle, the resources may seem scattered, or an unlikely fit, but with careful examination, we will find their niche within the picture as a whole. With thoughtful examination, research findings that sometimes seem irrelevant to daily practice can be translated[2] into accessible, applicable, evidence-based practices. Likewise, daily teaching activities, while sometimes appearing to lack any theoretical foundations or measurable impact, can be translated into viable research projects, easily evaluated and documented.

## Existing Evidence in Related Fields

Although the focus of this chapter is specifically focused on sign language interpreter education, it is valuable to look to related disciplines such as interpreting studies (IS) and spoken language interpreter education. An excellent resource is Pöchhacker's (2004) comprehensive and systematic examination of the diverse studies in the relatively young field of interpreting studies, which is essential reading for any interpreting educator. He reviews research about models, practices, and approaches in interpreting and interpreting education across both spoken and signed languages. His work presents a broad and insightful understanding of current evidence-based practices in interpreting, many of which have drawn directly from related fields as well.

Another excellent resource is provided by Sawyer (2004), who gives a comprehensive review of the history and practices of interpreting education. Like Pöchhacker, he highlights the research about interpreting pedagogy that has extended into related fields and demonstrated how interpreting has borrowed research methodologies and sound pedagogical practices in language acquisition, curriculum development, pedagogy, and assessment.

Based on his findings, Sawyer identifies three interdependent areas that interpreter education needs to address: (1) curriculum design, both for new programs and for existing programs; (2) assessment approaches that

---

2. Translation in this case refers to knowledge translation, the activity of making research findings applicable to the needs of practitioners in the field.

"appropriately, meaningfully, and usefully" address student performance across the curriculum; and (3) effective use of all aspects related to teaching, from the latest technologies to evidence-based teaching practices. He urges interpreter educators to focus on all three areas, advocating that, when considered together, "these measures enable the learner to develop expertise more rapidly and efficiently to the skill levels required at the top of the language industry" (2004, 5). Resources and evidence-based practices from related service professions, such as teaching second and foreign languages, education, nursing, and counseling, offer much from which we may learn. Drawing on these practices can, and has, informed the identification of evidence-based practices in sign language interpreter education.

## Evidence From Sign Language Interpreter Education

The history of teaching sign language interpreters is even younger than the fields of IS and interpreter education. However, some evidence-based practices have been assembled in sign language interpreting, and the foundations of evidence-based practices were set in place early.

## Early Foundations in Sign Language Interpreter Education

Perhaps because we tend to think of sign language interpreting education as a young field, it is easy to overlook—or underestimate—the mushrooming wealth of materials, research, and ideas that have grown up over the past 50 years. The focus on sign language interpreting education in the United States began in the mid-1960s, at times relying on related disciplines such as linguistics, psychology, education, and other fields for early knowledge and evidence. The need for research to inform the practice of sign language interpreter education in the United States was first put forth in 1979, when a national meeting called Interpreter Training: The State of the Art, was convened to "obtain complete, up-to-date information about current practices in interpreter training and future needs and directions" (Yoken 1979, 2). Forty-seven participants, all nationally recognized educators and researchers, contributed their insights and experiences to explore existing products, materials, and articles available to inform interpreter education practices. The results of that exploration included an annotated bibliography of 120 articles, books, and resources and an extensive listing of more than 200 articles and materials related to deafness and/or interpreting and interpreting education (Yoken 1979). In addition, the participants proposed a research agenda for interpreting education, identifying six areas needing immediate attention: (1) interpreters, (2) interpreter trainers, (3) administration of interpreter training programs, (4) methods and materials, (5) special issues, and (6) research (Yoken 1979, 2).

The excitement generated by this meeting resulted in an immediate follow-up conference, Interpreter Research: Targets for the Eighties, in 1980. Many participants from the initial meeting were joined by acknowledged researchers, linguists, and educators. The purpose of that conference was to synthesize and extend the research focus and topics identified during the first meeting. Two primary goals were identified: "to prioritize those previously identified [research] needs, and to develop the most important projects into specific research proposals" (Per-Lee 1980, 2). As a result, research proposals for the five most important research areas were created, which included work statements and rationales, manner and kind of research, time, cost, and potential applications for the results of the research proposed.

Areas of interpreter education that were identified as needing research at that conference were the following:

1. Profile of the competent interpreter. Identify factors related to aptitude, skill competency, and job satisfaction such as fatigue, memory, bias, knowledge of content, and lag time; as well as examine factors of discourse (rate, vocabulary, style, syntax, content), demographics, and the environment.

2. Evaluation/certification. Conduct a literature review of "reliable and valid" evaluation approaches for language, interpreting, and translating; inform Registry of Interpreters for the Deaf (RID) certification materials and approaches; and assess the reliability and validity of evaluations, including materials, reviewers, and criteria.

3. Entrance and exit criteria for interpreter trainees. Identify and research the screening processes of interpreter training programs of the time, as well as those of related fields, to inform curriculum design and instructional approaches for training.

4. Labor market analysis. Identify and understand the population to be served, including their needs, characteristics, and demographics.
5. Coursework and materials for a core curriculum for interpreter education programs (IEP). Compare results of differing factors (length-short term vs. long term; intensive vs. diffuse); assess entry requirements; and analyze resulting skills of students leaving these programs to determine their effectiveness. (Per-Lee 1980, 12–13)

Over the course of these two conferences, the participants described the state-of-the-art education environment in interpreter training at the time. Albert Pimentel, then director of the National Academy of Gallaudet College, described the results:

> As the conference revealed, a variety of interpreter training programs now exist. Geographically, they cover the country relatively well. Most programs, however, are still in the process of developing curriculums [*sic*] and refining methods, and thus there is considerable variety in program quality and sophistication. If the picture of the field provided by this document appears incomplete, it seems also to reflect the reality of present circumstances in a field that has made remarkable achievements in a short period of time. (Yoken 1979, 2–3)

The participants of the second conference unanimously recommended "a research center on interpreter training" (Per-Lee 1980, 26). Pimentel's description still applies and the final recommendation from the group holds true today. The call for identifying effective, evidence-based practices in interpreting education came early to the field of sign language interpreter education, yet much remains to be done.

## Continued Growth

Another comment on the body of knowledge amassed at the 1979 and 1980 conferences continues to haunt the field today:

> A literature search revealed a large body of opinion papers and some applicable research in the fields of linguistics and the language of signs. It uncovered no hard research that was systematically feeding into the overall long-range development of the area of interpreter training and the effective utilization of interpreters by deaf people. (Per-Lee 1980, 1)

Three decades later, some research in interpreter education exists, but there is no long-range development plan. While there has been continuous, if sporadic, growth and expansion of research in interpreting and interpreter education, it is not being used to inform decision making about curriculum, assessment, and the practices of interpreting educators in any systematic, long-term fashion. Programs, materials, discrete pieces of research, and isolated practices appear to be adopted or not, often based on little evidence of effectiveness. Much remains unknown and many valuable pieces of our practice are an unassembled puzzle—with pieces out of place, gathering dust, and easily lost. Newcomers to research are asking the same questions that were asked by the 1979 conference participants. Educators are parroting the techniques of their predecessors with no greater understanding of whether and how those educational practices are effective.

This assessment of sign language interpreter education is not intended to discount the advances that have taken place. Indeed, since 1980 much has been accomplished in the areas first outlined at those early meetings. It is beyond the scope of this chapter to provide a comprehensive review of these accomplishments but, along the lines of the work of Pöchhacker (2004) and Sawyer (2004), my intent is to reveal the tip of the "resource iceberg" that is already available to our field. As a starting point, Patrie and Mertz (1997) created an updated version of the original annotated bibliography from the 1979 meeting. Within this bibliography, various descriptions of the competent interpreter exist, ranging from descriptions of skills (Witter-Merithew and Johnson 2005) to discussions of cognitive aptitudes needed (Macnamara 2009). Further, there are now published studies of interpreter error (Cokely 1992), interaction (Hoza 2007), and the effect of the environment (Ramsey and Pena 2002). Discourse has been studied in American Sign Language (ASL) and interpreting (Roy 1993; Metzger 1999; Swabey 2002; Nicodemus 2009). Evidence-based teaching practices are available in a variety of volumes, including Roy's Interpreter Education series (2000–2009), Metzger's Studies in Interpretation series (2004–2009), and work by Marschark et al. (2005) and Napier (2009). There are also conference proceedings from organizations including the Conference of Interpreter Trainers (CIT) and Critical Link. The Commission on Collegiate Interpreter Education (CCIE) also provides standards for interpreter education programs that can inform the identification of evidence-based practices in our field.

In the area of evaluation and certification, information and research from various national certifying bodies, including the Registry of Interpreters for the Deaf (RID), the Association of Visual Language Interpreters of Canada (AVLIC), and the National Accreditation Authority for Translators and Interpreters (NAATI), now exists. In the recent past, intensive needs assessments surveys have been conducted, including the RID's *Research on Interpreter Shortages in K–12 Schools* (2007) and reports by the National Consortium of Interpreter Education Centers (NCIEC, 2007–2010).

Areas such as entrance and exit criteria have begun to receive more formal attention from researchers and educators. RID has made national certification contingent upon exiting a bachelor's program. Curriculum and materials used by programs can be found on program websites. Most of this information and these findings are grounded in sound theory, and some are supported by research findings, yet there remains room for much more research. Many existing studies would benefit from replication across audiences and settings.

In the more than 30 years since the original meeting, we have started to develop a body of information and knowledge that can inform decisions about curriculum, assessment, and teaching practices in interpreter education. However, if the goal of interpreter education is to prepare students to be successful in their chosen profession, it is time to move beyond the collection of these disparate pieces of information and establish a more rigorous study of their effectiveness, while simultaneously organizing and cataloging the results so that they are easily accessible to interpreter educators.

There are many challenges to be addressed before a coherent picture emerges from the mountain of pieces. This chapter is limited to only one— infusing effective practices into interpreter education—in the hope of offering ideas and suggestions that may contribute to the whole.

## Evaluating Educational Practices and Resources

The triple challenges of curriculum, assessment, and use described by Sawyer (2004) are far from discrete. These components overlap, inform each other, and evolve to present educators and researchers with new challenges. Evaluating current practices in interpreter education will lead to the identification of evidence-based practices. These practices will inform decisions about curriculum, which will then lead to their infusion into the teaching practices of educators. Integrating the pieces becomes an iterative, continuous process of innovation, assessment, infusion, and growth.

## Defining Evidence-Based Practice

To begin, we must first examine what is meant by *evidence-based practice* and what and who determines the types and levels of evidence required for a practice to be identified as evidence based. Although these terms are used frequently, finding a precise definition is elusive. Some disciplines define evidence-based practices in relation to a continuum of evidence types, as well as the quality and amount of that evidence. Interpreter educators need to do likewise, agreeing upon what constitutes evidence, determining how much evidence is needed, and dictating how strong that evidence must be. Finally, it is important to weigh other factors, such as practicality and accessibility, into decisions about using evidence-based practices.

## What Constitutes "Evidence"?

Evidence comes in many forms, some of which are more acceptable and compelling than others. In a scientific experiment, evidence may take the form of data borne from the manipulation of concrete variables that have tightly controlled measures. In education, evidence may be less tangible and it is more difficult to capture how a specific practice has "caused" improved learning or performance. For example, while it is possible to measure the number of correctly fingerspelled words in a target text, it is difficult to directly measure the learning that occurred that prepared a student to correctly fingerspell. The number of practice hours might be correlated to a specific level of fingerspelling mastery. Because of confounding factors, quantifying the impact of uncounted hours interacting with Deaf people is difficult, if not impossible, to measure with accuracy. Evidence in education may be evaluated in a number of ways and on a variety of levels. The questions needing to be addressed in interpreter education are what levels and types of evidence convince educators that they have a positive impact on the preparation of qualified interpreters?

To advance practice in interpreter education, I argue that it will be necessary for interpreter education to identify what is and is not acceptable evidence and to determine how much of which types of evidence make any given practice "evidence based." If interpreter educators are to infuse evidence-based practices into daily practice, we must establish guidelines and parameters about how those practices are defined and evaluated. Educators need to be aware of the types of evidence a given practice has generated and the strengths of each type of evidence as it is weighed in the whole. In reviewing data, documentation, and reports that serve as evidence of the impact or value of a teaching practice, we should explore other fields, including teaching and health care, where existing approaches for evaluating evidence can serve as examples.

As an emerging field within the human services professions, it may be necessary for interpreter educators to define evidence more broadly and flexibly than a long-established science such as physics. It may be that practices grounded in theory will be considered minimally evidence based. We may want to consider the extent to which a practice is used across institutions. We may want to accept the expert opinions of subject matter specialists as supporting evidence. Other factors to consider may be the way in which a practice has been implemented by educators and evaluated by researchers, the number of required replications, and the parameters of those replications. The goal of this chapter is not to provide definitive answers but rather to raise crucial questions and stimulate discussion by interpreter educators.

## How Strong Is the Evidence?

Evidence may come in many forms, but some is still considered to be more compelling than others. In addition to determining what is acceptable as evidence, interpreter educators need to identify criteria for evaluating the relative value, or strength, of each type of evidence. Given the types of evidence provided earlier in this chapter, greater weighting might be assigned to practices grounded in interpreter education theory than to those grounded in health care or early childhood education. If the number of institutions using a given practice is to be considered, factors in evaluating the evidence might be the reputation or standing of those institutions, the number of students graduated, and the length of time between their graduation and national credentialing. If expert opinion is to be considered, it will be important to determine which experts are more relevant to interpreting and interpreter education and, in the case of specialized practices, which experts are more relevant to the given specialization. If the number of replications of a researched practice is considered, it will be essential to identify whether the replications were implemented by the same researcher in all cases, by different educators and researchers, and across one or many target audiences (see Table 1).

Looking beyond evidence-based practices, it is important to consider other factors essential for effectiveness, in addition to evidence. It may be that evidence-based practices, while forming the kernel that informs interpreter education, are not sufficient to make decisions about interpreter education, curriculum, and assessment. A useful model comes from the Iowa Practice Improvement Collaborative on addictive substances. The Iowa collaborative went beyond the consideration of evidence when deciding which practices they wanted to be infused into their treatment agencies. They identified criteria that included practicality, availability of adequate materials, level of training needed by those using it, and feasibility of using it across different populations and regions (Iowa Consortium 2003). When extending this approach to sign language interpreter education, a researcher might develop evidence demonstrating that native or fluent bilinguals are most qualified linguistically as interpreters, but statistically, the number of native ASL users or fluent ASL–English bilinguals are simply insufficient to serve as the only individuals to recruit and train as interpreters. Choosing to accept only native ASL signers into interpreter education programs might be an evidence-based practice but implementing such a practice would not address the pressing need for more qualified interpreters. In fact, it would only exacerbate the need. It is essential, then, to pursue research to identify how to make less-perfect solutions (enhancing language skills of not-so-fluent bilinguals) workable. We need to develop an integrated system of evidence-based practices that are practical.

Table 1. Types and Levels of Evidence and Practicality

| Practice Is Evidence Based | *Questions to Ask* |
| --- | --- |
| Theory based | • *Is the study based on any theory?*<br>• *From a related field?*<br>• *From interpreter education?*<br>• *From sign language interpreter education?* |
| Used by institution(s) or individual(s) | • *Which institutions/individuals?*<br>• *How many institutions?*<br>• *How credible are they?*<br>• *How many graduates?*<br>• *How long between graduation and credentialing?* |
| Evaluated in research studies | • *Has the practice been evaluated/researched?*<br>• *What is the credibility of the methodology?*<br>• *Extent of audience?*<br>• *Number of replications (by whom; to whom)?* |
| **Practice Is Also Practical** | |
| Ease of use | • *How much training does an educator need to use the practice?*<br>• *Does it require equipment, resources, personnel (and how much?)* |
| Application in a range of settings | • *Can it be used for a range of audiences, in a range of settings?* |
| Associated methods of ensuring fidelity | • *If it is used, will it always be done appropriately?*<br>• *Will educators use it ineffectively?* |
| Associated materials for implementation (e.g., manuals, stimulus materials) | • *Are there materials available to use with the practice?* |
| Feasibility (e.g., high cost; limited resources) | • *How much will it cost?*<br>• *Are there adequate resources?*<br>• *Relevant value to cost/time?* |

# What Labels Should Be Used?

Finally, it will be important to categorize reviewed practices so that educators and researchers, as well as administrators and consumers, can find them, use them, and further add to the findings about them. Labels such as "gold standard," "promising," "best," and "effective" are frequently used to identify the extent to which a practice might be evidence based. One set of preliminary labels in sign language interpreter education has been introduced through the work of the NCIEC. The labels are (1) *standard practices*—practices that exist, with no evidence or theoretical foundation serving as a basis for predicting their success; (2) *best practices*—practices that are research verified, research based, or followed by exemplary institutions; and (3) *effective practices*—practices that are verified by research as yielding target outcomes (NCIEC 2010). While still new, this categorization offers one potential model to build upon as interpreter educators consider how to approach the challenge of infusing evidence-based practices into interpreter education.

In sum, it is essential to explore these questions and define evidence, evidence-based practice, and the criteria for evaluating our practices based on those definitions. As we develop an integrated matrix of effective evidence-based practices, we can also explore how these practices fit together to inform curriculum and assessment in interpreter education.

## DISSEMINATING THE PIECES

In the ideal world, with the pieces gathered into an easily accessible repository and our definitions of, and criteria for evaluating, evidence in place, the process of reviewing the many existing practices would begin, followed by categorizing, proposing expansions of some, and proposing new directions where gaps exist. A variety of options exist for this stage. Review panels can be convened to assess existing knowledge, articles, products, and research to identify which simply exist, which are promising, and which are best or effective. Experts in teaching, interpreting, and research can convene to identify priorities for replicating some studies, beginning research where gaps are found, preparing materials to support implementation of effective practices, and synthesizing and integrating the pieces and parts to shape a coherent whole.

Reviewing and categorizing is an essential stage in this endeavor. At the same time, it will be imperative to explore how this body of knowledge will be not only stored but actively disseminated in ways that are readily accessible. Research findings and evidence do exist to support some existing practices, such as the demand–control schema (Dean and Pollard 2001), discourse mapping (Winston and Monikowski 2002, 2005), consecutive interpreting (Russell 2005), and Deaf translation norms (Stone 2009). Recent publications, such as the *International Journal of Interpreter Education* (IJIE) and the Gallaudet Interpreter Education series in the sign language interpreting field, include more data-driven submissions. The work of Angelelli (2009) and Sawyer (2004) are two publications in the larger interpreting and translation field that proffer evidence-based practices to us. More research exists that might support existing or new practices (e.g., those in the Gallaudet Interpreting Research, *Sign Language Studies*, and Sociolinguistics in Deaf Communities series), if only educators could identify relevant ways of applying those findings. There exists a tremendous gap between published research findings and the application of those findings to interpreter education practice.

Likewise, many educators are employing practices that may seem effective. Educators believe that the practices produce positive changes in interpreting students and use them class after class, yet they have no evidence to substantiate their beliefs. They are hampered by a lack of training and practice in research often because they lack advanced academic degrees that develop research experience. With those skills, they might be able to bring more practices to the fore in interpreter education. The gap between teaching practices and the generated research looms large. For effective, evidence-based practices to become fundamental to interpreter education, researchers and educators will need to find common ground, translating their individual expertise and knowledge for each other.

## Narrowing the Gaps between Researchers and Educators

Beyond a systematic review and evaluation lies perhaps the greatest challenge for interpreter education: Once practices are identified and categorized according to the type and level of evidence that supports their use, they need to be infused into practice, not relegated to a new shelf to gather more dust. Many factors contribute to the success of infusing interpreter education with evidence-based practices. Support from institutions and organizations, and from the field as a whole, is essential. Stakeholders and consumers need to be an integral part of addressing the challenge from beginning to end. First and foremost, educators must infuse research into teaching and researchers must make their findings relevant and practical for educators.

The body of work of the 1979 and 1980 conferences serves as a prime example of the challenge of infusing evidence into interpreter education practice. Despite the valuable results of these two conferences, the results were not widely disseminated. In 2005, upon learning of the existence of documents from the 1979 and 1989 meetings, it required several months of searching for this author to locate them, using personal contacts, searching individuals' dusty shelves and boxes, and sending repeated requests to search archives in libraries. While much of the information was dated, and much newer, more relevant research has been conducted in some areas, the real surprise was the amount of still-relevant information and guidance the original documents offer. It is worth asking—how much of the knowledge they offered has been re-invented, rebuilt, or completely forgotten in our current practices? How much more effective might interpreter education be today had their work served more broadly as a foundation for future research and practice?

## Knowledge Translation

Knowledge translation is a phrase commonly used in business, government, and organizations. It refers to the need for making the abstract, sometimes esoteric, findings of various research projects easily understandable and relevant to the lay practitioner so that it can be infused into daily applications. It is described as "the middle, meeting ground between two fundamentally different processes: those of research and those of action" (Research Matters, n.d., 1). There is little disagreement from any quarter that this kind of translation from research to practice is essential.

In this chapter, however, I use *knowledge translation* in an extended sense, as the capturing of practitioner wisdom and knowledge by applying methodologically sound research approaches, thus translating it into evidence-based practice. Bringing together educators and researchers is not a new concept, as is illustrated by the proliferation of action research, but interpreter education is only beginning to combine the two activities and will benefit by active collaborations between educators and researchers. This kind of knowledge translation will begin to support the choices that interpreter educators and the administrators of programs make. Adopting evidence-based practices, within the realms of practicality, will result in more effective interpreting education. Educators who adopt an approach to teaching interpreting that always involves evaluation of impact and effectiveness learn more about their practice as they expand their knowledge and practices successfully.

The need to translate the implicit and tacit knowledge of interpreter educators into understandable, justifiable practices is pressing. Having evidence to support those practices that have impact and building them into a coherent body of knowledge is essential. While sign language interpreter education is continuing to expand, there is also a great danger of it withering and losing its history, wisdom, and experience. Surveys reveal that the number of interpreter educators retiring in the near future is greater than the number of interpreting educators being prepared to replace them. We know that interpreter education programs currently cannot fill the vacant faculty positions that are advertised (NCIEC 2007–2010). Many educators nearing retirement earned their wisdom and skills the hard way, by trial and error in the classroom. Must that same path to wisdom be imposed on the next generation of educators? Passing on existing knowledge to the next wave will enable them to build on what is already known. There remain bountiful opportunities for expanding the knowledge of interpreter education.

In a forward-looking manner, Pöchhacker writes about passing on of knowledge:

> New members of the interpreting studies community will interact with some old hands. It is when the latter find that the questions being asked are too clever and difficult for them to answer that all of us in this field may take heart from the realization that progress in interpreting studies is set to continue. (2004, 210)

In the subsequent sections, I offer a challenge—to educators, to researchers, and to the field at large—to begin to move out of the "comfort zone" of our classrooms, research laboratories, and interpreting practices to create new paradigms that will ultimately advance the profession of sign language interpreter education.

## Challenge to Educators

Many interpreter education practices remain untouched by any reference to, or reliance on, research. Speaking from my personal experiences as an interpreting educator for more than 25 years, I know this has been true in my own practice. From discussions with other educators, it is true for them as well. Often, as is the case in other educational environments, we teach the way we have learned, accepting the folklore of our field more easily than we accept evidence-based practices. Some practices may indeed be rooted in evidence of effectiveness, but how often are we, as educators, aware of the evidence, research, criteria, and standards that justify those practices? Programs may tout a specific philosophy or approach in their courses, yet, how many can explain the evidence that led to incorporating that philosophy or approach, the evidence that convinced them to choose it, and most important, the evidence being collected to verify that it works? How many students can recognize and explain the practices employed in their educations and the relative merits of one approach over another in effective interpreter education? Interpreter educators have a great deal of wisdom and knowledge to enrich the field, much of it implicit and internalized through long practice and much trial and error. That implicit knowledge and wisdom, translated into evidence-based practices, can serve students and consumers well.

There are several means for educators to reduce the practice-to-research gap, some easier than others. Learning more about the research process, understanding how to critically analyze research findings, and determining the relevance of research to interpreter education is a beginning. How can these challenges be addressed? Introductory research courses are readily available at most colleges and universities. Increasingly, discussion groups and communities of practice have been established to focus on specific topics. While face-to-face groups are inviting, there are also opportunities through online discussion groups. Educators can establish relationships with researchers interested in interpreter education in order to conduct research or simply to discuss complicated research findings and discover ways they can be made applicable to interpreter education. Collaborative relationships with researchers can inform their work as well. Helping researchers understand what interpreter educators need to know can inspire new research projects that will further inform educational practices.

Another way to ensure that educators' knowledge is translated into evidence-based practice is to become active researchers themselves. Asking questions about every process, activity, and decision we make as teachers opens up endless possibilities for research. For example, text selection for practice and assessment can inspire questions that range from narrow ("Why did I choose THAT stimulus text for interpreting practice today? And, did it achieve what I wanted it to?") to broad ("How and why do I choose texts for any of my courses? Are my choices effectively helping students increase their interpreting skills and abilities? Are there other ways to choose texts that would be more effective?"). Questions about program-wide decisions are as relevant as individual ones. Asking why a program has adopted role playing as an approach across the curriculum is as pertinent as asking if it would be effective in a single class session.

A critical question to explore is why we, as educators, are not enthusiastically bringing research, reflective practices, and evidence into our daily work. With a wealth of knowledge to share with the field, with each other, and with students, sharing this knowledge is essential.

Sharing this is difficult for many reasons. A lack of time, scarcity of financial resources, and limited knowledge about the research process may all be factors (see Swabey and Nicodemus 2011). For many, conducting research is most often difficult because of fear—fear of having a "stupid" idea, of not making sense, of feeling ridiculous among peers. Collaborative relationships with experienced researchers can address many of those difficulties, most especially fear.

## Challenge to Researchers

It is not only educators who bear the responsibility of infusing evidence-based practices into interpreter education. Researchers have a role to play as well. First and foremost, researchers can actively participate in the translation of their findings to accessible, practical practices. While not every researcher may be interested in finding direct educational applications for their work, partnerships and collaborations with educators can be both rewarding and enriching. Being available to talk about our research findings to classes, discussion groups, and teachers who might want to apply the findings into their daily practice are all avenues for making research findings more practically accessible to educators. With current technologies, participation and presentations to one group can be easily recorded and shared with others.

Beyond that, as researchers, we can encourage educators in their own research. Many may not know how to approach such an endeavor. The perceived activity of "research" is so big and daunting that many assume that they cannot do it or do it well. Reading research reports of studies that analyze hours of video or require the assistance of research assistants can make the activity of research seem far beyond the means of many interpreter educators. Having researchers serve as mentors to educators to replicate existing studies is another collaborative approach. Reviewing action research designs, discussing data collection strategies, and offering advice on the practical challenges to data collection in the everyday world of education all expand the research skills and potential of practicing interpreter educators. Many researchers already offer those services willingly to editorial boards, publishers, and professional organizations. In short, researchers can be transparent about research processes, so that educators who may have feared and resisted the research process will begin to look with excitement and anticipation at the prospect of conducting research about their own teaching practices.

A positive change in research is the growing acceptance of action research, the often individualized, self-reflective research practices that can be conducted without extensive funding, support, and technical expertise. Some established researchers and institutions have dismissed this type of research as "soft," too objective, and lacking in rigor. Yet, as more educators bring effective research practices into their classrooms, the findings become more valuable. Just as no single action research finding will be "generalizable" to every situation, no strictly controlled, quantitative set of research findings will ever be applicable to any single individual. The findings of action research, when done well, can lead to the development of more generalized questions to be researched in larger studies.

To reiterate, researchers can work closely with educators to strengthen methodologies and analysis, to narrow questions, and to link findings across several settings. These kinds of practices, formalized, categorized, documented, and reported in meaningful ways to educators that also satisfy the need for structured methodologies that are meaningful to researchers, have a rich potential for shifting current "seat-of-the-pants" teaching approaches to evidence-based practices that can enhance the field, students' skills, and ultimately, the interpreting services that are at the heart of our work.

## Challenge to the Field

The need to infuse evidence-based, effective practices in interpreting education extends far beyond those involved in the day-to-day teaching and research. Developing an integrated repository of our knowledge and practices requires a massive effort. Establishing a sustainable approach to reviewing and categorizing knowledge and practices is both expensive and long-term and requires a committed investment of time, effort, and money. It requires collaboration and support from a variety of institutions, organizations, and funding sources. In the United States, sign language interpreter education organizations such as CIT and RID need to come together to discuss how to organize the disparate pieces of information each currently maintains for its members. Institutions vested in supporting research in and about interpreting education will need to find ways of sharing their own repositories with outsiders. Ephemeral, grant-funded groups such as NCIEC and the National Clearinghouse need to collaborate closely with established institutions, organizations, and researchers to find enduring, sustainable homes for their work. Certifying and accrediting bodies need to share their findings and their approaches to enrich our knowledge; likewise, they need to infuse their evaluations with the evidence-based practices being generated. Publishers, institutions, and organizations need to explore the benefits of Open Access, which makes all published materials freely available for educators and researchers (Research Matters, n.d., 1). Arguing the pros and cons of an Open Access approach in higher education in the United States goes far beyond the scope of this essay; however, it is a pioneering innovation in a field such as sign language interpreter education, with its small audience, limited resources, and dispersed stakeholders. Funding agencies, both public and private, need to focus resources on this goal. Building a repository of evidence-based practices is a beginning; infusing an expectation that evidence-based practices are a minimum requirement in our interpreting education systems is the real challenge; and qualified interpreters will be the outcome.

## CONCLUSION: SYNERGY AND REJUVENATION

The trefoil knot (see Fig. 1) is often used to represent a dynamic integrated process, with pieces and threads constantly feeding into and growing out of the interactions and energies contributed to it. The pieces, disconnected and isolated, can be overwhelming and exhausting to comprehend, let alone master. Pulled together into a coherent, integrated whole, the pieces offer synergy and rejuvenation, bringing new excitement and discoveries to our work. With the trefoil knot as a metaphor, I suggest that it is time to gather the various and disparate pieces of knowledge about interpreter education into an intricate whole that is easily accessible, both in terms of practical understanding and easy accessibility. Addressing this challenge will benefit interpreter education within and across languages and modalities, in turn

Figure 1. Trefoil knot from Longtin 1996. Used with permission.

serving interpreting consumers who rely on qualified interpreting services to survive and thrive. These practices, this knowledge and information, once reviewed and categorized, can be offered in support of decisions faced by interpreter educators and administrators about curriculum, assessment, investment in technology and resources, and professional development for faculty. They can provide interpreting educators with a rich selection of practices that have been systematically scrutinized, based on evaluation of evidence provided. Identifying practices that are effective will also help identify areas where gaps in practice exist and where new approaches and innovative strategies may need to be developed. Finally, it is vital to ensure that the pieces, as well as the whole, are accessible to others and practical to use.

Achieving this goal necessitates long-term collaborative efforts among researchers, educators, and stakeholders. Infusing evidence-based practices into interpreter education means much more than simply developing an intellectual understanding of effective evidence-based practice. It means that we as educators willingly replace ritualistic, commonly accepted practices with reflective, well-considered practices grounded in research. Moreover, it means that educators begin conducting research about the practices they routinely use. Likewise, we as researchers need to translate our findings into useful and practical educational strategies. Shifting from a stance of "them" and "us" (researchers and educators) to one of "we" will encourage collaborative projects that bring the rigors of research to the demands of practice. Such collaborative projects will lead to improved interpreter education, and ultimately, to more qualified interpreters.

## REFERENCES

Cokely, Dennis. 1992. *Interpreting: A sociolinguistic model.* Burtonsville, MD: Linstok.
———. 2005. Shifting positionality. In *Educational interpreting and interpreting education*, edited by Marc Marschark, Rico Peterson, and Elizabeth A. Winston, 3–28. New York, NY: Oxford University Press.
Hoza, Jack. 2007. How interpreters convey social meaning: Implications for interpreted interaction. *Journal of Interpretation* 39–68.
Iowa Consortium for Substance Abuse Research and Evaluation. 2003. *Evidence-based practices.* Accessed July 5, 2010, from http://www.uiowa.edu/~iowapic/files/EBP%20Guide%20-%20Revised%20 5-03.pdf.

Longtin, Tom. 1996. *Trefoil puzzle* (image 2). Accessed July 5, 2010, from http://homepages.sover.net/~tlongtin/puzzles/puzzles.html.

Macnamara, Brooke. 2009. Interpreter cognitive aptitudes. *Journal of Interpretation* 9–32.

Marschark, Marc, Rico Peterson, and Elizabeth A. Winston, eds. 2005. *Sign language interpreting and interpreter education*. Oxford: Oxford University Press.

Metzger, Melanie. 1999. *Sign language interpreting: Deconstructing the myth of neutrality*. Washington, DC: Gallaudet University Press.

Metzger, Melanie, and Earl Fleetwood, eds. 2000–2010. Studies of Interpretation Series. Washington, DC: Gallaudet University Press.

Monikowski, Christine, and Rico Peterson. 2005. In *Educational interpreting and interpreting education*, edited by Marc Marschark, Rico Peterson, and Elizabeth A. Winston, 188–207. New York, NY: Oxford University Press.

Napier, Jemina, ed. 2009. *International perspective on sign language interpreter education*. Interpreter Education Series, vol. 4. Washington, DC: Gallaudet University Press.

NCIEC. 2007–2010. *NCIEC needs assessments reports*. Accessed August 20, 2012, from http://www.tiemcenter.org/?page_id=786.

———. 2008a. *NCIEC interpreter referral agency needs assessment report*. Accessed June 4, 2013, from http://www.tiemcenter.org/?page_id=786.

———. 2008b. *NCIEC deaf consumer needs assessment report phase 1*. Accessed June 4, 2013, from http://www.tiemcenter.org/?page_id=786.

———. 2009a. *NCIEC deaf consumer needs assessment report phase 2*. Accessed June 4, 2013, from http://www.tiemcenter.org/?page_id=786.

———. 2009b. *NCIEC deaf consumer comparison needs assessment report phase 1 and 2*. Accessed June 4, 2013, from http://www.tiemcenter.org/?page_id=786.

———. 2009c. *NCIEC vocational rehabilitation needs assessment report*. Accessed June 4, 2013, from http://www.tiemcenter.org/?page_id=786.

Nicodemus, Brenda. 2009. *Prosodic markers and utterance boundaries in American Sign Language interpretation*. Studies in Interpretation Series, vol. 5. Washington, DC: Gallaudet University Press.

Nicodemus, Brenda, and Laurie Swabey, eds. 2011 *Advances in interpreting research: Inquiry in action*. Philadelphia: John Benjamins.

Patrie, Carol, and Julie Mertz, eds. 1997. An *annotated bibliography on interpretation*. Washington, DC: Gallaudet University.

Per-Lee, Myra S., ed. 1980. *Interpreter research: Targets for the eighties*. Washington, DC: Gallaudet University.

Pöchhacker, Franz. 2004. *Introducing interpreting studies.* New York: Routledge.

Ramsey, Claire, and Sergio Pena. 2010. Sign language interpreting at the border of the two Californias. In *Interpreting in multilingual, multicultural contexts,* edited by Rachel Locker McKee and Jeffrey E. Davis, 3–27. Studies in Interpretation Series, vol. 7. Washington, DC: Gallaudet University Press.

Registry of Interpreters for the Deaf. (2007). *Research on interpreter shortages in K–12 schools.* Accessed July 5, 2010, from http://www.rid.org/aboutRID/grants/#Research%20Grant%20Program.

Research Matters, International Development Research Centre. n.d. *Knowledge translation toolkit.* Accessed July 5, 2010, from http://www.idrc.ca/en/ev-128908-201-1-DO_TOPIC.html.

Roy, Cynthia B. 1993. A sociolinguistic analysis of the interpreter's role in simultaneous talk in interpreted interaction. *Multilingua* 12 (4): 341–63.

———, ed. 2000–2009. Interpreter Education Series. Washington, DC: Gallaudet University Press.

Sawyer, David B. 2004. *Fundamental aspects of interpreter education.* Amsterdam: John Benjamins.

Swabey, Laurie. 2002. Beyond he said, she said: The challenge of referring expressions fo interpreting students. In *Advances in teaching sign language interpreters,* edited by Cynthia B. Roy, 78–99. Interpreter Education Series, vol. 2. Washington, DC: Gallaudet University Press.

Witter-Merithew, Anna, and Leilani J. Johnson. 2005. *Toward competent practice: Conversations with stakeholders.* Alexandria, VA: Registry of Interpreters for the Deaf.

Yoken, Carol, ed. 1979. *Interpreter training: The state of the art.* Washington, DC: National Academy of Gallaudet College.

COMMENTARY

# Convergence and a Call to Action
## Debra Russell

THE CHAPTER written by Elizabeth A. Winston entitled "Infusing Evidence into Interpreting Education: An Idea Whose Time Has Come," is another reasoned argument about the need to include research and evidence-based teaching practices within interpreting education. Winston identifies a road map for delineating criteria upon which evidence can be examined and stresses the need for educators to engage in collaborative efforts to infuse evidence widely into interpreter education.

Winston helps the reader understand that as a relatively young profession, many of the practices that have shaped signed language interpreting and interpreter education may not be grounded in research and as such are not based on evidence. This is an important element of the chapter that has also been discussed by Gile (2011), Nasr (2010), and Moser-Mercer (1994). I also addressed how to examine the quality and appropriateness of the research methodology used in interpreting studies in a keynote address at the Conference of Interpreter Trainers (Russell 2008). However, as Gile (2011) reminds us, we need research training if we are to enhance the amount and quality of empirical research available in our field. As Winston stresses, educators must be able to discern evidence from existing practices. Such a shift has the potential to move us beyond teaching based on what we have always done or on the latest commercial product that may have little or no research underpinnings. Winston provides a cogent review of existing research, highlighting findings that stem from other fields of study, including language acquisition, curriculum development, pedagogy, and assessment and in doing so identifies key connections among the value of solid research, gaps in our existing knowledge, and ways in which we might engage in cyclical practices to see educators as creators of research.

The chapter also highlights a model for determining which evidence-based practices might be selected for use in interpreter programs, based on practicality, availability of adequate materials, training required by those using the materials, and feasibility of use across different demographics. This proposed integrated approach is an important and innovative contribution in leading our field forward in addressing the gap between published research and the application of the findings to our educational practices.

As a field, we have an opportunity to embrace Winston's message about understanding our knowledge base, including important research contributions that may have been lost over the years, only to be reinvented or rebuilt. As Winston argues, this will require a new approach to capturing the existing research in a systematic way that allows the broadest group of educators access to the repository and ensures knowledge transfer becomes part of the fabric of our field. Her emphasis on using technology to build a research network that can both nurture new researchers and hold collective conversations about assessing research and its application to practice is an exciting proposal. While these networks exist informally, and formally among small pods of researchers, the power of this has yet to be extended to building larger international knowledge networks that are focused on research-to-practice conversations, mentoring new scholars, and identifying research topics that would enhance our current understanding of interpreting.

As our field gives increased attention to the pressing need to develop a practice-oriented research community, we see a tangible example of building a collaborative research community through the European Master in Sign Language Interpreting (EUMASLI), which is doing just as Winston encourages: addressing the gap between researchers and teachers. Napier (2009) reminds us of the power of debating ideas, sharing research, and reflecting on our knowledge by publishing in peer-reviewed journals such as the *International Journal of Interpreter Education*, and graduates of the EUMASLI program will be well positioned to share their findings and contribute to our field's burgeoning scholarship. Additionally, Nicodemus and Swabey (2011) compiled an excellent selection of papers from a range of scholars from spoken and signed language interpreting, to guide aspiring researchers as they grapple with methodological challenges. This convergence of authors, including Winston, who support the need for research training, research networks, greater institutional collaboration, and principled approaches to applying evidence to our diverse teaching contexts, is exciting. If all of these aspects were realized in North America, our field would benefit tremendously. More important, students and ultimately consumers will be true beneficiaries of a profession informed by rich and robust research contributions, educators who are both critical consumers of the literature and creative facilitators who can bridge research and bring it to bear on their program design, curricula decisions, and teaching strategies (Russell 2011).

## REFERENCES

Gile, Daniel. 2011. Preface. In *Advances in interpreting research*, edited by Brenda Nicodemus and Laurie Swabey, vii–ix. Amsterdam: John Benjamins.

Hessmann, Jens, Eeva Salmi, Graham Turner, and Svenja Wurm. 2011. Developing and transmitting a shared interpreting research ethos. EUMASLI—A case study. In *Advances in interpreting research*, edited by Brenda Nicodemus and Laurie Swabey, 177–98. Amsterdam: John Benjamins.

Moser-Mercer, Barbara. 1994. Paradigms gained or the art of productive disagreement. In *Bridging the gap: Empirical research in simultaneous interpretation*, edited by Sylvie Lambert and Barbara Moser-Mercer, 17–23. Amsterdam: John Benjamins.

Nasr, Marion. 2010. La didactique de la traducion—une etude scientometrique. Unpublished doctoral dissertation, ESIT, Universitye Parie 3, Sorbonne Nouvelle.

Napier, Jemina. 2009. Editorial: The real voyage of discovery. *International Journal of Interpreter Education* 1:1–6.

Nicodemus, Brenda, and Laurie Swabey, eds. 2011. *Advances in interpreting research*. Amsterdam: John Benjamins.

Russell, Debra. 2008. *Linking pedagogy and research: The road ahead*. Keynote address presented at the biennial Conference of Interpreter Trainers, San Juan, Puerto Rico.

———. 2011. Designing a research project: Beginning with the end in mind. In *Advances in interpreting research*, edited by Brenda Nicodemus and Laurie Swabey, 27–46. Amsterdam: John Benjamins.

# Big Elephants in the Room
*Claudia V. Angelelli*

THE CHAPTER entitled "Infusing Evidence into Interpreting Education: An Idea Whose Time Has Come" is an invitation to pause and analyze concepts that may have different meanings in different fields, such as "evidence" and "evidence-based pedagogy." Elizabeth A. Winston ponders questions about evidence: what evidence is, what constitutes evidence, how compelling evidence needs to be, and if the amount of evidence that exists in translation and interpretation (T&I) is sufficient be considered evidence. These are not simple questions. Winston offers us the opportunity to continue discussions on a series of complex and controversial issues. Arguing for evidence-based interpreter education is one step toward opening up a closed circle, which I have discussed elsewhere (Angelelli 2004, 25). This circle, formed by associations, practitioners, and schools, constructs and co-constructs discourse on interpreting that, if not based on research and theory from interpreting studies (IS) and the various disciplines that inform IS, risks perpetuating the status quo and hindering the progress of a field of study. In this commentary I present only a few of the complex and controversial issues raised by Winston's work after I share some reflections on evidence.

## REFLECTIONS ABOUT EVIDENCE

Evidence allows researchers and teachers to justify their choices. Winston's discussion on the types of evidence contributes to the conversation that originated in the nineties and raises several important issues. Among them is the timeliness for evidence-based interpreter education, given the state of IS. In her chapter she addresses the plausibility of an inventory of evidence. This would facilitate access to and sharing of evidence and enhance the credibility of such evidence. Perhaps it would be useful to look into other service professions to understand their approaches to evidence-based practice, their definitions of evidence, their types of acceptable evidence, and relative strengths of the various types of evidence. If this were to be done, the next logical step would be the creation of a taxonomy. This taxonomy could present evidence types in terms of how they were collected and analyzed, their contexts, other potential analyses, applications, and their strengths and weaknesses. These are just some of the criteria according to which evidence could be classified. Perhaps if interpreter education, and the field of IS as a whole, had a taxonomy of evidence, it would be more feasible to collaborate with other fields, as researchers from other disciplines could look at data from new angles using different lenses and methods. This interactive and interdisciplinary approach would generate a larger body of knowledge from which we would all benefit. However, the questions remain: In interpreter education, who benefits from this knowledge, what motivation exists for accessing it, how likely it is that this new knowledge will be treated differently than current knowledge, and finally how is this knowledge made available and accessible to instructors?

Looking at existing practices is important and, in Winston's words, it constitutes the first step in this process. Winston's overview of research in education of both spoken and signed languages contributes to the conversation on interpreter education. In addition it allows us to reflect on the interaction between spoken and signed languages. Although it would not make sense to overlook their uniqueness, one wonders if such a separation really needs to exist, if we need to compare and contrast spoken and signed languages and cultures, or if spoken and signed languages and cultures can converge in discussions under umbrella terms of *multilingualism* and *communication*. One wonders what points of convergence and divergence exist between them and how evidence-based education plays out in each of them.

In terms of the amount of evidence present in interpreter education, Winston discusses the reason for a relatively small amount of evidence, especially when compared to evidence from other fields. This scarcity might explain why discussions on issues of teaching interpreting are seldom based on research. Winston states the relatively newness (or youth) of IS as one of the possible explanations for the relatively small amount of evidence-based pedagogies produced in the field (an issue that has been raised several times before). While this "youth" of IS may certainly be one of the factors, one wonders for how much longer IS is going to hide under the veil of "youth" to justify the status quo. Research in IS and in interpreter education, while not abundant, is solid, is theoretically or empirically based, and many times presents an interdisciplinary approach. So, it appears then that the issue is not so much that research in IS or interpreter education is of limited amount but rather that the amount of research that exists does not seem to permeate practice. Therefore, some of the big elephants in the room are related to disconnects between research and practice, as well as to mapping what can be done about it. These issues may not have a straightforward solution, but we need to face them if we want the field to move forward. In other words, what do we do about this? Who does it? And how do we get it done?

If interpreter education and interpreting pedagogy are going to be evidence based, then a culture of evidence needs to be embraced by all stakeholders. From this question, various others derive: How do *we* make that happen? *Can* we make it happen? Who is the "*we*"? Who are the stakeholders? What steps need to be taken? What factors get in the way? What educational contexts are more conducive to an evidence-based education? I will discuss these questions,[3] not necessarily in order of importance. They emerge from diverging conceptualizations of interpreter, interpreter education, and teacher education, to name only a few.

The first is interpreter education. When the various stakeholders (practitioners, professional organizations, industry, and academia) discuss education or educational opportunities, do they all conceptualize education in the same way? What really is interpreter education for each of them? Currently interpreter education occurs within academia[4] (ranging from full-fledged programs to isolated courses), as well as in professional organizations (in the form of continuing education during annual meetings or special seminars) and industry (through training courses and seminars for specific market needs). The goals and approaches of all of these pro-

---

3. Given space constraints only a few examples are discussed in this commentary.

4. Given this venue it is not necessary to discuss educational opportunities in academic settings in detail.

grams and courses are different. In many cases education gets confused with training on the tricks of the trade.

Professional organizations and companies offer educational programs so that interpreters can stay current in the field. There is nothing wrong with this, except that these organizations make assumptions as to what an interpreter is and what makes an interpreter. These assumptions take us to the second big issue: the interpreter. Specifically, how do conceptualizations of an interpreter from professional organizations and industry differ from conceptualizations of an interpreter in academia? Are interpreters only those who hold a degree? Are interpreters those who can perform some interpreting tasks based on their life experiences? Conceptualizations about interpreters dictate the kind of professional development and continuous education available for them. As I have argued elsewhere (2004b, 91–97) the "education" of interpreters is multifaceted, nontraditional, and therefore not consistent with other professional areas. While the only path to become an engineer is to pursue a degree in engineering, interpreters in many cases do not need a degree [the exception being in American Sign Language (ASL) / English interpreting as required by Registry of Interpreters for the Deaf (RID)] to perform interpreting tasks. Therefore, the term *interpreter* is used for both persons who hold a degree in interpreting and those who do not hold a degree. These profiles have very different needs when it comes to professional development. While the former attends conferences to stay current in the field, the later attends conferences to seek information about everything and anything related to interpreting because it is through those meetings and short workshops that the latter becomes an interpreter. Therefore, as we discuss interpreter education we should face the third issue: teacher education. Who teaches what to whom?

As I have discussed elsewhere (Angelelli 2004, 91–97; 2005; 2008), the backgrounds and knowledge of instructors in interpreting classes vary. Therefore, their approaches to teaching range from a practice based on pedagogical principles grounded on research and theory to a series of unrelated tasks based on their practical experience. Teaching practice needs to be informed by research and cannot be based solely on personal experiences and anecdotes. As valuable as those may be to illustrate specific points, they are simply isolated examples and cannot drive the curriculum. Teaching is based on much more than experience. Teaching is based on pedagogical principles (Brown 2007) and is not random. Interpreter education (like interpreting itself) cannot be discussed in terms of an art or a craft. It has a foundation. It is a field of inquiry based on research and principles. It is this foundation that makes for a sound practice and allows teachers to justify their choices. Interpreter teachers should stay current with relevant theory and research. They may participate or lead projects of action research. In this way their practice would be aligned with research and theory. This alignment will begin to replace a closed circle with an ecological circle grounded on evidence.

## References

Angelelli, Claudia V. 2004. *Re-visiting the Interpreter's Role*. Amsterdam: John Benjamins.

———. 2005. Healthcare interpreting education: Are we putting the cart before the horse? *ATA Chronicle* 34 (11): 33–38, 55.

———. 2008. The role of the interpreter in the healthcare setting: A plea for a dialogue between research and practice. In *Building bridges: The controversial role of the community interpreter*, edited by Carmen Valero Garcés and Anne Martin, 139–52. Amsterdam: John Benjamins.

Brown, D. H. 2007. *Teaching by principles: An interactive approach to language pedagogy*. New York: Pearson Longman.

# INDEX

*Figures are indicated by f following page numbers.*